More Than Black?

More Than Black?

Multiracial Identity and the New Racial Order

G. Reginald Daniel

TEMPLE UNIVERSITY PRESS

PHILADELPHIA

Temple University Press, Philadelphia 19122
Copyright © 2002 by Temple University
All rights reserved
Published 2002
Printed in the United States of America

⊛ The paper used in this publication meets the requirements of the American National
Standard for Information Sciences—Permanence of Paper for Printed Library Materials,
ANSI Z39.48-1984.

Library of Congress Cataloging-in-Publication Data

Daniel, G. Reginald, 1949–
    More than Black? : multiracial identity and the new racial order / G. Reginald Daniel.
        p.   cm.
    Includes bibliographical references and index.
    ISBN 1-56639-908-4 (alk. paper) — ISBN 1-56639-909-2 (pbk. : alk. paper)
        1. United States—Race relations.   2. Racism—United States—History.   3. Racially
    mixed people—United States—Race identity.   4. African Americans—Race identity.
    5. Whites—United States—Race identity.   6. Eurocentrism—History.   I. Title.

E184.A1 D243 2002
305.8'04–dc21   2001027643

For Aunt Kay, who knows what it took to get here

Contents

Preface

On December 2, 1955, my first-grade teacher began class by saying, "Yesterday, in Montgomery, Alabama, a colored women, Mrs. Rosa Parks, was arrested for refusing to let a white passenger have her seat on the bus. It's time we colored people stood up for our rights!" The question of "rights" went over my head. I was especially confused by the phrase "we colored people." I knew that everyone was "colored." Some people were brown. Others were pink (which I knew to be a blend of red and white), and others beige or tan (which were blends of brown and white). I remember how excited I was that year when Crayola came out with a box of crayons that included pink, beige, and tan, although I was somewhat perplexed by the flesh crayon. It was similar to tan but I knew that everyone was not "flesh"-colored. Nevertheless, I was happy to see my own tan color among the crayons. Up until then, crayon boxes had included only the basic colors and I had been unable to get pink, beige, or tan, except when I did water colors and had access to white paint to blend with red or brown.

In reponse to my teacher's pronouncement, I raised my hand and asked who "colored" people were. "Everyone in this school!" she replied, startled. "What color are they?" I asked. "We're brown! We're Negroes!" I had seen brown people; in fact, there were many at my school. I also knew that my own tan-colored skin was part brown. But I had never heard of the color "Negro" before, much less come across it among my crayons or paints. The whole discussion left me quite confused. At the end of class, my teacher gave me a note to take home to my mother, instructing her to have a talk with me about being Negro and about segregation. Many years later, my mother told me that she had avoided the subject up until this point because she did not want me to develop a sense of inferiority. Now, however, she tried to explain the absurdity of segregated schools, water fountains, public parks, theaters, restaurants, hospitals, funeral homes, and cemeteries. She agreed that our family was "tan" rather than "brown." (There were some pink and beige family members, however, who I later discovered were not pink or beige at all but looked "white." I had never seen anyone the color of the white crayon or blackboard chalk).

My mother went on to explain how we came to be "tan" Negroes, throwing in details about African slavery and about our Irish, English, French, American Indian, Asian Indian, and possibly German-Jewish ancestry. She concluded by saying that we were a blend of many things, and thus only part Negro. But we were still members of the Negro race—which was another word for colored people—because of our African ancestry. This logic struck me as somewhat dubious, and I objected, "But, Mommy, when you mix brown and white, you don't get brown or white, you get tan." She told me it was not the same with people. Outwardly I acquiesced but was confused and disturbed by the conversation. I could not understand how I could have Asian Indian and African and Native American and several European backgrounds and be "Negro." How could you take one part of my whole background, the African part, and ignore the rest? "That's stupid," I thought. "That doesn't make any sense. One plus one equals two, not one."

I shelved the issue until 1965, when I stumbled upon an article in *Ebony* magazine that discussed race relations in Brazil. As I browsed through the article, my eyes fell upon a passage that spoke of these mysterious creatures called "mulattoes." They were the products of racial blending between Africans, Europeans—primarily Portuguese—and Native Americans, and were intermediate to these groups—"Just like me! Just Like Tabitha on *Bewitched*. Like Mr. Spock on *Star Trek!* Like twilight, that zone between day and night we all pass through at dusk and dawn." From that point on I sought to find ways of embracing "blackness" while at the same time identifying with my other backgrounds. In this odyssey the classroom became not merely an academic arena but a path to self-discovery, transformation, and personal liberation, even if these things were pursued under the often mocking or disapproving scrutiny of my peers and superiors.

I wanted to gain insight into why multiracial individuals of partial African American descent were prevented from embracing their other racial backgrounds in the United States. I discovered part of an answer in a social code called the "one-drop rule of hypodescent," which held that the offspring of interracial unions were to be defined racially as African American, regardless of the racial identity of their other parent. And not only the children of interracial unions, but the grandchildren and great-grandchildren and great-great-grandchildren—in fact, anyone who had any traceable African descent, anyone with so much as "one drop of African blood," was designated as black under the one-drop rule. European Americans concocted this rule so as to maintain social distinctions between themselves and African Americans, their subordinates. The dominant whites used the one-drop rule to justify legal prohibitions against interracial sexual relations, and especially interracial marriage, in order to preserve white racial and cultural "purity." The rule also, conveniently, served to increase the number of slaves and exempted white landowners (particularly slaveholders) from the legal obligation of passing on inheritance and other benefits of paternity to their multiracial offspring. Moreover, the rule helped maintain white racial privilege by supporting other legal and informal barriers to racial equality in most aspects of social life—both public barriers (e.g., political, economic, educational) and private ones (e.g., residential, associational, interpersonal). The one-drop rule did not become a normative part of the legal apparatus in the United States until the early twentieth century (circa 1915), but it gained currency as the informal or "commonsense" definition of blackness over the course of the seventeenth and eighteenth centuries. (Other rules of hypodescent that used different formulas to define legal blackness had existed since the colonial period.) This was increasingly the case during the nineteenth century and definitively so by the 1920s, by which time the one-drop rule had become an accepted part of the U.S. social fabric.

Most people are unaware that the one-drop rule is unique to the United States and applies specifically to Americans of African descent. Vast numbers of individuals—except perhaps African Americans—remain equally uninformed about the rule's oppressive origins. There is an even greater lack of awareness of the oppressive effects this mechanism of social control has had on multiracial-identified individuals. Most people in the United States never question the rule's "illogic." They thus reinforce, if only unwittingly, the notion that blackness and whiteness are mutually exclusive, if not hierarchical, and objective categories of experience.

The issues surrounding multiracial identity in the United States are not, however, limited to the experience of individuals of predominantly African American and European American descent. And during the past decade the adequacy of the black-white paradigm for understanding the past, the present, and particularly the future of U.S. race relations has been challenged from many quarters. Nevertheless, there are several salient reasons for focusing specifically on the significance of multiracial identity as it relates to the construction of racial blackness.

First, for generations African Americans have been the largest designated racial "minority" in the United States. Second, while the law has been preoccupied with race in general, the place of blackness in U.S. jurisprudence (including post–civil rights challenges to formal expressions of racism) makes a contemporary examination of the progeny of black-white unions particularly significant.

Furthermore, I contend that the black-white paradigm has been the touchstone for the treatment of all racialized "Others" in the United States. Despite its limited application to the experience of those racial "Others," the black-white paradigm has provided the context in which those experiences have been grounded historically—and it continues to do so today. Unless otherwise indicated, therefore, the words "mulatto,"[1] "multiracial," and "biracial" are used interchangeably in this book to refer to individuals of predominantly European American and African American descent, although other backgrounds—particularly Native American—may be included in their lineage. "Black" generally refers to individuals who are considered

to be predominantly African American in racial makeup, although the term is sometimes used as a synonym for "African American" and "African-descent American,"
categories that encompass both "black" and "multiracial" individuals.

Given that the genetic, archaeological, and linguistic evidence indicates that the
first human communities evolved in Central Africa millennia ago, everyone in the
United States is in some generic sense an African-descent American. Between 90,000
and 180,000 years ago, populations in Africa spread throughout Africa, Asia, Europe,
and the Pacific; perhaps as early as 30,000 years ago but at least as recently as
15,000 years ago, they migrated to the Americas. Through adaptation to various
environments they evolved into geographical aggregates of populations displaying
differences in skin color, hair and facial morphology, and other physical features
commonly referred to as "racial traits." These physical differences (phenotypes)
reflect variations in genetic information (genotypes) that are transmitted through
one's ancestors. Nevertheless, human beings as members of the same species *Homo
sapiens sapiens* share 90 to 95 percent of their genes.

If geno-phenotypical diversity in the form of racial traits is a biological fact, the
boundaries delineating geno-phenotypical subgroupings are not discrete or fixed
entities. These boundaries have always been eroded by contact—through migration,
trade, and war—which has inevitably set into motion a countertrend toward "racial
entropy." Over time racial entropy levels out absolute differences by diffusing
common genetic information—and ultimately common phenotypical traits—
throughout the general population if no forces intervene to prevent this process.
Consequently, the 5 to 10 percent of total genetic information that determines phenotypical traits associated with racial differentiation is itself the product of millennia
of genetic "blending."[2] Indeed, considering how long *Homo sapiens* have inhabited
the planet earth, a "multiracial" lineage is the norm rather than the exception
among humans. Anthropologist Jack Forbes has calculated that all humans have
about 32,000 "statistical" ancestors over the previous fifteen generations, which is
approximately 300 to 375 years. Trace a person's lineage back even further, and the
number of ancestors is staggering.[3]

Generally speaking, the smaller the proportion of any given ancestry the more
probable it is that the number of genes inherited from that ancestry is also pro-
portionately smaller. Yet it is not the case that individuals will necessarily inherit a
genotypical blueprint that is in direct proportion to their fraction of a specific ancestry. Genes are randomly distributed in individuals such that although it is highly
unlikely, an individual with, for example, one European and one West African parent may in fact inherit no genes from West African forbears. Such a person would
not only appear phenotypically European but would in fact be genotypically European as well. There is no guarantee that a person with one or more West African
ancestors will inherit genetic information from those forbears or exhibit discernible
West African phenotypical traits.[4]

In individuals whose ancestry is three-fourths or even one-half West African who are phenotypically able to "pass" as European, there are, presumably, fewer Africoid genes than would be expected.[5] Yet individuals whose ancestry is one-fourth or less West African are rarely if ever phenotypically distinguishable from Europeans. In these cases, there is the "illusion" of complete "whiteness" despite their partial African ancestry. Only at the genetic level, in the DNA itself, would we be able to see such an individual's Africoid and Europid ancestors. Nonetheless, the one-drop rule designates as black any individual of any traceable West African ancestry, regardless of geno-phenotype.

The biological concept of race attempts to explain geno-phenotypical differentiation as it is perceived and interpreted. But racial boundaries are illusive. Phenotypical traits are not transmitted in genetic clusters but vary independently. This fact has led some people to assert that there is no such thing as race. They view race as an unfortunate legacy of the past five hundred years of human history and recommend that we discard the concept of race altogether. Others argue that race has a social reality, even if the concept has no valid scientific basis. Those who hold that race is a social construction point out that race has historically been a powerful force in Western thought and behavior, one embedded in the structure of social institutions. Even people who maintain that race is an illusion recognize the social reality of race in the West and cannot avoid using the term even as they deny its existence.[6]

Like the larger educated community, scholars have reached no consensus on the definition of race, although they generally agree that the concept should be regarded as a neutral classificatory term. One could argue not that we need to dispense with the concept of race—i.e., geno-phenotypical diversity—but that race is simply one of many differentiating categories, like sex, class, and so on, that influence human experience. Rather than reject the concept out of hand, we should transcend essentialized notions of race and deal more forthrightly with racism and racial inequality. Racial discrimination, oppression, hatred, and other odious forms of human thought and behavior have less to do with race than with abuses and atrocities that have been committed in the name of race.

Any attempt to use the term "race" in an objective, scientific, and functionally neutral manner is nevertheless undermined by unavoidable complexity and contradiction. Despite its supposed neutrality as a biological concept, race has historically been (and continues to be) inextricably intertwined with a society's distribution of wealth, power, privilege, and prestige, and therefore with inequality. In the national consciousness of the United States, race has almost always had priority over socioeconomic class, sex/gender, age, or religion as an indicator of social and economic inequality. In fact race has often served to disguise, or deflect attention from, other types of social division (as, for example, when poor white farmers in the post-Reconstruction South were encouraged to identify with wealthy white planters rather than with the poor blacks with whom they had more in common economically). The concept of racial difference has created a chasm of social distance expressed both explicitly and implicitly in all kinds of social intercourse. And it is this social construction of race, not the biological concept, that has had such a deleterious effect on the social order, in this country and elsewhere.[7]

The social sciences attempt to explain the sociopolitical reality of race quite apart from its use as a concept in the biological sciences. Accordingly, racial formation theory challenges the position that race is an illusion, that race is something that we can and should move beyond. It also rejects the position that race is an "objective reality," the essentialist formulation that views race as absolutely fixed in biological datum. The racial formation paradigm acknowledges that race is a social construction: The concept of race is based on biological characteristics, but the selection of particular human features for purposes of racial signification has changed over time and is necessarily a sociohistorical process.[8] This process groups different geno-phenotypical features for social and ideological, not scientific, purposes. The resulting racial categories affect a given society's allocation of wealth, power, privilege, and prestige. In fact racial categories are "unstable" and "decentered" complexes of sociocultural meanings that are continuously being created, inhabited, contested, transformed, and destroyed.[9]

Racial formation thus plays an important role in structuring and representing the social world, despite the unavoidable contradictions inherent in the concept of race and the somewhat arbitrary nature of biophysical racial groupings and boundaries—not to mention the abuses and genocidal practices that have been committed in their name. Race may be thought of not only as an element of social structure but also as a dimension of human cultural representation and signification. This does not mean it is an illusion—far from it. Race is both a microlevel phenomenon of the individual psyche and interpersonal relations, and a macrolevel component of collective identities, from the "intrapsychic to the supranational."[10]

By recognizing race as a social and historical construct, racial formation theory makes it possible to analyze the process by which a society determines racial meanings and assigns racial identities. At any given moment in space and time many interpretations of race exist in the form of "racial projects." Every racial project is necessarily a discursive or cultural initiative. Such an initiative involves an interpretation, representation, or explanation of racial dynamics by means of identity politics that attempts to rescue racial identities from their distortion and erasure by the dominant society. At the same time, each racial project is also a political initiative. Its goal is to organize and redistribute resources, a process in which the state is often called upon to play a significant role. The state has historically exercised power not only in the politics of racial exclusion (and inclusion) but also in enforcing racial definition, classification, and, ultimately, identification.[11]

Racial formation theory suggests that the articulation of racial meanings is a multidimensional process of competing "projects" that may stem from a variety of potential sources. These may include "subjective" phenomena such as racial identities, religion, and popular and elite culture. They may also involve "objective" social structural phenomena such as political movements and parties, state institutions and policies, market processes, and so on.[12] The pattern of racial meanings and identities, the racial dimensions of social inequality, and the degree of political mobilization based on race, therefore, all display instability and flexibility. Consequently, the logic of race is determined in multiple ways at any given historical moment. For the majority of people in any given society, race may be understood uncritically and defined on the basis of simple "common sense." Racial identities are reproduced by their own "naturalness" and "taken-for-grantedness" in the daily lives and conversations of the society. In such a context, there would be minimal contesting of the meaning of race and it would be limited to a few marginalized racial projects at most. In another social context, race might be highly politicized and the site of significant social mobilization. Here we would expect to see a high degree of racial contestation. In such a setting we would expect national debate about race and a great deal of popular uncertainty about the significance of race in everyday life.[13]

Some scholars, as well as many members of the public, not only view "ethnicity" as a less "problematical" concept—and thus as a suitable substitution for race—but also erroneously view racial and ethnic lines as critically different from each other. Ethnicity generally refers to a social subset whose members are thought by themselves and others to share a common culture that sets them apart from other groups in the society. These individuals also share a common ancestry or origin (real or imagined)—and thus may have similar or common geno-phenotypical traits—that also distinguish them from other social groups. In addition, they may participate, in varying degrees, in shared activities in which their common origin and culture are significant.[14]

Because ethnic formation includes notions of both race and culture, the term "multiethnic" might seem more descriptive than "multiracial." "Multiethnic" might seem to lend itself to a more nuanced discussion of identity, that is. The notion of ethnicity experienced as culture—the "culturalization" of ethnicity—is, nevertheless, different from the experience of racial or geno-phenotypical and ancestral differentiation—the "racialization" of ethnicity. This does not mean that ethno-cultural differences between groups that are ethno-racially similar (for example, English Americans and Irish Americans) have not been the source of prejudice and discrimination. But it does mean that the overriding structural wedge in the United States, in terms of the distribution of wealth, power, privilege, and prestige, has been based primarily on notions of ethno-racial difference and only secondarily on differences of an ethno-cultural nature.

Acknowledgments

Neither time nor space allows me to acknowledge the countless acts of support and encouragement I received from hundreds of individuals who helped bring this book to fruition. I would like to extend a special thanks to Sylvia Brown, Victoria Beardon, and Mary Crain, who knew about this book before I did and encouraged me to write it. Paul R. Spickard, Maria P. P. Root, and Teresa K. Williams-Leon provided personal and professional support and encouragement over the past ten years—and chided me when I needed it—which made it possible to carry on in the face of obstacles that at times seemed insurmountable.

Gary Nash read part of the manuscript and saved me from historical errors. Paul R. Spickard, Maria P. P. Root, and F. James Davis also read the manuscript and provided very constructive and supportive feedback. David Estrin and Connie McNeely helped me make important cuts on early drafts that tightened the manuscript without sacrificing my ideas. José Garcia provided invaluable research assistance. Miki Goral and Norma Corral, who are the backbone of the Reference Department at the UCLA Research Library, provided invaluable assistance on this and other projects over the years and left no stone unturned in helping track down obscure sources. I am also indebted to Grafikart Copy Shop for its stellar technical support; to Hana Fujii, for her input on the cover design; and to Lori Pierce, Josef Liles, and Lars Linton, who helped me proofread the manuscript.

My thanks to the University of California, Santa Barbara, for awarding me an Academic Senate grant to do research for the book, and a Faculty Career Development Award for release time from teaching in order to complete it. I owe a special debt to my colleagues and the staff in the Department of Sociology at UCSB, who have created a uniquely stimulating and supportive environment in which to work.

Special thanks go to the many individuals who have been my friends and comrades in the struggle over the past thirteen years: Nina Gordon, Ramona Douglass, Levonne Gaddy, Carlos Fernández, Nancy and Roosevelt Brown, Steve and Ruth

White, Faye Mandell, Ron Vidal, B. J. Winchester, Edwin Darden, Steve and Celesta Cheney-Rice, Irene Carr, Eamon Buehning, Susan Graham, Francis Wardle, and Roberta and Clifford Brown. Others contributed directly or indirectly to this project and deserve mention. I think particularly of Catherine ("Katia") Squires, Adam Gottdank, Lorene Boudaghians, Cynthia Nakashima, Elaine Minor, George E. Brooks, Karen Gatchel, Kaylynn Ewing, Lucinda and Therman Newsome, Kerry and Mathew Iadarola, James Wallace, Jennifer Gong, Greg Tanaka, Ari Rosner, Kim Williams, Jonathan Cordero, Kim da Costa, Rebecca Chiyoko-King, Thomas López, Paul Sachet, Mary Beth Crain, Audrey Chang, Carlos Alberto Torres, Beatrice McHenry, Susan McHenry, Cleo Reynolds, Kimberly Jones, Ken Wilber, Stephen Cornell, Mary Britton, Theo Mitchell, James U. Collins III, Maureen Silos, Rani Bush, Nina Moss, Leon Ferder, Ludwig and Francis Lauerhass, Ray Vagas, Ayuko Babu, Angela Alvarez, Karen Moeck, Terry Wilson, Kook Dean, Greg Mayeda, Uriah Carr, Daphne Bell, Yolande Bell, Carol Clark, Tiffany Rocquemore, Marian Ferreira, Donna Johnson, Carrie Jones, Carol Carnes, Paula Moore, Diane Watanabe, Ladeen Werden, Norman Guy, Ronald Tiggle, Barbara Hand Chow, Sheila Gardette, and Davey Silverman.

I must also thank my "Montecito cousins," Nicole, Kelly, Chris, David, Hana, Alex, Chomper, and Oscar, for their moral support, and Paulette Haban and Jeremy Busacca, as well as Roger Friedland, who provided me with shelter and transportation, respectively, during my "migrant faculty" days. I will also be eternally grateful to Nadia Kim, Julie Silvers, and Shadi Alai, along with the hundreds of other students who have enrolled in my classes at UCLA and UCSB and who have had faith in my vision when others have not.

Janet Francendese of Temple University Press is an exemplary editor, as anyone who has worked with her knows. I am grateful to her and to the readers recruited by the press to review the book.

I hope that my many unnamed friends, colleagues, and relatives will take whatever profit or pleasure they may derive from this book as partial repayment for their steadfast love and friendship. Each contributed to making this a better book. Of course, I alone am responsible for the shortcomings that remain.

More Than Black?

Introduction

In 1931 George Samuel Schuyler (1895–1977) published the first successful satirical novel in African American literature. Entitled *Black No More*, the novel centers around Dr. Junius Crookman, an African American doctor who invents an electronic treatment that will "change Black to White in three days,"[1] and promises, in Crookman's view, to cure the race problem in America. A former numbers racketeer, Hank Johnson, helps the doctor promote his invention. Together they establish a chain of extremely successful "Black-No-More" clinics throughout the United States. As the African American population begins to vanish, entrepreneurs of both races face potential economic ruin because slums cease to be profitable business investments. It is no longer necessary to enforce the Black Codes, and poor white southerners awaken to the sudden reality that they are at the bottom of the social hierarchy.

As the months and years pass and the African American population becomes almost extinct, black children are born to ostensibly white couples with greater and greater frequency. Although these offspring can themselves be transformed into whites through Dr. Crookman's treatment, their black infancy is a source of embarrassment to many of their parents. The rapid disappearance of African Americans causes social, political, and economic upheavals that lead to panic and paranoia across the nation. Meanwhile rabid racists go insane trying to determine who is a former black. Eventually the Black-No-More organization is pressured into shutting down.

The climax of Schuyler's satire comes when Dr. Crookman, appointed Surgeon General by a Republican administration, publishes the results of his study comparing "original" whites with "converted" whites. To Dr. Crookman's amazement his findings indicate that it is still possible to distinguish between the two types of whites: The "converted" whites are "two to three shades lighter" than the "original" whites. Schuyler comments on the irony of the situation and offers a rationale for the demise of the Black-No-More organization:

To a society that had been taught to venerate whiteness for over three hundred years, this announcement was rather staggering. What was the world coming to, if the blacks were whiter than the whites? Many people in the upper class began to look askance at their very pale complexions. If it were true that extreme whiteness was evidence of the possession of Negro blood, of having once been a member of a pariah class, then surely it were well not to be so white! . . .

A Dr. Cutten Prodd wrote a book proving that all enduring gifts to society came from those races whose skin color was not exceedingly pale, pointing out that the Norwegians and other Nordic peoples had been in savagery when Egypt and Crete were at the height of their development. Prof. Handen Moutthe, the eminent anthropologist (who was well known for his popular work on *The Sex Life of Left-Handed Morons among the Ainus*) announced that as a result of his long research among the palest citizens, he was convinced they were mentally inferior and that their children should be segregated from the others in school. Professor Moutthe's findings were considered authoritative because he had spent three entire weeks of hard work assembling his data. Four state legislatures immediately began to consider bills calling for separate schools for pale children. Those of the upper class began to look around for ways to get darker. It became the fashion for them to spend hours at the seashore basking naked in the sunshine and then to dash back, heavily bronzed, to their homes, and, preening themselves in their dusky skins, lord it over their paler, and thus less fortunate, associates. Beauty shops began to sell face powders named Poudre Negre, Poudre le Egyptienne and L'Afrique.[2]

Now the roles in the racial hierarchy are reversed; the "converted" whites have become pariahs and the social apparatus created to deal with the "Negro Problem" has to be reconstructed to deal with the "white problem." Schuyler wryly suggests that the solution is quite simple: African Americans must not only adopt European American culture but must literally disappear as a distinct racial group. Unfortunately, because American culture depends on racial hierarchy for its very identity, it is necessary to create a new racial hierarchy in order to maintain the nation's social, political, and economic equilibrium.

The Eurocentric sensibility that Schuyler satirizes emerged with Europe's rise to global dominion in the fifteenth century and has dominated Western thought and behavior ever since. Part I of this book, "White over Black," examines the relationship between modernity, colonialism, and the emergence of the Eurocentric paradigm, which is based on European scientific and technological domination on an unprecedented scale. Beginning in the fifteenth century, Europe became the center of a global civilization through its imperialist program of exploration and exploitation of non-Western "Others." The ideology underlying this program of expansion and domination presumes the superiority of European values and customs, and rationalizes their imposition on "the Other" as a beneficial "civilizing" process.

Chapter 1 explores the relationship between modernity and the Eurocentric paradigm and emphasizes the implications of white racism and white supremacy for the non-Western "Other," particularly people of African descent. Chapter 2 discusses the impact of white supremacy on racial formation in the United States, where European Americans, in order to preserve both their cultural and racial "purity" and their dominant status, enforced the one-drop rule. This social mechanism relegated multiracial individuals to the subordinate group by designating as "black" all those with any African ancestry. The one-drop rule perpetuated a binary racial system in which people are defined as either/or, black or white. The impact of the one-drop rule reached a draconian extreme with the institutionalization of Jim Crow segregation in the late-nineteenth-century American South.

Historically, the one-drop rule has created unique identity issues for people of both European American and African American traceable descent. Most of them, having been designated "black" by the social and cultural norms of white society, have identified themselves as black, although a significant minority has resisted this designation. European American control over the boundaries between black and white, between dominant and subordinate, has therefore been relative. I examine this "resistance" and provide the first in-depth study of multiracial identity as part of the ongoing sociohistorical process of racial formation, as outlined by sociologists Omi and Winant's *Racial Formation in the United States from the 1960s to the 1990s* (1994). Drawing on this racial formation theory, I propose multiracial identity as a racial "project" that is simultaneously a cultural and political initiative directed at challenging institutions, polices, conditions, and rules directly and indirectly based on the one-drop rule.

The formation of a multiracial identity can be characterized broadly according to two basic strategies of resistance, both of which challenge the dichotomization of blackness and whiteness that originates in Eurocentric thinking. Both of these strategies also resist institutional policies and structures and challenge social attitudes that uphold the one-drop rule and the binary racial project. However, one strategy uses Eurocentric dynamics to its own advantage by maintaining the hierarchical valuation of whiteness over blackness. The other strategy reflects a "new multiracial identity," which deconstructs the Eurocentric dichotomy as well as the hierarchical valuation of blackness and whiteness as mutually exclusive and unequal. Given the longstanding tension in black-white relations, this new multiracial identity may be viewed as a positive development as the United States enters the new millennium.

Part II, "Black No More," analyzes resistance tactics that have maintained the hierarchical valuation of whiteness over blackness. The "Black-No-More" strategy was motivated by the legal system of segregation that sought to control the potential threat to white dominance posed by individuals of African descent. Generated by racist pressure that has rewarded whiteness and punished blackness, this strategy therefore has been a means of avoiding racial social stigma and a reaction to the denial of white racial privilege that comes with European ancestry. I argue, nonetheless, that this strategy brings into sharp focus the illogic of the one-drop rule, which deemed as inferior individuals who were culturally, and in many cases phenotypically, different from whites in name only.

Chapter 3 examines strategies of resistance such as "passing." This is a radical form of integration whereby individuals with a European phenotype and cultural orientation turn their backs on their African heritage, temporarily or permanently, in order to enjoy the privileges of "whiteness." Compared to overt battles against racial inequality, passing may appear to be a form of opportunism, or selling out. When viewed on a spectrum of tactics, however, it is clear that passing is an underground tactic, a "conspiracy of silence" that seeks to beat racial discrimination at its own game. This chapter also explores such forms of resistance as the formation of blue-vein societies, which were pluralistic elites within the African American community. Membership in these societies was determined by individuals' phenotypical and cultural resemblance with European Americans. By re-creating the dominant European American image within the subordinate group, these societies sought to distance themselves from common stereotypes of blacks. At best these societies created the illusion of having escaped the taint of subordinate group status; they never actually achieved equality with whites. Yet both the formation of blue-vein societies and the strategy of passing contested the black-white dichotomy and thus subverted the one-drop rule, even if neither actually overturned it.

Chapter 4 looks at other strategies of resistance, including the formation of enclaves on the periphery of both the African American and European American communities, such as "triracial isolates" and Louisiana Creoles of color. The term "triracial isolates" refers to some two hundred rural communities scattered throughout the eastern United States, particularly the South, inhabited by people who are a blend of European, African, and Native American ancestry. Like the blue-vein societies, they are pluralistic in nature. But while the blue-vein societies formed an urban elite within the African American community, triracial isolates live apart from both blacks and whites in communities on the fringes of villages and towns, or in isolated rural enclaves. What these triracial communities have in common are less actual cultural bonds than their refusal to accept the one-drop rule. Most of them affirm only two components—Native American and European American—if they acknowledge their multiracial ancestry at all. In this sense, their self-definition appears to be more reactionary than revolutionary.

During the colonial period, the experience of multiracial individuals in the lower South ("Latin" North America), particularly Louisiana, differed from that in the North and upper South (Anglo-North America). This region, which was settled by the French and Spanish, was more tolerant of miscegenation. Although there were legal barriers to interracial marriages, rape, temporary extramarital relations, and extended concubinage and common-law unions between white men and women of color were approved, if not encouraged, by prevailing, unwritten mores. In addition, Europeans in the region granted multiracial individuals (commonly referred to as Louisiana Creoles of color) an intermediate status and privileges inferior to those of whites but superior to those of blacks. These comparatively more favorable circumstances changed when Louisiana was annexed by the United States in 1803. The U.S. occupation of Louisiana, and the implementation of the one-drop rule in that region, reversed the intermediate status Creoles of color had maintained under the French and Spanish regimes. With Anglo-North Americanization, Creoles of color began the long quest to preserve their intermediate status, as they watched Louisiana's racial order become polarized into black and white.

Ultimately multiracial individuals in Louisiana were relegated to the subordinate status of blacks, deprived of citizenship, politically disenfranchised, and eventually segregated from European Americans. It is no accident that the implications of blackness in U.S. jurisprudence played themselves out in Louisiana in the landmark 1896 Supreme Court decision involving a Creole of one-eighth African American descent, Hommeré Plessy. In *Plessy v. Ferguson* the Court conceded that the legal definition of blackness varied from state to state and was thus beyond its jurisdiction. It nevertheless took brief "judicial notice" of what was assumed to be racial common sense: An African American was anyone with any amount of African American traceable descent. *Plessy* set a judicial precedent for future rulings on legal definitions of blackness. It also established Jim Crow segregation in public railway transportation and, shortly thereafter, in public facilities and schools.

The Louisiana Creoles of color and triracial isolates challenged the social inequities associated with being designated African American, as did the blue-vein societies. But they often sought to achieve this goal through the formation of communities "outside" the social and cultural parameters of the African American community. The blue-vein societies used their racial and cultural whiteness to challenge the legal liabilities that came with being designated black. But these elites did see themselves, however tenuously, as part of the larger African American community. They sought to maximize legal rights for African Americans without at the same time necessarily seeking to overturn official definitions of race. Their goal, though this was not always made explicit, was to redistribute resources and social goods (e.g., educational, political, and economic benefits) along racial lines. In their pursuit of this goal individuals contested the construction of blackness and whiteness but supported the racial hierarchy in order to maintain their own racial privilege. In addition, the triracial isolates and Louisiana Creoles of color created alternative third identities (or ternary racial projects) that actually destabilized the American binary racial project. Although these communities did not in fact dismantle the one-drop rule they were successful, to varying degrees, in breaking it.

The purpose of the one-drop rule was to draw boundaries between black and white, assert the superiority of whiteness, and deny equality to African Americans. It also had the unintended consequence of encouraging group identity among those designated as black, which enabled blacks to organize and eventually culminated in the civil rights movement of the 1950s and 1960s. The civil rights movement dismantled Jim Crow segregation and achieved the passage of historic legislation that dissolved legal (if not de facto) racial discrimination and inequality, including the last laws against interracial intermarriage in 1967 (in *Loving v. Virginia*). The *Loving* decision and the comparatively more fluid social relations that followed it led to growth not only in the number of interracial marriages but also to the birth of "first-generation" (or biracial) offspring. Eventually many interracial couples began challenging the one-drop rule by instilling pride in their children about their multiracial identity.

The carriers of this new identity are primarily these "first-generation" individuals, but they also include a smaller number of "multigenerational" persons. "First-generation" individuals have one parent who is both socially and self-designated as black and one who is socially and self-designated as white, regardless of these parents' actual racial genealogy. "Multigenerational" individuals have parents, or even generations of ancestors, who have been viewed as black by society although their backgrounds include African American, European American, and other ancestries (particularly Native American); these individuals, and/or their parents and ancestors, have resisted identifying solely with the African American community. By the 1990s, the growing population of black-white interracial couples, as well as "first-generation" and "multigenerational" individuals of African American and European American descent—along with other intermarried couples and multiracial-identified individuals from various racial backgrounds—began lobbying for changes in official racial designations that would make possible a "multiracial" identification.

Part III, "More Than Black," describes the configuration of this new multiracial identity. In Chapters 5 and 6 I argue that the motivation behind this identity differs significantly from previous strategies of resistance. In previous racial projects individuals subverted or broke the one-drop rule by embracing their European American ancestry as a means of gaining social advantage. The "more-than-black" strategy reflected in the formation of a new multiracial identity seeks to dismantle the one-drop rule altogether. This identity thus deconstructs the dichotomization of blackness and whiteness, as well as the hierarchical relationship between these two categories of experience. Its goal is to rescue racial identities from distortion and erasure by incorporating both African American and European American backgrounds. Individuals who display this identity recognize the commonalities between blacks and whites (integration), but at the same time appreciate the differences (pluralism). The new multiracial identity, as one of the fruits of the civil right movement of the 1950s and 1960s, thus builds on the egalitarian, pluralist tenets of the racial movements of the 1960s, which sought to achieve the equality of difference. It also resuscitates the integrationist goals of the 1950s—which were rejected because of their assimilationist implications—by simultaneously seeking to replace this hierarchical integration with a more egalitarian dynamic.

Chapter 7 analyzes the debate that emerged between 1988 and 1998 surrounding multiracial identity, generally speaking, and, more specifically, the collection and reporting of data on multiracial-identified individuals on the decennial census. Some of the most important information relating to that discussion is presented for the first time in this book in the form of data collected through observation of the public behavior of students at the University of California at Los Angeles, Santa Barbara, and Santa Cruz, and that of individuals in attendance at support group meetings and conferences on the subject of multiracial identity. It also includes data obtained through observation as a member of the advisory board of the Association of MultiEthnic Americans (AMEA) and former advisory board member of Project RACE (Reclassify All Children Equally, 1992—1997). These two organizations have sought to revise the collection of official racial and ethnic data to make possible a multiracial identification. My analysis also draws on secondary literature, along with data obtained from academic journals, the popular print media—newspapers, magazines, and the internet—television and radio, U.S. Congressional hearings on racial census categories, *Federal Register* reports, and 1990 census data tabulations (available through the Statistical Information Office, Bureau of the Census).

In particular, my analysis of the census debate takes up the question of African American opposition to multiracial identity. Many African Americans have argued that the one-drop rule, although originally oppressive, has been a means of mobilizing African Americans in the struggle against white racial privilege. These people also view the rule as a means of preventing erosion in the number of individuals who under the current system are counted as black. These numbers, they argue, are needed to enforce and support civil rights legislation and claims aimed at tracking historical and contemporary patterns of discrimination, and in arriving at goals for achieving social and economic equity. African American concerns about multiracial identity are not limited to the potential impact it may have on the collection of data needed to support civil rights legislation and other claims aimed at tracking patterns of racial discrimination. They also fear that many individuals will designate themselves as "multiracial" rather than as black in order to escape the social stigma associated with blackness. This would undermine the integrity and solidarity of African-descent Americans just as "passing," blue-vein societies, Louisiana Creoles of color, and triracial isolate communities have done.

Those multiracial identity projects, the thinking goes, were not only products of the Eurocentrism in the larger society but were also responsible for a divisive and pernicious "colorism" that grew up between multiracial individuals and blacks. By granting the preferential treatment of the former over the latter, the phenomenon of colorism has historically created a divide between the less privileged black masses and the privileged few. Some critics maintain that multiracial individuals—particularly those who physically approximate European Americans—would be co-opted into the mainstream of society as provisional whites (as has been the case in Brazil). Others assert that multiracial individuals would be granted a structurally intermediate status separate from and subordinate to dominant whites, but also separate from and superior to that of African Americans (as has been the case in South Africa).

Part IV, "Black No More or More Than Black?" considers the new multiracial identity as it relates to these larger social concerns. In Chapter 8 I address some of these questions by examining larger contemporary trends in black-white relations and race relations generally. I argue that the new multiracial identity as a racial project is not synonymous with the psychosocial pathology of colorism. I point out, however, that this identity is not inherently immune to the lingering effects of insidious toxins in the racial ecology. The desire to embrace a European ancestral/cultural background as a way to affirm a more egalitarian identity could be subverted by larger social forces. Multiracial individuals could be granted the status of new "insiders" who are rewarded with greater opportunities to achieve wealth, power, privilege, and prestige. The "outsiders," the black masses, would be pushed further onto the periphery of society. This new politics of racial inclusion could undermine the very gains in civil rights that now make the recognition of multiracial identity a possibility. Racial status would remain essentially unchanged, although the relationship between race and opportunity would be modified. There would be an illusion of power sharing without any power sharing in fact.

The fact is that racial integration has allowed only a select few African-descent Americans to gain access to wealth, power, privilege, and prestige—and even in many of those cases the gains are circumscribed and may be easily eroded. Furthermore, the privileged few tend to be disproportionately of more "visible" European ancestry and share social and cultural values with affluent whites because of class identity. The black masses, along with darker-skinned individuals in other communities of color, remain disproportionately in blue-collar jobs and among the ranks of the underemployed and unemployed. The one-drop rule has ceased to be the primary factor determining the social location of African-descent Americans, but the politics and ideology behind it have not gone away. Phenotype—particularly skin color—is still a form of racial capital, in combination with the increasing significance of culture and class.

Contemporary black-white relations have thus shifted away from the racial apartheid of the past. Although this transition has been uneven, formal exclusion and coercion have been replaced with more informal dynamics. At the same time, we have witnessed another trend toward white hegemony in the form of inegalitarian integration, or assimilation. This half-hearted attack on white racial privilege merely weakens the black-white dichotomy while leaving the hierarchical structure intact. Assimilation, moreover, reflects the conservative political, social, and cultural agendas that have undermined the integrity of the African American community since the 1980s.

The shift from white domination to white hegemony indicates, however, that the criteria for racial whiteness may be expanding in the United States, as we see in the assimilation of select African-descent Americans who approximate the European American ideal. Theoretically, this process could increase the number of individuals with "insider" status and maintain the United States as an ostensibly "white" nation. A politics of racial inclusion would also be of strategic value given that the "white" or European American population in the United States will lose its numerical majority status in this century. If European Americans appear to have become more willing to bend the one-drop rule, African Americans, paradoxically yet understandably, hold on to this device ever more tenaciously, for the reasons noted above.

The use of the one-drop rule for cultural and political mobilization is most obvious in currents of Afrocentric discourse and in other racial projects that rely on the notion of a primordial African "race" and nation. Accordingly, some proponents of Afrocentric thought—particularly its more radical variants—have argued that multiracial identity is inimical to their goal of uniting African Americans as a cohesive force. Chapter 9 offers an examination of the deeper meaning of Afrocentric thought and its compatibility with the new multiracial identity. I argue that radical Afrocentrists ignore the potential that a multiracial identification may hold for challenging the imposition of what Victor Anderson calls a myopic and constricting "ontological blackness."[3] This is not to suggest that we should dismiss Afrocentric concerns about identity politics. Given the pervasiveness of white racism and supremacy, which have sought to prevent a radical African diasporic subjectivity, the strengths of Afrocentric discourse are undeniable: the fostering of group pride, solidarity, and self-respect among African-descent individuals; the challenging of the assimilationist strategy; and the perpetuation of differences in the manner of inegalitarian pluralism (apartheid).[4] But radical Afrocentrism also has its contradictions and weaknesses—notably, that its exponents often criticize the validity of the concept of "race" on the one hand while reinscribing essentialist notions of black identity on the other.[5]

One factor that divides Afrocentrism from the new multiracial identity is that "Afrocentrism" means different things to different people, and this has obscured its deeper significance. Although Afrocentrism is significantly related to African history and originated in Black Nationalist thought, it is more appropriately described as a paradigm that places African-descent individuals at the center of their analyses. In addition, Afrocentrism rejects the Eurocentric paradigm that has perpetuated the hierarchical ranking of racial difference. Moreover, Afrocentrism acknowledges a common cultural inheritance that all humans share as descendants of the first diaspora out of Africa. Yet many radical Afrocentrists' inclusive application of the term "black" to anyone and anything of African ancestry, no matter how remote in space or time, ignores the complex ancestral, genetic, and cultural diversity and blending that has taken place over the eons. One could argue, therefore, that some strains of radical Afrocentrism reaffirm the same oppressive mechanism inherent in the one-drop rule. If Afrocentric discourse is to dismantle Eurocentrism it must also deconstruct the "either/or" paradigm. More moderate variants of Afrocentrism are compatible with the new multiracial identity, as both are engaged in a critique of the pathologies of Eurocentrism and modernity but also challenge rigid essentialist notions of identity.[6] They point to more inclusive constructions of self and community that are absent from more radical Afrocentric discourse and could provide the basis for new forms of integration. The various types of African-derived subjectivity would be accommodated without at the same time negating a larger African-derived plurality or maintaining that plurality as a complete antithesis of whiteness. Part of the struggle for a radical African American collective subjectivity that furthers black liberation must necessarily be grounded in a process of decolonization. It must continually challenge and go beyond racial essentialism and the reinscription of notions of authentic identity.[7] This process should include ways of constructing self and community that oppose the either/or representation of blackness and whiteness created by the one-drop rule.

Chapter 9 also provides an analysis of the new multiracial identity within the general theoretical frameworks of "hybridity" and multiple identities. In particular, I draw on analyses of the relationship between Eurocentrism and modernity, and of racial identity politics discussed in postcolonial and postmodernist studies. I argue that the new multiracial identity has the same impetus that lies behind the linking of the Afro-Asian world with the formation of Western Europe in postcolonial (and Afrocentric) discourse. What are generally considered the "borders" between the West and the larger non-Western world are actually porous "frontiers." They have been more blurred and permeable than Eurocentric rhetoric and imagery have acknowledged. In addition, Western European domination of others through apartheid and assimilation is only one, albeit important, side of the historical narrative.[8] The other side of the coin is the hybridization that originated in the European absorption and adaptation of "others" in the form of egalitarian cultural and, frequently, racial integration. To a significant degree, what we refer to as European civilization "is actually a universal human heritage that for historical, political, and geographical reasons" has been bequeathed to the modern world "in the guise of a European or Western synthesis." It is significant that the synthesis and stamp are uniquely European, but the fact that the sources are plural and intercontinental is equally meaningful.[9] This is particularly so when we consider that the racial and cultural narcissism that buttressed Eurocentrism and European imperialism has deliberately obscured these connections.

As part of the general assault on Eurocentrism, postcolonial discourse not only challenges notions of racial purity but also questions the notion that race is an objective reality absolutely fixed in biological data. Because modern science has been unable to produce empirical data to confirm clearly delineated biophysical racial boundaries, many "deconstructive" postcolonial thinkers recommend that the concept of race be dispensed with altogether. They tend to present race as a problem, a legacy of the past, and a misconception that should be consigned to the dustbin of history. Many also argue that any kind of racial identification—multiracial or otherwise—is fraught with irreconcilable contradictions. I note, however, that this opposition to a multiracial identity does not originate simply in the conviction that race is a false concept but in the misinterpretation of the discourse on multiracial identity as grounded in biological rather than ancestral notions of race. Biological notions of race and those based on ancestry may overlap but are not synonymous. The former are based on one's genetic inheritance irrespective of ancestral background. The latter are grounded in the backgrounds in one's lineage or genealogy, irrespective of genetic concerns, and are the basis of the new multiracial identity. Exposure to these backgrounds enhances and helps to concretize a feeling of kinship.

Such critics also dismiss claims that the new multiracial identity is "new" at all because everyone is in fact "multiracial." This "deconstructive" postcolonial perspective seeks to "transcend race" altogether in pursuit of a universal humanism. Individuals who support this position believe that all categories and identities—racial and otherwise—are largely sociocultural constructs (or mere "fictions") that have no basis in "reality." Any notion of transcending race by reifying it through a multiracial identification is thus hopelessly naive, if not politically regressive. The proponents of the "constructive" postcolonial perspective, however, posit a multiracial identity as a form of "racial transcendence" that acknowledges a more inclusive identity based on a multiplicity of ancestral backgrounds. While it is true that a multiracial lineage or background is normative among humans, this perspective argues nevertheless that most individuals display single-racial (or monoracial) identities despite the many backgrounds that may make up their genealogy. The new multiracial identity is embraced by individuals who seek to ground their sense of "we-ness" in more than one community and feel a sense of kinship with several communities. Moreover, this identity challenges the legitimacy of racial hierarchy in determining the distribution of social wealth, power, privilege, and prestige. I contend that the new multiracial identity is part of a broader postcolonial social transformation and consciousness, although it does not in and of itself dismiss the concept of race. It does, however, challenge essentialist and reductionist notions of race and de-centers racial categories that originate in the dominant Eurocentric paradigm by pointing to the ambiguity and multiplicity of identities.

Today's more iconoclastic attitudes toward racial identity—particularly the new multiracial identity—seem themselves to reflect an even more fundamental shift in consciousness, frequently referred to as postmodernism. The goal is to move beyond the either/or paradigm of dichotomous hierarchical ranking of differences and instead incorporate concepts of "partly," "mostly," or "both/neither." This thinking has made itself felt not only in new models of multiracial identity but in a variety of disparate, yet ultimately related, phenomena. Included among these are the environmental, feminist, and holistic health movements, interdisciplinary thinking in universities, and Gestalt therapy in the field of psychoanalysis, to mention only a few examples.

Chapter 9 examines the new multiracial identity as part of this more fundamental postmodern shift. Much like postcolonial thinkers, postmodernists frequently seek to deconstruct dichotomous and hierarchical thinking by exhibiting "marginal" or "hybrid" phenomena that are indecipherable with reference to the dichotomy and hierarchy. This demonstrates the difficulties of defining one category of experience without including elements of the other. Rather than reverse the dichotomy, however, this strategy questions the hierarchical grounds on which the dichotomy is erected. Accordingly, phenomena are seen as relative and complementary rather than as hierarchical and exclusive categories of experiences. In addition, postmodern thinkers interrogate the conception of a linear connection of subjects to an objective world. This has led them to dismiss the notion that the "truth" can be found in any absolutely impartial sense. They have been instrumental in pointing out that all concepts and categories, racial and otherwise, are largely sociocultural constructs grounded in cultural and historical circumstance.

In the Epilogue I posit that the new multiracial identity, as part of this postmodern (and postcolonial) turn, is a compelling development as the United States enters the new millennium. It remains to be seen how many individuals imbued with this new identity will actually live out its full implications by helping to transform the United States into a more racially democratic order. Yet individuals are active agents in constructing, maintaining, reconstructing, and deconstructing their own identities. And identities are capable of reconstructing circumstances via the actions they set in motion. Sociologists Fenstermaker and West point out that race is much more than an individual characteristic or some vaguely defined set of role expectations. Rather, it is an ongoing phenomenon that is accomplished in interaction with others and must be situated in social situations. The accomplishment of racial identity normalizes and naturalizes the social dynamics based on race, that is, it legitimizes ways of organizing social life. This in turn reaffirms institutional practice, the racial order, and the respective power relations associated with them. The accountability of individuals to race categories is the key to understanding the maintenance of these dynamics. It is a mechanism whereby situated social action reproduces racialized social systems whose entrenched ideas, practices, explicit decisions, and procedures construct dichotomous racial hierarchies that exclude, control, and constrain human agency.[10]

Because the racial order in the United States, along with its dichotomous racial categories, boundaries, and hierarchies, is continually constructed in everyday life, it follows that under certain conditions, individuals acting as singular agents or as collective subjectivities resist pressures to conform to these social forces. The assertion of the new multiracial identity represents just such a form of resistance to the U.S. racial order—particularly to commonsense notions of a black identity based on the one-drop rule—that precludes the simultaneous affirmation of a white, or any other racial, identity. Although it should not be viewed as a solution in and of itself to racial inequality, the new multiracial identity's radical potential should not be underestimated. It signifies the formation of a cluster of new possibilities or a new archetype in the nation's collective racial consciousness. Its goal is to transform traditional American racial categories and boundaries, as well as to challenge racial hierarchies, by expanding definitions of blackness—and whiteness—to include more multidimensional configurations.

An examination of multiracial identity can increase our understanding not only of trends in black-white relations but of similar trends in other groups as well. Indeed, rules of hypodescent have been applied to the first-generation offspring of interracial unions between the dominant European Americans and other subordinate groups of color (e.g., Native Americans, Asian Americans, Pacific Islander Americans, Latino Americans). Racial group membership has historically been assigned to these first-generation offspring based exclusively on the subordinate "background of color." Generally speaking, however, successive generations of individuals whose blended lineage has included a particular background of color, along with European American ancestry, have not invariably been designated exclusively, or even partially, as members of that group of color if the background is less than one-fourth of their lineage. Instead these individuals have been given a white racial identity and the privileges that accompany whiteness. When such people identify themselves as people of color, this is their choice, not something imposed on them from outside. This has been the case with celebrities like Kevin Kostner, Kim Basinger, Cher, and others who have acknowledged their Native American ancestry. For all intents and purposes these individuals are considered white—or at least not people of color—even if their personal identification is at odds with a white racial designation.[11]

This flexibility has not been extended to the offspring of interracial relationships between African Americans and European Americans. To the contrary, these individuals have been the targets of the longest-standing and most restrictive rule of hypodescent, which has not only denied them the power to choose how to describe their racial identity but has ensured that their African American ancestry is passed down in perpetuity. All future offspring are thus socially designated as black and subjected to attitudes and policies that deny them equal status with European Americans and other racial groups as well.

The Anglo-North American annexation and colonization of "Latin" North America, including the Southwest, Louisiana, and the Gulf Coast, is an excellent case study. The social position that the Mexican population would occupy in the American Southwest was largely unscripted. Although most Mexicans were dark-complexioned mestizos who were phenotypically more Native American than Spanish,

African ancestry was widely dispersed among all social classes, including the elite. Yet in colonial Mexican society, multiracial individuals could purchase certificates of "whiteness" that erased their Native American or African origins. This certification not only gave them legal status as *Españoles* and greater opportunity for vertical social mobility; it also enhanced the comparatively more fluid racial demarcations between "pure" Spaniards (or whites), light mestizos, and mulattoes. Consequently the memory of African forbears eventually was lost and forgotten, if not deliberately and successfully concealed, by the many light-skinned, Spanish-identified descendants of the Southwest's first families.

This tendency makes it difficult to determine whether and to what extent the African ancestry of the Mexican population was known by the Anglo-North American colonizers and European-descent immigrants after annexation; or whether and to what extent knowledge of that ancestry simply had little or no impact on attitudes toward Mexicans because their African ancestry was not significantly distinguishable phenotypically from the Native American ancestry (the largest subordinate population in the region was Native American rather than African). What seems clear is that Mexicans were widely considered to be mestizos of predominantly European and Native American descent irrespective of any African ancestry or phenotypical traits they might have had.

After the conquest, annexation, and subsequent colonization of the Southwest during the U.S.-Mexican War of 1846, Mexicans—who are largely multiracial individuals of predominantly Native American and European American descent (mestizos)—were legally guaranteed their rights to citizenship and suffrage by the Treaty of Guadalupe Hidalgo of 1848 and the U.S. Constitution. Thus Mexican Americans were extended an official white racial identity, despite the fact that they were not "white" in the Anglo-Saxon or Northern European sense.[12] It is true that the Mexican Americans' legal status as whites, like their rights to U.S. citizenship, was frequently disregarded in practice. And the extension of white privilege was not necessarily intended to include the entire Mexican American population. Rather, the prime beneficiaries of that privilege, and those deemed most worthy of integration into the new racial order, were members of the light-skinned *Tejano, Hispano,* and *Californio* ranchero (and merchant) elite in Texas, New Mexico (and Arizona), and California, respectively. Those individuals not only boasted of their "pure" Castilian ancestry—and thus identified themselves as *Españoles* (Spaniards)—but also were considered white under the racial policies that had prevailed during Mexican rule. A "white" designation was logical given the limitations of the U.S. racial order, which necessarily made definitions of Native American or African American comparatively less applicable. (Of course, if the rule of hypodescent had been applicable to indigenous ancestry in the same way it was to African American ancestry, the entire Mexican population could have been designated as Native American.) Ultimately, multiracial individuals in the Southwest came to be designated more in terms of their national ethno-cultural origins as Mexican Americans than in terms of their ethno-racial origins as mestizos.

Despite their contradictions and inconsistencies, these attitudes and policies contrasted sharply with those displayed toward multiracial individuals of African American and European American descent (mulattoes) in the lower southeast after France and Spain ceded to the United States their territory in Louisiana and the Gulf ports through the Louisiana Purchase Treaty of 1803 and the Adams-Onís Treaty of 1819, respectively. Under the French and Spanish regimes in that region—much as in other areas of the Americas settled by the French, Spanish, and Portuguese—multiracial individuals maintained an intermediate racial identity and were accorded a racial status inferior to that of whites but somewhat superior to that of blacks. In Louisiana, however, multiracial individuals were not typically extended a white racial identity, as was frequently the case with very light-skinned mulattoes in other parts of Latin America. With Anglo-North Americanization of Louisiana and the Gulf region, multiracial individuals—who formed the largest percentage of the population referred to as Creoles of color—lost their intermediate status and privileges when the racial order began to polarize into either black or white. However, many Creoles of color felt that the Louisiana Purchase Treaty with France assured them equal citizenship in the United States. When they petitioned for equal citizenship and civil rights, U.S. authorities not only denied their appeals but also, slowly but systematically, began to erode the few privileges they had maintained under French and Spanish rule. More important, Anglo-North Americans showed no desire to extend to even the wealthiest and lightest-skinned of the multiracial elite a legal white racial identity or any of the privileges associated with that status.[13]

Unlike the Louisiana Purchase Treaty, the Adams-Onís Treaty between Spain and the United States was meant to protect the entire population that Spain left behind in Mobile, Alabama, and Pensacola, Florida. Creoles of color in that region who by treaty became citizens of the United States were, therefore, initially exempted from restrictions later enacted by the United States against free people of color. During the 1840s and 1850s, the legislatures of Alabama and Florida reversed their earlier actions and began enacting restrictive laws aimed at free people of color that did not specifically exclude Creoles of color.[14] Multiracial individuals in Louisiana and the Gulf ports thus came to be viewed less in terms of their national ethnocultural origins as French or Franco-Hispanic Americans, and more in terms of their ethno-racial origins as African-descent Americans. Consequently, they were not only redefined as black but also denied rights to citizenship and suffrage until the passage of the Reconstruction amendments between 1865 and 1868 after the U.S. Civil War. Ultimately, even these legal rights were circumvented in practice and rendered practically null and void by the rise of Jim Crow segregation at the turn of the twentieth century. They were not fully regained legally until the civil rights acts of 1964 and 1965.

The uniqueness of the one-drop rule becomes more apparent when one considers the attitudes European Americans have displayed toward multiracial individuals of European and African descent who immigrate to the continental United States from Latin America (e.g., Puerto Rico, Cuba, and the Dominican Republic). Racial dynamics in that region have been characterized by pervasive miscegenation and the validation of this blending by a ternary racial project that differentiates the population into whites, multiracial individuals, and blacks. "Multiracial" has thus been both an official designation and a personal identification since the colonial period. Blackness and whiteness are relative, representing merely the polar extremes—negative and positive, respectively—on a continuum in which physical appearance, in conjunction with class and culture rather than ancestry, has come to determine one's racial identity and status in the social hierarchy. Admittedly, in the continental United States, designators indicating the national-cultural origins of these populations as Latinos (or "Hispanics") to some extent gain in importance over those specifying their racial background. Nevertheless, the experience of groups such as Puerto Ricans, Dominicans, and Cubans (who for the most part are predominantly of Spanish and African descent, with some degree of Native American ancestry), indicates that U.S. attitudes and policies toward multiracial individuals from Latin America have been inconsistent and differ somewhat from those displayed toward multiracial individuals of African American and European American ancestry. At times multiracial individuals from Latin America who combine African with European ancestry have been extended, however begrudgingly and selectively, an official white racial identity, as well as some of the privileges accompanying that designation.[15]

Attitudes toward the offspring of unions between African Americans and other groups of color have varied, although these individuals, more often than not, have been subject to the one-drop rule, as we see in the public and media response to golfer Tiger Woods, whose father is black, Chinese, and Native American and whose mother is of Thai, Chinese, and Dutch descent. After winning the Masters Golf Tournament in 1997, Woods responded to the media comments that he was the first African American to win the tournament, "My mother is from Thailand. My father is part black, Chinese, American Indian. So I'm all of those. It's an injustice to all my heritages to single me out as black." This response set off a firestorm of controversy among African Americans. Later, on *The Oprah Winfrey Show*, Woods stated that as a youngster he invented the term "Cablinasian" in order to embrace a racial identity that captured respectively his European, African, Indian, and Asian backgrounds. Nevertheless, Woods is most frequently referred to in the media as an African American golfer.[16]

Some of the inconsistency in attitudes displayed toward offspring of blended ancestry is due to the fact that the positioning of these other groups of color in the racial hierarchy has been more ambiguous than that of African Americans. In addition, membership in other groups—except in the case of Native Americans—has been less clearly defined in U.S. jurisprudence. Intragroup experiences among subordinate groups of color have varied, and their experiences of subordination by European Americans, while similarly oppressive, have not been exactly the same. Nevertheless, groups of color in the United States share a common history of racial subordination to European Americans and therefore to some extent have experienced the rule of hypodescent.

The Black-Chinese in Mississippi are an excellent case study that not only highlights this issue but also provides a broader basis for understanding the unique implications of the social construction of blackness (and whiteness) as it relates to the rule of hypodescent. Chinese were recruited to replace African American labor in Mississippi after the Civil War and the abolition of slavery, but the binary racial order in the South necessitated that they be classified as either black or white. Although the Mississippi Chinese had no African ancestry, southern whites originally defined them as closer to blackness than to whiteness by virtue of the similarity between their social position and that of African Americans and the fact that they were not of European descent. (Had there been more Native Americans in that region, European Americans might have classified them as "American Indian," as they initially did with Chinese immigrants in California.)

The Mississippi Chinese succeeded locally in moving their racial positioning out of a social space near blackness to one that was near whiteness, thus achieving a sort of situational, if not actual, racial whiteness. This came about as a result of various changes that elevated the socioeconomic status of the Mississippi Chinese, as compared to that of African Americans, as well as changes in their social relations with African Americans. As part of this process the Chinese community disowned Chinese-black interracial couples, as well as biracial Chinese-black offspring.[17]

Among the first social scientists to discuss the uniqueness of the one-drop rule and its consequences are Edward Byron Reuter (*The Mulatto in the United States*, 1918; *Race Mixture*, 1931), Robert Park ("Human Migration and the Marginal Man," 1928), Everett Stonequist (*The Marginal Man*, 1937), E. Franklin Frazier (*The Free Negro Family*, 1932; *The Negro Family in the United States*, 1939), and Gunnar Myrdal (*An American Dilemma*, 1944). By the 1950s and 1960s, however, the question of racial definition was eclipsed by the civil rights and black consciousness movements. A notable exception to this trend was the work of Brewton Berry (*Almost White*, 1963), which examined racially blended communities of African, European, and Native American descent scattered throughout the eastern part of the United States referred to above as triracial isolates. Gist and Dworkin (*The Blending of Races*, 1971) provided a comparative global study of multiracial populations but devoted little attention to the impact of the one-drop rule on race relations in the United States. It was not until the late 1970s that this topic reemerged as an area of study in the works of literary historian Judith Berzon (*Neither White nor Black*, 1978), historians John Mencke (*Mulattoes and Race Mixture*, 1979), Joel Williamson (*New People*, 1984), and in works on Louisiana Creoles of color by anthropologist Virginia Domínguez

(*White By Definition*, 1986), and historians James Haskins (*The Creoles of Color of New Orleans*, 1976) and Gary Mills (*The Forgotten People*, 1977).

Although work on the one-drop rule had been done before, it is only in the past decade that we have seen the emergence of groundbreaking research on the subject of multiracial identity generally, and on its implications for multiracial identification (e.g., Spickard's *Mixed Blood*, 1989; Root's *Racially Mixed People in America*, 1992, *The Multiracial Experience*, 1996; Zack's *Race and Mixed-Race*, 1990, *American Mixed Race*, 1995; Funderburg's *Black, White, Other*, 1994; J. M. Spencer's *The New Colored People*, 1997; R. Spencer's *Spurious Issues*, 1999; Azoulay's, *Black, Jewish, and Interracial*, 1997; Korgen's *From Black to Biracial*, 1998; Kilson's, *Claiming Place*, 2000; Brown's *The Interracial Experience*, 2000; Krebs's *Edgewalkers*, 2000; Wallace's, *Relative/Outsider*, 2001).

The surge of interest in this subject can be largely attributed to increased interracial marriage and the growth in the number of multiracial offspring since the overturning of the last antimiscegenation laws in June 1967. These more recent studies have not only explored the implications of the one-drop rule; many also examine the positive benefits of being multiracial (e.g., increased appreciation of differences, a wider worldview and range of sympathies). They have challenged the conclusions of previous research—particularly misinterpretations of Robert Park's theories of marginality—that characterized multiracial individuals as psychologically dysfunctional and unstable, due to the "mutually exclusive" natures of their black and white backgrounds. However, with the exception of Spickard's comparative and historical study, much of this research has been confined to psychological and social psychological analyses.

Contemporary sociologists in particular have tended to overlook the continuing significance of the one-drop rule. They have paid even less attention to its impact on multiracial-identified individuals of European American and African American descent. Order theories foresee the eventual integration of African-descent Americans into the secondary (political, economic, educational), and primary (residential, associational, interpersonal) spheres. These theories also envision the cultural (beliefs, ideals, meanings, values, customs, artifacts), and racial (geno-phenotypical/ancestral) absorption of African-descent Americans into the larger society, following the same pattern of European origin immigrant groups. This pattern has also been displayed by successive generations of individuals whose blended lineage has included a particular background of color, along with European American ancestry.[18]

It is apparent that the physical and ancestral criteria for integration into Anglo-Protestant culture—and the accomplishment of a white racial identity—has expanded dramatically over the course of U.S. history. Although white racial identity—and the privileges that go with it—and European ancestry have historically been intertwined, they are not synonymous. Irish, Italian, and Jewish immigrants from Eastern Europe were not initially extended the full benefits of white racial identity and white racial privilege, even though they, like Protestant Anglo-Americans, were European in origin and thus white. They succeeded in accomplishing that designation and achieving those privileges only after a protracted struggle, which was aided in no small part by varying degrees of cultural integration and socioeconomic mobility that distanced them from their original status as pariahs.

But order theories have not taken into consideration the fact that no matter how well African Americans are integrated into the primary structural sphere through racial intermarriage, the one-drop rule guarantees that African ancestry is passed on in perpetuity as a means of racially designating all future multiracial offspring as black. As long as this device remains intact, whether formally or informally, it precludes a multiracial identification. This mechanism also reproduces an African American plurality that is distinct from, even if on equal terms with, European Americans in the larger society. This, in turn, precludes the racial absorption of African Americans in the manner of European immigrants and their descendents, as well as the multiracial descendents of European Americans and various other groups of color.[19]

The thesis of African American exceptionalism espoused by power-conflict theories challenges the conclusions reached by order theorists. The focus is on the historical and contemporary structural disadvantages that keep African Americans disproportionately at the bottom of society occupationally, educationally, and politically. Accordingly, the experience of African Americans (and people of color generally speaking) is significantly different from that of European-descent Americans.[20] Power-conflict theories also call into question whether African Americans actually desire the racial and cultural integration extended to European immigrants and their descendents even if this type of integration were available to them. Nevertheless, these theories have ignored the oppressive effects of the one-drop rule on multiracial-identified individuals of African American and European American descent. In addition, they have focused little attention on the role this social device has played in forming a separate African American community. The formation of a distinctive African American culture and institutions hinders the structural inclusion, and ultimately the cultural and racial absorption, of African Americans along the lines followed by European immigrants and their descendants.

A notable exception to the neglected study of these topics is F. James Davis (*Who Is Black? One Nation's Definition*, 1991), who has provided the most recent and by far the most thorough and insightful sociological analysis of the one-drop rule. Davis points out that the one-drop rule has become such an accepted part of the U.S. fabric that most individuals—except perhaps African Americans—are unaware of its oppressive origins.[21] In recent years U.S. institutions have generally repudiated the notions of racial "purity" that previously supported the ideology of white supremacy. As a result, the legal definition of blackness based on rules of hypodescent has been removed from the statutes of all fifty states.[22] Many European Americans nevertheless reinforce notions of white racial exclusivity and superiority that were codified in the one-drop rule. Black and white racial identities in the United States have been so well crafted that they reveal little evidence of their construction. They are embraced and often celebrated by those who carry them—and by the society at large—as if they were objective facts of existence rather than socially constructed ideas.

The continuing significance of the one-drop rule was underscored in a 1983 Louisiana court case filed as *Jane Doe v. State of Louisiana*. Until 1970 a Louisiana statute had defined as African American anyone with a "trace of black ancestry." Then, in response to a 1970 lawsuit brought on behalf of a child whose ancestry was allegedly only $1/256$ African American, the legislature redefined as black anyone whose ancestry was more than $1/32$ African American. Jane Doe (Mrs. Susie Phipps) had been denied a passport because she had checked "white" on her application even though her birth certificate designated her race as "colored." She was, in fact, the great-great-great-great granddaughter of a French planter named Jean Gregoire Guillory who in 1770 took his wife's African American slave, Margarita, as his mistress. Apparently, the "colored" designation on Mrs. Phipps's birth records was based on information supplied by a midwife, who presumably relied on the parents' or family's status in the community. Mrs. Phipps and all of her siblings were phenotypically indistinguishable from European Americans.[23]

In 1982–83, Susie Phipps sued the Louisiana Bureau of Vital Records to change her racial designation from "colored" to "white." The lawyers for the state claimed to have proof that Mrs. Phipps was $3/32$ African American. That was enough ancestral blackness for the district court, in May 1983, to declare her parents, and thus Mrs. Phipps and her siblings, to be legally African American. Assistant Attorney General Ron Davis thus upheld the law designating Susie Phipps as African American.[24] Phipps's attorney argued, however, that the assignment of racial designators on birth certificates was unconstitutional. He also disputed the accuracy of the $1/32$ designation and called on the expertise of anthropologist Munro Edmonson to testify on Mrs. Phipps's behalf. According to the *Tribune*, Edmonson stated that there was no way of determining Mrs. Phipps's slave ancestor's exact percentage of African American ancestry, and consequently no way of determining hers. Also, while acknowledging the "impressive" genealogy compiled by the bureau to support its case, Edmonson was quoted in *People Magazine* as saying that none of these data said anything at all about Mrs. Phipps's "race." Since genes are distributed randomly before birth, it was at least theoretically possible for children to inherit all of their genes from just two grandparents. In addition, Edmonson is reported to have testified that modern genetic studies indicate that in terms of gene frequencies, African Americans on average inherit 25 percent of their genes from European American ancestors while European Americans on average inherit 5 percent of their genes from African American ancestors. More importantly, the article stated that according to the $1/32$ ancestral rule defining legal blackness, statistically speaking the entire native-born population of Louisiana would be African American.[25]

Although Phipps lost her case in the lower courts, in June 1983 the legislature unexpectedly abolished its statute defining as black anyone with 1/32 African American ancestry. It implemented instead a new ruling that gave parents the right to designate the race of newborns, and even to change classifications on birth certificates if they could prove the child was white by a "preponderance of the evidence."[26] The new 1983 statute, along with the 1970 ruling, marked a shift from the previous Louisiana standard of racial definition based specifically on the one-drop rule. This change in policy supposedly grew out of an attempt to reflect a "more reasonable" or "modern" standard in keeping with the "liberalization" of the racial ecology in the post–civil rights era.[27]

Yet each time the Phipps decision was appealed to higher courts in 1985 and 1986, the state's Fourth Circuit Court of Appeals upheld the district court's decision. They argued that no one could change the racial designation of his or her parents or anyone else (479 So. 2d 369). Said the majority of the court in its opinion: "That appellants might today describe themselves as white does not prove error in a document which designates their parents as colored" (479 So. 2d 371).[28] Of course, if the parents' designation as "colored" could not be changed, it follows that their descendants would necessarily be defined as black by the "traceable amount rule." In addition, the appellate court concluded that the preponderance of evidence clearly indicated the Guillory parents were "colored." The court also affirmed the necessity of designating race on birth certificates for public health and other important public programs. It also held that equal protection of the law had not been denied as long as the designation was treated as confidential.[29] The Phipps case was appealed to the Louisiana Supreme Court in 1986, but the court declined to review the decision and gave no explanation other than it concurred in the denial for the reasons assigned by the court of appeals on rehearing (485 So. 2d 60). Similarly, in December 1986, the U.S. Supreme Court refused to review the decision: "The appeal is dismissed for want of a substantial federal question" (107 Sup. Ct. Reporter, interim ed. 638). Thus both the final court of appeals in Louisiana and the highest court of the United States upheld the application of the rule of hypodescent, if not the one-drop rule itself.[30]

Anthropologist Virginia Domínguez points out, however, that the issue in this case was not racial designations per se but rather the role of law, as interpreted and arbitrated by agents of the state. The question was whether the 1970 statute infringed on the Equal Protection Clause of the U.S. Constitution and, if so, whether one of those rights was the freedom to choose what one is. Here, however, the state played two seemingly contradictory roles as both counsel and prosecution. On the one hand, it became the institution restricting Susie Phipps's right to choose her racial identity. On the other hand, it provided the only avenue through which she could appeal for the right to exercise that choice. The plaintiff was thus simultaneously pitted against the state as the agent of society at large, and forced to seek redress through the very legal system that was the original perpetrator of the "injustice."[31]

Part I

White Over Black

CHAPTER ONE

Eurocentrism: The Origin of the Master Racial Project

From Ideational to Sensate: Science, Modernity, and the Law of the Excluded Middle

Racial formation is a specifically modern phenomenon that coincided with the colonial expansion of various West European nation-states—specifically Spain, Portugal, Italy, France, Germany, Holland, Denmark, and England—beginning in the late fifteenth and early sixteenth centuries. It was an outgrowth of encounters between Europeans and populations that were very different culturally and, above all, phenotypically, from themselves as they established colonial empires in the Americas, Asia, and the Pacific Islands. More important, racial formation was instrumental as the justification for a unique form of slavery. Although expansion, conquest, exploitation, and enslavement had characterized the previous several thousand years of human history, none of these things had been supported by ideologies or social systems based on race. Beginning in the sixteenth century, increased competitiveness among European nation-states, as well as the consciousness of their power to dominate others, influenced European perceptions of all non-Europeans, and ultimately laid the foundation for the formation of the concept of race.[1]

A corollary to the rise of European nation-states to global dominion was a Eurocentric worldview. Eurocentrism emerged during the Renaissance in the fifteenth century, reached maturity during the Enlightenment in the late eighteenth century, and has been a dominant mode of consciousness in Western civilization ever since. It is a peculiarly narcissistic form of knowledge that views Europe as a self-contained entity and as the transcendental nexus of all particular histories, by virtue of its unprecedented accomplishments in the realms of materialist rationalism, science, and technology. European accomplishments in these realms enabled the exploration of remote areas of the globe and the exploitation of the resources, including human beings, that Europeans found there. The colonization of these areas, although it was an extremely complicated process fraught with deeply conflicted aims and motives (and not without its European dissenters), brought European nation-states to a position of global preeminence and turned fledgling nation-states into commanding imperial powers that could dominate non-European others. The ruling classes of Western Europe, in their progressive evolution toward "enlightenment," tended to see the process of conquest and colonization as a contest between "civilization" and "barbarism."

The epistemological underpinnings of the Eurocentric paradigm, and ultimately of the entire modern worldview, originated in what sociologist Pitrim Sorokin called the "sensate" sociocultural mode. This paradigm supported the belief that the external world has a logical order and is the result of an interplay of calculable forces, discernible rules, and measurable bodies—the empirical, rational perspective on nature. Mechanical principles were seen to govern the structure and movement of the planets, the changes on earth, and the structure of the smallest insects alike. Once grasped, these laws could also be manipulated for human gain.[2] This materialist-rationalist conception represented a fundamental reorientation toward the cosmos and was a radical shift away from what Sorokin called the "ideational" sociocultural mode that prevailed during the medieval era. During that period spiritual and metaphysical beliefs gave rise to the conviction that the structure of the universe was divinely ordained and that the religious authority of the Church prevailed over natural knowledge.[3]

By medieval reckonings, the physical world was seen to have a moral plan and all bodies, from the smallest particle up through humanity and beyond to the heavens and the Godhead, had their fixed and "natural" place in a hierarchy.[4] It was understood that changes undergone by bodies on earth were parallel to and controlled by movements in the heavens. Although the heavenly bodies were considered to be of a "higher" order than terrestrial ones in this Great Chain of Being, all creation was linked in a tightly knit world that displayed a careful gradation of ranks accompanied by a detailed catechism of instructions governing mutual responsibilities and obligations in the grand hierarchy. In this medieval worldview there could be no ultimate distinction between, or dichotomization of, physical events, truths, and spiritual experiences. Indeed, the underlying principles of the Great Chain of Being have much more in common with what Ken Wilber has defined as holarchy than with hierarchy. Differential function, responsibility, and rank are not necessarily equivalent to differential value and worth. In other words, the Great Chain viewed all growth processes, from matter to life to mind, as occurring via holarchies, or orders of increasing holism and wholeness. Wholes then become parts of new wholes, each of which transcends and includes its predecessor. The whole is greater than the sum of its parts; that is, the whole is at a higher or greater or deeper level of organization than the parts alone.[5]

By contrast, the Renaissance worldview—embodied in the sensate mode (and represented in the persons of Galileo and Francis Bacon)—was based on an almost sacred "Law of the Excluded Middle" that supported an "either/or" paradigm of dichotomous hierarchical ranking of differences. Accordingly, the spiritual or metaphysical universe and the world of natural phenomena were viewed as mutually exclusive, if not antagonistic, phenomena. The natural environment had until then been experienced as an organic unity of spirit and matter. They were now viewed as a composite of lifeless material bodies, acted upon by immaterial forces and energies that were distinct from humanity. Taken to its logical conclusion, the natural and physical worlds ceased to be an "inspirited" domain with which humans felt a sacred kinship. Instead, they were reduced to a secular terrain subject to objective laws. The latter were to be discovered by logical deduction and careful empirical observation.[6] The humanity that knew and worked to discover these laws was a dematerialized mind that was distinct from the body and the rest of the objective world it observed.

It is in this context that the services of technology itself not only received an entirely new emphasis but also gained preeminence over other types of invention and cultural expression.[7] This shift was accompanied by the further detachment of human beings (creatures of reason and intellect) from nature (that which the Godhead controlled), although it was man who had been provided with reason in order to serve as the Godhead's steward of the earth's resources and make the fullest use possible of the gifts of nature. Nature, along with woman (as well as human traits such as feeling and intuition, which were deemed more reflective of the female value sphere), was to be dominated and rendered submissive to the rational will of man (and, indirectly, the Godhead).[8]

The "City of God" and the "City of Man"

The growth of Western science and technology, which was a catalyst for the rise of sensate sociocultural dominance, was the result of a combination of favorable factors.[9] The relatively even distribution of rainfall in Western Europe throughout the year meant that extreme periods of dryness and flooding were infrequent and precluded the need for complex irrigation systems. This in turn diminished somewhat the need for political rule to sustain economic prosperity. The herds of European farmers were spared tropical diseases, and once livestock were built up and farmers developed the technology to plow the heavy soils, agricultural improvements followed. As a result, European farmers could produce a relatively large agricultural surplus, which led to an increase in urban populations and the rise of new cities. Moreover, a secure and growing urban merchant tradition and a multiplicity of political units and classes fighting with each other for supremacy—feudal lords, centralizing kings, and the Church—thwarted political unity and provided leeway for commerce and independent urban life. Urban merchants could bargain for considerably greater freedom and self-government than elsewhere, which in turn provided more room and greater reward for independent thinkers. In no region outside Western Europe was this combination of circumstances more favorable for the development of an autonomous urban tradition whose practitioners were allowed to pursue their work unhampered. Rationalism, science, and a new kind of philosophical speculation flourished, and the sensate sociocultural mode became deeply rooted.[10]

The paradigmatic shift to the sensate sociocultural mode in Western consciousness, having separated the physical from the moral world, led to a decline in the Church's authority, which ultimately served as a catalyst for the disintegration of the relationship between church and state. This was paralleled during the Reformation of the sixteenth century by a breaking away of the religiously deviant and defiant—particularly the Protestants of the Anglo-Germanic cities of Northern Europe. These individuals pushed the farthest this rationalization and eventually broke with the authority of the Church of Rome. This in turn helped nurture the belief that the entire history of Europe necessarily led to the blossoming of capitalism—the ultimate economic expression of the sensate mode—to the extent that Christianity (particularly Protestantism) was more favorable than other religions to the flourishing of individual over collective concerns.[11]

In subsequent social changes the merchant class replaced the nobility and hereditary monarchies with the principles of liberal democracy. This was the ultimate political expression of the sensate mode, as was Protestantism its religious expression and the capitalist mode of organization its expression in the economic domain. Yet capitalism would take acquisitive property-based individualism and freedom in the marketplace to unprecedented extremes. The capitalist orientation would involve the investment of capital in the production of commodities for the market, while profits were created by extracting surplus from labor by having laborers work longer hours than was necessary for their own subsistence. Consequently, more often than not, capitalism would undermine the egalitarian principles of democracy and become a mechanism for the exploitation of the weak by the powerful in both the economic and political domains.[12] Nevertheless, new modes of production and exchange unleashed by capitalist dynamics provided the foundation for less constrained social relations and restrictive political institutions than those that had prevailed under medieval feudalism, which were rigidly and hierarchically structured.[13] Indeed, the sense of mutual obligation and the thoroughgoing influence of the Church and religious belief held medieval society together. This helped to prevent, for the most part, the kind of resistance and revolt that began to characterize Western culture when the Renaissance concept of individualism began to take hold and ultimately became a license for the unbridled pursuit of freedom.

The feudal order began to weaken as early as the thirteenth century, after the Crusades and the discovery of new markets in China following the journeys of Marco Polo. By the end of the fifteenth century, feudal laws of mutual obligation no longer restricted social relations. Commercial or fiduciary relations originating in the new money economy and mercantile classes were replacing them. In addition, merchants, bankers, and manufacturers were no longer tied to local markets but were free to make the entire world their domain. They could transform anything and everything into commodities that could be sold on the market for profit.[14] The desire for profit was not, however, merely a reflection of the longstanding human desire to have the most or to take the most from others. Rather, the pursuit of profit was a new passion in which the goal was the progressive and insatiable accumulation of the medium of exchange. This process of accumulating more and more wealth was a rationalized, abstract pursuit in which the passion for the process of accumulation itself replaced the passion for the object of desire. Everything, including human life, was subordinated to the quest to extract value, exchange commodities, and accumulate wealth.[15]

Europeans and "Others": Racial Formation and Racial Difference

By the fifteenth century, the drive to accumulate more and more wealth had reached the point where Western culture was coming to view the entire world, including human beings, as objects to be used to create that wealth, or to be disposed of if they stood in the way of acquiring it. This view was behind the conquest of the Americas, the extermination of Native Americans, the African slave trade, and the rise of plantation slavery in the American South. These developments comprised the Eurocentric master racial project from which all other racial projects originate. Racialized thinking reached maturity during the eighteenth and nineteenth centuries and received new impetus in the last third of the nineteenth, when the European powers scrambled madly to divide up Africa in a new burst of imperialist acquisition. A massive expansion of African slavery was one result.

Never before had the opportunity for seemingly unlimited wealth and resources seemed so great as during Europe's imperialist expansion. The conquest of the Americas was of particular importance. The New World exceeded the wildest dreams of European explorers and merchants seeking new venues for trade. But the New World—like Africa, Asia, and the Pacific Islands—contained not only natural resources to exploit but human populations as well, populations that were phenotypically and culturally different from themselves.[16] These differences challenged European understandings of the origins of the human species and raised disturbing questions as to whether these strange peoples could even be considered part of the same human family. Perhaps the differences of these Others—not only the physical but, more importantly, the cultural ones—could justify their exploitation and even enslavement. Given the scope of the European onslaught—the Europeans' advantages in military technology, their religious conviction of their own righteousness, and their lust for new goods and new markets—the division between the "civilized" world of white European culture and the "primitive" world of black, red, and brown "savages," seemed a "natural" consequence.[17]

The breaking of the "oceanic seal" separating the "old" and the "new" worlds, which began with the European "discovery" of the Americas, was paralleled by a break with the previous "proto-racial awareness" by which Europe had contemplated "Others." The conquest of the Americas was not simply an epochal historical event; it also marked the beginning of modern racial awareness and formation. This awareness was first expressed in religious terms, and soon also in political and scientific ones, as a rationale for the exploitation, appropriation, domination, and dehumanization of people of color. Racial formation was grounded in and used to justify oppressive and exploitive economic relations and was sanctioned by the state. It emerged in the twin policies of extermination of Native Americans and enslavement of Africans, and was used to sanction the dehumanization of people who were phenotypically and culturally different from their oppressors.[18]

Racialized thinking thus served not only as a justification for African slavery but also for the conquest and control of "Others" through occupation and settlement of their land.[19] During the last third of the nineteenth and early part of the twentieth centuries, this way of thinking was used to justify the partition of Africa and, to a lesser degree, the colonization of parts of Asia and the Pacific. Racialized thinking underlay the Anglo-North American annexation and incorporation of Mexican territory into the United States and the expansion into the Philippines and the Pacific, as well as into Latin America and the Caribbean under the banner of "free trade" on the one hand and the Monroe Doctrine on the other.[20]

Eurocentrism and white racism are not merely forms of ethnocentrism—that is, racial and cultural chauvinism in which one's own group is considered the standard against which all others are measured—which exists in almost every culture that has ever existed. Eurocentrism is more extreme than the mere racial and cultural chauvinism that applies almost universally, because it is based on a more systematic, comprehensive, integrated, and reciprocal set of ideological beliefs. All of the major European philosophies, social theories, and literary traditions of the modern age have been implicated in this system. Even the antagonism that Christian Europe displayed toward the two most significant non-Christian "Others"—the Moslem and Jewish populations—cannot be considered more than a "dress rehearsal" for racial formation. Despite the chauvinism and atrocities of the Crusades, these hostilities were universally interpreted in religious terms even when they had racial metaphors.[21]

The Curse of Ham

The religious explanation for the blackening and banishing of Noah's son Ham and his offspring is widely considered to be the original rationalization for the enslavement of blacks. The "curse of Ham" seems a disproportionate punishment for the offense: Noah cursed Ham's son for Ham seeing Noah naked, condemning him and his progeny to be servants of servants (Genesis 9:20–25). The descendants of the son of Ham, according to theological interpretations of the story, were the inhabitants of Africa, including the Egyptians, who at the time the myth began to circulate had fallen from their pinnacle of power.[22] The curse, ordained by God as an eternal punishment for Ham's disobedience, was said to be the curse of blackness, which in turn was the badge of slavery.

The symbology of blackness was significantly intensified when Europeans observed that Africans pursued an "uncivilized" way of life in which the ideational and sensate worlds were seen not as antithetical but as complementary opposites. Even worse, to European minds, Africans went about in states of nakedness and semi-nakedness and had no apparent sense of modesty about their bodies. The Africans' nakedness, their sexual mores, and above all their blackness, served to set them off as a profoundly distinct form of humanity from the Europeans, if they were even human at all. That all too human anthropoid apes were also discovered in Africa did nothing to diminish the suspicion that perhaps Africans were not really human at all.[23] Evil forces, and whatever was forbidden and horrifying in human nature, were personified as black and could be projected onto the African. Death and unconsciousness were blackness, and so were Africans; and if their skin was not in fact absolutely black, it was close enough. God (or nature) had conveniently seen to it that Africans came to represent blackness, darkness, and the unconscious, which would become the "nuclear fantasy," or nightmare, of its polar opposite—the whiteness, lightness, and rational consciousness that were personified by Europeans.[24]

With the growing need for a cheap, dependable source of plantation labor in the New World, the notion of the black Hamite as slave gradually became an accepted part of secular culture in support of the legal justification for African enslavement. Although some form of color prejudice against blacks had existed in various places since antiquity, it had never before been institutionalized in a system of racialized slavery, nor had it been justified by an elaborate racialized ideology of white superiority and black inferiority. Moreover, slavery had never been a permanent condition before the European enslavement of Africans, but a temporary status; slaves in other cultures were generally granted their freedom after serving an allotted time. Nor had color (or phenotype) been a crucial factor in determining an individual's social location before European enslavement of Africans.

Beginning in the sixteenth century, however, black Africans bore the ancestral stigma of Ham's curse, which conveniently served the economic, political, and religious interests of white Europeans. The biblical sanction dispelled moral concerns about the economic exploitation of blacks but kept Africans within the human family.[25] But European slavers did not simply own the body of the black slave. They went further, reducing the slave to a body without a mind. By objectifying black slaves, European slavers made them quantifiable and more easily absorbed into a rising world of productive exchange. Slaves were chattel (from the Middle English for *property*, derived from the medieval Latin for *cattle*), and thus were equivalent to four-legged beasts of burden, and in certain key respects no different from the rest of the mindless universe of objective matter.[26]

From Eurocentrism to Scientific Racism

Racial oppression was, therefore, grounded in exploitive economic relations and was sanctioned by the state. Eurocentric values permeated the major institutions of society by structuring the ways individuals thought about race.[27] The social and political activities of the dominant class played a major role in the construction of Eurocentric culture.[28]

Eurocentric racial formation is based on particular assumptions about human difference, but it is not a unified set of ideas. Eurocentrism evolved under the influence of "the material conditions, the cultural and naturalistic knowledge, as well as the motivations, objectives, and levels of consciousness and comprehension of those individuals who formulated the concept of race and first imposed racial classifications on the human species."[29] As a cultural initiative the concept of race had no basis in natural science but was the culmination of popular beliefs about human differences. Beginning in the mid- to late eighteenth century, however, the concept of race was embraced by naturalists and other learned individuals who gave it credence and legitimacy as a supposed product of scientific investigation.[30]

Racial formation not only underpins a social order that has historically divided the world's peoples into biologically discrete and exclusive groups; it also became a way of categorizing what were already conceived as inherently unequal populations. More important, racial formation supports the notion that these groups are by nature unequal and can be ranked on a continuum of superiority and inferiority.[31] The concept of race became so widely used that it began to replace other classificatory terms. Indeed, had the concept of race never been invented it is likely that people would have continued to be identified by their own name for themselves or by other categorizing terms such as people, group, society, and nation, or by labels derived from the geographic region or locales they inhabited.[32]

Racist ideology was so universal and infinitely expandable that by the nineteenth century all human groups of "varying degrees of biological and/or cultural diversity could be subsumed arbitrarily into some 'racial' category, depending upon the objectives of those establishing the classifications."[33] By borrowing the methods of animal classification and transferring them from Linnaeus and Curvier to Darwin, Gobineau, and Renan, nineteenth-century European savants contended that the genetic variants of the human species called races inherited innate characteristics that transcended social evolution. "Races" were accordingly conceived as "naturally" immutable and heritable status categories linked to visible physical markers. Racial formation not only served to justify the dominance of certain socioeconomic classes or ethnic elements but also became a new dimension of social differentiation that superseded socioeconomic class.[34]

Races, which were formed by the landscape and climate of their homelands, retained permanent and pure essences, although they took on new forms over time. History became the biography of races and consisted of the triumph of strong and vital populations over weak and feeble ones. Victors were seen as more advanced than and thus superior to the vanquished. It was self-evident that the greatest race in human history was the European or Aryan one. It alone had, and always would have, the capacity to conquer all other peoples and to create advanced and dynamic civilizations. European identity, constructed to distinguish it from the identity of "Others," led necessarily to a ranking among Europeans themselves based on their closeness to or distance from the Western European ideal.[35]

By the early decades of the nineteenth century, the concept of race generally contained several ideological ingredients—beliefs, values, and assumptions generally unrelated to empirical facts—that served to guide individual and collective behavior.[36] The first and most basic ingredient of "race" was the universal classification of human groups as discrete, mutually exclusive biotic pluralities. Racial classifications were based not on objective variations in culture but on subjective and arbitrary judgments that reflected superficial assessments of phenotypic and behavioral variations. A second ingredient was an inegalitarian ethos that ranked these biotic pluralities hierarchically, with white Aryan Europeans at the top of the pyramid.[37]

A third ingredient was the belief that superficial physical characteristics reflected behavioral, intellectual, temperamental, moral, and other qualities. It followed that the culture of any given "race" was a reflection of its biophysical form. A fourth ingredient was the notion that biophysical characteristics, behavioral attributes and capabilities, and social status were inheritable.[38] Finally, and perhaps most important of all, was the belief that each exclusive racial plurality was created by God or nature as unique and distinct from all others. Imputed differences could never be altered, bridged, or transcended. Christians saw racial inequalities as divinely ordained, and the nonreligious rationalized them as the product of natural laws. "Scientific" inquiry confirmed the inequalities between races in a way that supported Europeans' conviction of their own superiority. And the state ultimately gave this structural inequality official sanction. White racism and white supremacy were institutionalized as systematic components of European social structure.[39]

CHAPTER TWO

Either Black or White:
The United States and
the Binary Racial Project

The Colonial Foundation of the Racial Order:
The Origin of the Binary Racial Project

The Anglo–North American racial order, like other racial orders in the Americas, originated in the Eurocentric paradigm. In the United States as in Europe blackness and whiteness represent the negative and positive poles of a dichotomous hierarchy premised on the "Law of the Excluded Middle." Racial formation in Latin America, particularly in places like Brazil, however, has involved a less rigid implementation of the "Law of the Excluded Middle," which is reflected in Latin America's pervasive miscegenation and the relative absence of social stigma attached to it. In places like Brazil, racial blending is sanctioned by the implementation of a ternary racial project that differentiates the population into whites, multiracial individuals, and blacks. Blackness and whiteness represent polar extremes on a continuum where physical appearance, class, and cultural attributes, rather than racial signifiers per se, determine one's identity and status in the social hierarchy. The region is marked by notable fluidity in racial/cultural markers and by the conspicuous absence of legal barriers to equality in both the public and private spheres.

As a result, select multiracial individuals have historically been allowed token vertical socioeconomic mobility into the bourgeoisie on the basis of how closely they approximate what Dutch sociologist Hoetink calls the "dominant somatic norm image," that is, phenotypical approximation to the European standard.[1] However, somatic (external) characteristics of a cultural and economic nature (e.g., speech, mannerisms, attire, occupation, income) and psychological (internal) factors (such as beliefs, ideals, values, and attitudes) are also taken into consideration. Consequently, a few exceptional blacks have gained vertical mobility on the basis of their economic and cultural, if not their phenotypical, approximation to the dominant "psychosomatic" norm image. The inegalitarian nature of this type of integration is captured in Figure 1*b*. Both the gray and black circles are in a subdominant position. However, the positioning of the gray circle is not only intermediate, and thus

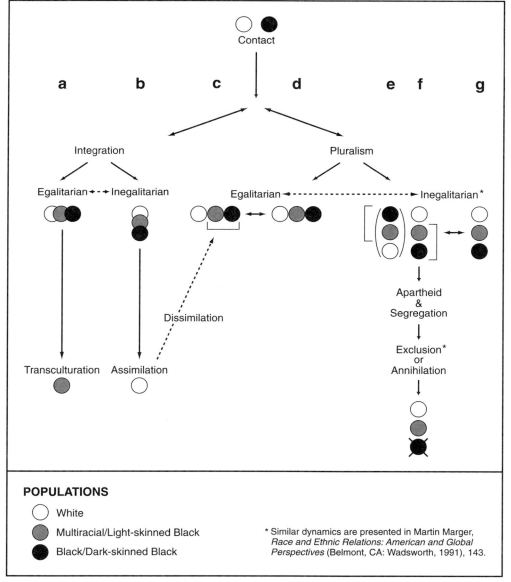

FIGURE 1. Pluralist and integrationist dynamics.

comparatively less subdominant than the black circle, but also linked with the dominant white circle due to its closer somatic approximation to the latter.

The possibility for upward mobility, which historian Carl Degler calls the "escape hatch," does not imply, as many have argued, that masses of mulattoes in countries such as Brazil gain easy access to the prestigious ranks of whites because they are mulatto rather than black. Rather, Degler's central argument is that the escape hatch is an informal social mechanism by which a few "visibly" multiracial individuals, for reasons of talent, culture, or education, have been granted situational whiteness.[2] This has made it possible over time for millions of individuals whose ancestry has included African forbears but who are phenotypically white or near-white to become officially white.

The social construction of whiteness in Latin America is thus more inclusive than that in the United States. And multiracial individuals occupy an intermediate position in the racial hierarchy. Yet, collectively speaking, their location is much closer to that of subordinate blacks than to that of dominant whites. In keeping with Eurocentric dynamics, the primary racial divide in terms of the distribution of wealth, power, privilege, and prestige is between whites and non-whites, and only secondarily between the black and multiracial populations.[3] In contrast to Latin American race relations, U.S. Anglocentrism is an extreme form of Eurocentrism that has recognized no intermediate or multiracial identity or status, although both patterns of race relations originate in the Eurocentric paradigm. That said, U.S. Anglocentrism perpetuates a binary racial project based on the one-drop rule that designates as black all individuals of African descent, and this binary racial project requires that individuals be categorized as either African American or European American.

Until the 1960s scholars explained the striking differences between the binary U.S. and ternary Latin American racial projects as a product of a greater racial altruism on the part of Portuguese and Spanish colonizers compared with the racial attitudes of the English colonizers of North America. But research since the 1960s has found that European colonial attitudes were motivated primarily by self-interest, regardless of the nationality of the colonizers. The social conditions that prevailed in the Americas were the determining factors. And the rate of miscegenation and social differentiation of multiracial individuals from whites and blacks were largely determined by the ratio of European men to women and the number of whites to blacks.[4]

Colonial race relations in "Anglo" North America (the North and the upper South of the United States) differed markedly from those in South America, Central America, the Caribbean, and "Latin" North America (the lower South). The relative balance between European males and females in North Carolina and the area northward and westward made possible the reestablishment of European patterns of domestic life. Consequently, the white family formed by legal marriage remained the standard social unit and permissive attitudes toward miscegenation were discouraged. This was particularly true of New England. In that region Europeans tended to immigrate as families, and single males found a sufficient number of white females. In New England more than any other region parity between the sexes was established quickly and continued throughout the colonial period.[5]

If demographics in Anglo-North America made racial and cultural blending less common than it was in Latin America, they did not prevent it altogether. Although whites dominated the thirteen colonies, there were also African American centers of reference that were smaller but of equal demographic significance, and at times, of necessity, accommodated differences in beliefs, values, customs, and artifacts. These same factors also allowed a significant blending in perceptions of time, aesthetics, and approaches to ecstatic religious experience in the manner of egalitarian cultural integration. Even the distinctive linguistic features of the southern dialect are a Creolization of West African and Old English speech patterns.[6] The integration of beliefs, values, and customs through intermarriage or social intercourse, however, certainly did not extend to equitable treatment in the educational, political, and economic arenas, which tended to follow the pattern of inegalitarian pluralism typified by apartheid. Nevertheless, by the end of the colonial period blacks and whites had forged a new southern culture that was a transcultural blend of both.

Also, during the early seventeenth century the number of blacks in the New World was comparatively small, and the distinction between white indenture and black slave was less precise than that between bonded and free. Consequently, a number of African-descent Americans were able to enjoy a measure of freedom in the public sphere and in some cases become independent landowners and employers of servants and owners of slaves. In the private sphere, phenotypical differences were accommodated in the manner of egalitarian pluralism, and there were no laws prohibiting the comingling of ancestral lines despite strong social prejudice against miscegenation. This is indicated by the small but significant number of blacks and whites of both sexes who intermarried or formed common-law unions of some duration, and had legitimate offspring, alongside more widespread clandestine and fleeting liaisons that involved births out of wedlock. Many of these liaisons took place between white masters and indentured or slave women of African descent and involved extended concubinage and rape.[7]

Given the initial shortage of women, both African and European American, as well as the harsh realities of frontier life in sixteenth-century North America, marriages and other sexual relationships were frequently formed out of simple opportunity, which contributed to widespread miscegenation. This was particularly true of relationships between European American servant women and African American men, both slave and free, who were the largest source of multiracial offspring in the early colonial period. In addition, free white men also married African slaves, who were often the only women they knew. Irrespective of the ratio of blacks to whites, both African Americans and European Americans exhibited a remarkable capacity over the course of the eighteenth century to achieve a balance between the sexes in their respective communities except in areas on the newly opening frontier. The tendency of both African American and European American women to survive at a higher rate than men, despite their initially smaller numbers, was counterbalanced by the continuous flow of European males into the free population, as well as of African and European males into the population of bond-laborers. This was due to the larger ratio of men to women imported as indentures and slaves.[8]

Over the course of the seventeenth century, African slaves replaced European indentures as bonded labor to the degree that slavery became an entrenched fact of colonial life. As the African-descent population expanded to meet labor needs, barriers were erected between African Americans and European Americans, particularly indentured white servants. Codes were promulgated to solidify the distinction between slave and free, which ultimately came to mean the distinction between black and white. Simultaneously, several of the southern colonies and some northern colonies began enforcing laws that criminalized sexual relations and intermarriage between whites and blacks.[9] It is highly significant, however, that the first antimiscegenation legislation passed by Virginia and Maryland in the 1660s and 1680s was largely concerned with regulating interracial sexual relations and marriages between European women—particularly indentures—and slave men of African descent. The earliest laws did not actually forbid interracial unions but sought to discourage miscegenation by imposing stiff fines or severe penalties ranging from banishment to whippings, or locking white indentured women into additional terms of servitude. They also stipulated that children born of these relationships would be held in bondage for extended periods of time. With the passage of these and similar statutes, white slave owners actually had an economic incentive to coerce black slave men and white indentured women into marriage, in order to increase the number of bound servants, despite the social antipathy toward such unions. So widespread was this abuse that in 1681 an act was passed in Maryland that imposed stiff fines on masters and ministers performing such marriages.[10]

Later statutes stipulated that free white men who married interracially or became sexually involved with African American women, slave or free, were to incur the same fines and penalties imposed on free white women. By the middle of the eighteenth century, laws did not merely discourage interracial sexual relations and marriage but outlawed these relationships altogether.[11] This was particularly the case with black male–white female unions, whether marriages or sexual relations outside wedlock. To some extent these relationships were less common and carried a greater social stigma because of the initial shortage of available white women. Even after the number of white women in all colonies—particularly in the upper South—approached that of white men, however, black male–white female unions were frowned upon in practice even when they were not forbidden by law. These relationships threatened the sanctity of white womanhood and the integrity of the white family, both of which were pivotal to preserving the racial purity of the European American community and to perpetuating the transmission of white wealth, power, privilege, and prestige down through the generations.[12] Even in those colonies—and eventually those states—where interracial unions between blacks and whites were allowed, these relationships, whether informal unions or legal marriages, carried painful social consequences.

Such restrictions alone did not markedly decrease the rate of miscegenation, however. The key change was a shift in public attitudes. Rape and extended concubinage involving white slave masters (or overseers) and women of African descent, whether slave or free, continued to be tolerated. These relationships had no legal standing, posed little threat to the slave system, and would become the source of most subsequent miscegenation. The Anglo-North American patriarchy thus established an economic and political system, as well as a cultural ideology, grounded in racial, gender, and class oppression. White male slave owners had the power to control not only the productive labor of African American men but also the productive and reproductive labor of African American and European American women.[13] If legislation and public pronouncements were relatively unsuccessful at controlling miscegenation, there was little cause for real concern so long as it was restricted largely to white male exploitation of African American women, especially when these men disowned their mulatto offspring, which they usually did.[14] This practice had the dual advantage of divesting the mulatto offspring of white slave masters of the privileges associated with paternity and increasing the number of individuals held in bondage.

White Domination and the One-Drop Rule

The early balance between European males and females in Anglo-North America (the North and upper South), coupled with the overwhelmingly large percentage of whites, precluded the pervasive miscegenation that typified Latin America. These same factors also diminished any need that the dominant whites might have had for the collaboration of multiracial individuals in maintaining the racial status quo, and thus made social differentiation of multiracial individuals from whites and blacks largely unnecessary. Although Free Coloreds in Anglo-North America tended to be disproportionately multiracial and occupied important roles in the skilled trades, there was generally an abundant supply of poor European immigrants to fill less desirable economic occupations. If the predominantly mulatto Free Coloreds often functioned as "situational whites" in Latin America and in the lower South ("Latin" North America), European immigrants to some extent functioned as "situational mulattoes" in the North and upper South and were frequently the source of economic competition with Free Coloreds during the nineteenth century, which almost always had a racial cast.[15]

Compared to blacks, multiracial individuals were disproportionately represented among free people of color in all regions of the North and South. Yet their status in Anglo-North America differed significantly from that in Latin-North America. There is insufficient data to determine the exact size and status of the multiracial segment of the Free Colored population prior to the 1850 census because until then the U.S. census did not distinguish between black and multiracial individuals.

In 1850, for the first time, federal enumerators were instructed to designate whether African Americans (Negroes) were black or mulatto by marking a person either "B" or "M" on the census schedule. According to the 1850 data, mulattoes made up a much larger percentage (24.8 percent) of the African American population in the North than they did in the nation as a whole (11.2 percent).[16] Free Coloreds in the upper South (203,702) exceeded those in the lower South (34,485) and made up a larger percentage of the total population of African descent in the upper South (12.5 percent) than in the lower South (3.5 percent).[17] Yet only a small percentage of mulattoes lived in the North, and the multiracial segment of the Free Colored population in the upper South was predominantly rural, of humble European American origins, and of modest means. Furthermore, there was a larger number of blacks in the ranks of Free Coloreds in the upper South (78,556 mulattoes and 125,146 blacks) than in the lower South (23,683 mulattoes and 10,802 blacks), due to large-scale manumissions that took place around the time of the American Revolution.[18] Although the number of Free Coloreds and mulattoes, as well as the number of mulattoes *among* Free Coloreds, were larger in the upper South, multiracial individuals made up only 38.6 percent of the total Free Coloreds in that region. In the lower South multiracial individuals were 68.7 percent of the total Free Colored population. Accordingly, the percentage of mulattoes in the ranks of Free Coloreds in the upper Southeast was only little more than half of the percentage of mulattoes among Free Coloreds in the lower South. In addition, Free Coloreds in the lower South were not only overwhelmingly multiracial but also from comparatively well-to-do European American origins and tended to be urban.[19]

The majority of these Free Coloreds lived in precarious economic circumstances and sometimes in grinding poverty, and inhabited an ill-defined penumbra between servitude and fettered freedom. Nevertheless, the ternary racial project prevailed in the lower South, especially in the urban centers. The experience of Free Coloreds, then, was similar to that in continental Latin America and the Caribbean, although Free Coloreds in the lower South were fewer in number and had little opportunity for social elevation. They were allowed just enough room to carve out a sense of dignity in a world that tolerated (while exploiting) them but was essentially hostile to their existence. The populations of Charleston, Savannah, and of gulf ports such as Natchez, Mobile, Pensacola, and New Orleans included many skilled and prosperous Free Coloreds who achieved a degree of education and accumulated some property. These circumstances granted them the most secure position of free people of color anywhere in North America despite the generally deplorable conditions in which they lived. The privileged status of Free Coloreds in the lower South is all the more significant given that most people of any African descent in both the upper and lower South were slaves.[20]

The legal status of free mulattoes was ambiguous at best up to the time of the American Revolution, although European Americans had begun to chip away at their rights as early as the 1660s. Yet when slaves began pouring into the colonies in the early eighteenth century and the number of Free Coloreds began to expand, their status rapidly deteriorated. Some southern legislatures began to make their emancipation by slave owners more difficult, imposing discriminatory taxes on free mulatto women and denying equal rights to free mulattoes in a wide range of categories—including the right to vote and carry a firearm. Other states barred Free Coloreds from holding office, serving in the militia, or testifying against whites, placed restrictions on interstate travel and migration, and required them to carry passes proving their free status or risk being fined, expelled from the state, or kidnapped and reenslaved.[21]

These changes in the post-revolutionary era were accompanied by increasing concern about precise legal definitions of race. During the colonial era only Virginia and North Carolina had legislated the definition of blackness, designating as black any individual with African American ancestry back three generations (North Carolina legislators sometimes also investigated the fourth generation removed). Any free person with an African American parent, grandparent, great-grandparent, and sometimes a great-great-grandparent—in other words, anyone with up to one-eighth or one-sixteenth African American ancestry—was deemed black and subject to laws regulating Free Coloreds. Other colonies appear to have implemented similar policies but none seems to have made them part of the legal structure.[22]

Yet as the status of Free Coloreds declined in the late eighteenth century, the distinctions between their status and that of free whites had more serious social implications than before. If the legal definition of blackness prevented the infiltration of white society by light-skinned African Americans, it also threatened to condemn "swarthy" whites to the subordinate status of Free Coloreds. In order to prevent such a mishap, in 1785 Virginia lowered the racial divide and defined as black anyone having one African American forebear in the previous two generations, i.e., anyone with a black parent or grandparent. States in the upper South, such as Kentucky and Missouri, generally adopted the Virginia rule. North Carolina implemented a similar statute, except when interracial marriage was proposed, in which case blackness was defined into the third generation. Two states in the lower South—Florida and Mississippi—implemented the Virginia standard based on the second generation removed.[23]

While most of the states in the upper South defined blackness by tracing African American ancestry back two generations, a stricter law, extending the line back three generations, was eventually adopted in Georgia, Tennessee, Alabama, Texas, and much of the lower South. Georgia lawmakers in particular took measures against the potential infiltration of the white population by light-skinned mulattoes. In that state individuals enjoying the rights and privileges of free whites could be taken to court if their ancestry was in any doubt. Should it be proved that these individuals were of more than one-eighth African American ancestry, they were pushed into the community of Free Coloreds. No other state enacted a similar measure, but many legislatures in the lower South would follow Georgia's lead and eventually raise the racial divide one notch. Some northern states also established legal definitions of blackness, usually going back to the third generation. It was a fine legal distinction, usually without much practical significance. Informally, whites generally considered as black anyone with any African American ancestry at all, no matter how remote.[24]

These attitudes and policies had especially egregious consequences for multiracial individuals in those parts of the lower South that had previously been under Spanish or French jurisdiction. Anglo-Americanization brought about a significant erosion of their privileged position. Over the course of the nineteenth century the Latin American ternary racial project was gradually replaced with a binary racial project, which by the early twentieth century designated as black all individuals of any African descent. The legacy of these policies lasted well into the twentieth century apart from a brief period during Reconstruction (1865–1879). During the first decades of the twentieth century, the one-drop rule became accepted as the legal definition of blackness in some southern states and as the "commonsense" definition throughout the United States.[25] State after state enacted legislation to prevent interracial sexual relations and marriages by imposing heavy fines and penalties, and also made such marriages null and void when they did occur.

Scientific Racism and the Rise of White Supremacy: Consolidating the Binary Racial Project

According to the Swedish social scientist Gunnar Myrdal, the racist attitudes and practices that systematically prevented equality between African Americans and European Americans in most aspects of social life comprised a racial creed that was a flagrant breach of what he defined as the "American creed." This creed was based on the egalitarian principles enshrined in the Declaration of Independence and the U.S. Constitution and Bill of Rights. The American creed proclaimed that all individuals were born equal with inalienable rights to "freedom, justice, and fair opportunity."[26] The contradiction between the American and racial creeds was exacerbated over the course of the eighteenth and nineteenth centuries by the increasing demand for cheap labor and the ensuing expansion of African slavery. But if racial differences could be said to indicate different species of humans rather than superficial geno-phenotypical variations within a single species, then the American creed and its promise of constitutional equality did not have to apply to people of African descent.[27] In support of this position a number of prominent European American thinkers sought to prove that Africans were a subhuman species. They became part of a concerted effort among Western intellectuals who attempted to replace the doctrine of monogenesis (one human species) with the theory of polygenesis. Polygenesis was premised on the inegalitarian pluralist creation of races that deemed Africans and their descendents to be a separate, different, and inferior species.[28]

White Supremacy and the "Aryanization" of Greece

As the debate raged on over the "humanness" of Africans, European and European American thinkers were especially concerned with distancing the origins of Western civilization as far as possible from any association with individuals of African descent. Egypt became a focal point of this debate by virtue of its location on the African continent and long history of racial and cultural contact with the European and Asian worlds. Egypt, after all, had given rise to one of the earliest recorded civilizations. Bernal's "Ancient Model" has represented Greek culture, beginning around 1500 BCE, as the direct result of Egyptian and Phoenician colonization. This information was derived from the writings of Greek philosophers—particularly Herodotus and Deodorus—who obtained their information largely from the oral accounts of Egyptian priests.[29]

With the concomitant expansion of African slavery, however, it became increasingly unpalatable that Greek civilization could have been the result of the blending of indigenous Europeans, Africans, and Semites. The Ancient Model was therefore eclipsed by a racist view of history that flourished in Europe during the eighteenth and nineteenth centuries. In order to support the autonomous, "immaculate" conception and "purity" of Western origins, Romantic nationalists and racists replaced the Ancient Model of Greek history with what Bernal calls the "Aryan Model" (the currently accepted version of Greek history).[30] These scholars discarded the accounts of the Egyptian basis of Greek civilization as fanciful notions, as out of place in serious history as Greek myths of sirens and centaurs.

The notion of the Greek ancestry of Western Europe—which underlies the Eurocentric paradigm—thus performed an essential function in the assertions of Europe's superiority over Africans and "Others." Greece became the source of rational philosophy and presaged the triumph of reason that characterized Enlightenment thought (the sensate mode).[31] But in order to incorporate Greece fully into Western Europe's lineage, the differences between Greece and the ancient Afro-Asian world had to be accentuated. And in order to support the ancestral connection with the Greeks—who were highly "civilized" at a time when most Western Europeans were still "barbarians"—it became necessary to emphasize, if not invent, commonalities between these Greeks and modern Europeans. Those who supported this historical revisionism resolved the contradiction between anecdotal accounts of Egyptian colonization and their more scientific chronicles by treating those accounts as exceptional departures from otherwise rational Greek thought, as products of "Egyptomania."[32] This delusion supposedly served the nationalist pride of both Egyptian priests and Greek thinkers.[33]

White Supremacy and the "Aryanization" of Egypt

The discovery of the antiquity of Egyptian civilization during Napoleon's expedition into North Africa in the early nineteenth century, which raised the possibility that Africans could have contributed significantly to Egypt's development, represented a major obstacle to the claim that Africans were inferior to Europeans. European scholars in the nineteenth century may have felt certain that Greek civilization was essentially self-generated and owed nothing to Egypt. They could not, however, convincingly argue the inherent and permanent biological inferiority of African-descent individuals as long as Egypt remained an African civilization. Christian theologians began to argue, therefore, that Noah had cursed only Canaan, the son of Ham, and his progeny, which included all black (sub-Saharan) Africans and their descendents. Another son, Mizraim, had not been cursed and was the progenitor of the gifted, dark-skinned white (or "Caucasian") Egyptians, the creators of one of the earliest recorded civilizations.[34] Consequently, a population that was Afro-Eurasian in ancestry—and in many respects predominantly African in origin—was given a berth among the Aryan races, not in first class, but in the escape hatch section reserved for whites of questionable ancestry. The creation of two lineages—a servile, cursed Africoid branch and a gifted and blessed Caucasoid branch—thus neatly resolved the problem of the Hamitic curse and allowed the Christian conscience to rest peacefully once again.[35]

This "whitening" of Egypt in the context of nineteenth-century Anglo-North American racial theory was an attempt to justify and rationalize slavery in the years leading up to the Civil War, as well as the ruthless exploitation and domination of blacks during Jim Crow segregation after Reconstruction. For it was in the United States that the most concerted "scientific" effort took place to prove that Egyptian civilization had not been African in origin.[36] The primary focus was on the question of miscegenation and the devastating effect it could have on Anglo-North American civilization. Throughout the nineteenth century the scientific establishment of Europe and the United States tried to prove that the Egyptians were and always had been white. They did not deny that blacks were numerous in Egypt, but they argued that their social position had not changed significantly from ancient times to the present, that is, that Egyptian blacks had always been servants and slaves, while Egyptian kings, priests, and military had always been white.[37] Egypt, then, served as an ancient historical precedent for a white society with black slaves, which justified the "natural" place of blacks in the American South. Researchers used this evidence not only to support claims that the races were permanently different and mutually antagonistic, but also to advance policy recommendations that would maintain their permanent separation. That the contemporary Egyptian population was clearly made up of a blend of Arabs, Africans, and Afro-Arabs did not disprove the "Caucasian thesis," they argued. It only explained Egypt's long decline. Aryans alone created Egyptian civilization, and the subsequent blending of the races debased it and brought about its degeneration, infertility, barbarism, and ultimately its fall.[38]

It was likewise maintained that any breakdown of the social divisions between blacks and whites in the United States promised the decline and fall of the entire nation. Those who maintained this belief argued that the differences between the species of humans is permanent and that this permanence is preserved thorough the laws of hybridity by the degeneration and eventual infertility of any hybrid crossing between them. They emphasized the idea that miscegenation between Anglo-North Americans and African-descent Americans would cause whites as a race to decline and eventually die out altogether. The term miscegenation, in fact, originated in the United States in 1864 during the Democratic Party's campaign for the presidency; it was coined in a pamphlet entitled "Miscegenation: The Theory of the Blending of the Races," published anonymously but later attributed to David Croly and George Wakeman. Inflaming racial fears was necessary to gain support for the continued enslavement of African Americans and the segregation (or repatriation to Africa) of those who were free.[39]

Many people assume erroneously that the term *miscegenation* is derived from adding to "cegenation" the prefix *mis-*, from the Anglo-Germanic for ill, wrong, or unfavorable. The word is actually derived from the Latin words, *miscere* (to mix) + genus (race). In addition, miscegenation between blacks and whites has mistakenly been used to suggest the genetic crossing of different species that are in fact merely geno-phenotypical variations of the same species, *homo sapiens sapiens*.

These arguments were in no small part supported and justified by the founders of American anthropology Josiah Nott, George Gliddon, and Samuel G. Morton. From the 1840s onwards these men and others presented their claims as scientific truth and were instrumental in promoting in Europe and the United States the Anglo-North American ideology of race.[40] Their sentiments were perhaps the clearest indication of the gradual broadening of the ideology of white racism, which had been used to support African enslavement and the systematic subordination of blacks after slavery. Now, however, this ideology was expanded to include notions of white supremacy, which were grounded in "scientific" arguments that perpetuated the fiction of the genetic superiority of Europeans and the genetic inferiority of Africans in order to preserve white privilege.

Part II

Black No More

CHAPTER THREE

White by Definition: Multiracial Identity and the Binary Racial Project

Passing: Going Underground

In the United States, multiracial individuals of African American and European American ancestry for the most part have internalized the one-drop rule and have identified themselves as black. Various forms of resistance to rules of hypodescent, however, have always challenged both legal and commonsense constructions of blackness. European American control over the boundaries between black and white has always been relative rather than absolute.

One historical form of resistance has been "passing," a radical form of integration in which individuals of a more European American phenotype and cultural orientation make a clandestine break with the African American community, temporarily or permanently, in order to enjoy the privileges of the dominant white community. Compared with frontline battles against racial inequality, passing may seem to be mere opportunism, a way of selling out or accepting the racial status quo. If viewed on a spectrum of tactics, however, passing may be seen as an underground tactic, a conspiracy of silence that seeks to beat oppression at its own game.[1] As a form of racial alchemy, passing exposes the political motivations behind racial categories and seeks to turn oppression on its head by subverting the arbitrary line between white and black.[2]

Discontinuous Passing

As a form of radical integration, passing has meant deliberately shifting one's racial reference group from black to white and should not be confused with situations where racially blended individuals are mistaken for white. Cultural factors are important in the phenomenon of passing, but not as important as phenotypical (and thus genotypical) factors.[3] Those unable to pass as European Americans have often adopted Latin or other non-English names; some have passed as members of other groups of color, such as Asians or Native Americans, that are perceived to have a more privileged status in the racial hierarchy.

It is difficult to say whether passing has actually decreased since the civil rights victories of the late twentieth century. But it is clear that these legislative and judicial victories have given Americans of African descent greater access to sectors of society from which they were previously barred. The most immediate impetus behind passing has thus been removed. It is interesting to note that during the era of segregation the most common form of passing was the discontinuous type.[4] Whether for reasons of practicality, revenge, or amusement, discontinuous passing was a brief trip across the racial divide for an evening in a white restaurant or theater or a more comfortable seat on the train. Sometimes people of African American descent have migrated to other parts of the country, where they have passed as white, but have continued to identify themselves as black when they return to visit friends and family in their hometown. Many held day jobs as whites, returning to the African American community at night. And some passers became "white liberals," opening doors that otherwise would be closed to individuals of African descent. In the 1920s, Walter White (1893–1955) became an undercover operative for the National Association of the Advancement of Colored People (NAACP) and temporarily crossed the racial divide in order to accomplish the dangerous task of investigating lynchings in the South.[5]

All have experienced the anxiety of operating in two different and antagonistic worlds, while at the same time struggling to keep each world separate. Precautions had to be taken against the possibility of exposure, deliberate or unwitting, by an acquaintance, although African Americans typically honored an unwritten code of silence on this score. Individuals sometimes displayed an evasiveness or aloofness in public that might indicate they were seeking to conceal their "real" racial identity.[6] Several women who obtained jobs normally closed to African Americans, such as stenographer, telephone operator, receptionist, and floorwalker in department stores, reported the complications that could arise from discontinuous passing. One woman said that when friends at work invited her to their homes or wanted to visit hers, she fabricated excuses as to why she could neither accept their invitations nor extend invitations to them. Eventually the stress of keeping up the masquerade became too great, and she resigned her job. At her new job she made a strict habit of not forming friendships with coworkers.[7]

Another woman, who lived in Washington, D.C., in the early 1920s and frequently took her two daughters to white movie theaters, expressed the need for vigilance in these matters. She was less concerned about bumping into acquaintances than about successfully escaping the scrutiny of "spotters." These were African Americans whom theater owners hired as racial detectives, in the belief that one African American could always spot another, no matter how phenotypically white that individual might be. In order to evade these spotters the woman would apply several layers of powder to the face of the one daughter whose skin tone might have aroused suspicion. This same woman would also routinely board her two daughters on the "white" train car whenever she sent them off to visit relatives in Richmond, Virginia.[8]

During the early 1950s, a woman who was passing as white in Los Angeles secured employment as a buyer with an exclusive Beverly Hills clothing store, a position she certainly would have been denied had her employers known she was descended from African Americans. This woman socialized only with whites and lived in a fashionable two-bedroom home in an upscale white neighborhood in the old Wilshire area. (At the time there were covenants that sought to prevent blacks from owning property in the area). But she went to a black beautician in the African American community under an assumed name in order to have her hair straightened. Not only was she afraid of being "found out" in a white beauty salon, she also felt that a black salon would know exactly how to make her hair appear as naturally straight as possible.

This was particularly important because the hot comb, or curling iron, was the primary tool for straightening the hair of African American women. The results were less natural looking, and significantly less long-lasting, than the chemical straightening that became popular beginning in the 1960s. Also, the hair could more easily revert to its natural state when exposed to humidity or perspiration. Once given a professional styling, the woman's hair looked naturally straight, except perhaps to a very discerning African American eye. During the summers, she wore her hair in a tightly coiled French bun in order to prevent frizzing, particularly at the nape of the neck when she perspired.[9] Even this precaution did not prevent her from making several anxious trips to the ladies' room at social gatherings to monitor the situation.

Continuous Passing

Continuous passing, which involves a complete break with the African American community, has been the most sensational sort of crossing over, although it has been studied far out of proportion to the number of individuals who probably practiced it prior to the civil rights era of the 1950s and 1960s. Because passing was a clandestine, closeted affair, it is not possible to pinpoint its origins in the United States or to know for sure how many people engaged in it, whether sporadically or permanently.[10] It is possible that a few offspring of the first contact between African Americans and European Americans in the early colonial period passed as white. Most of these first-generation individuals, however, would have had enough discernible African ancestry to prevent their passing as white even if they had wanted to. It is likely that passing became easier for successive generations of multiracial individuals, as procreation with each other and with whites decreased the number of "African genes" and increased phenotypical approximation to European Americans. For the most part, individuals who have passed as white have inherited few if any genes from West African ancestors. Only about 1 percent of the genes of European Americans are derived from African American antecedents, although the total of European Americans with West African forebears numbers in the millions.[11]

Passing in general, and continuous passing in particular, became a more appealing prospect as legally sanctioned discrimination increased, first with the codification of slavery in the late seventeenth century and then with the restrictions on manumission and on free people of color in the late eighteenth century, which continued through the nineteenth. Throughout the antebellum period, runaway mulatto slaves with no phenotypically discernible African traits were often able to pass as free people of color, if not as whites—in part because whites associated freedom with mulattoes and slavery with blacks. The near-white appearance of many multiracial slaves made it possible for them to escape from slavery into the population of Free Coloreds and from there into the population of European Americans.[12] President Thomas Jefferson's son Beverly and daughter Harriet, conceived with his multiracial slave Sally Hemings, supposedly ran away from the Monticello estate where they had been slaves, and passed as white in Maryland and Washington, D.C. Two more of Jefferson's sons with Hemings—Eston and Madison—were freed by the third president's will and eventually vanished into white society in Wisconsin and Ohio, respectively. John Wayles Jefferson, Eston's son, served as a white lieutenant colonel of the Eighth Wisconsin during the Civil War. Madison established himself in the African American community in Ross County, Ohio, and remained there until his death. His son, William Beverly Hemings, crossed the racial divide and served in a white regiment—the Seventy-third Ohio.[13]

The "great age of passing," particularly of continuous passing, occurred between 1880 and 1925 and was no doubt a direct response to the Jim Crow laws that were passed at the end of the nineteenth century.[14] Because of the need for spatial mobility and anonymity, continuous passing was more common among men than among women, and occurred more frequently in the urban North (particularly during the first great migration of 1900–1925), than in the rural South.[15] It is impossible to come up with hard numbers, however, and estimates are based largely on conjecture. Some sociologists have placed the number of passers during this period at 10,000 to 25,000 per year; others put the figures significantly higher, at over 100,000 annually.[16] European American alarmists of the era, fearing "racial mongrelization" and the decline of Anglo-North American civilization by "crytomelanism" (or invisible blackness),[17] tended to exaggerate these figures. Certain African American leaders used these numbers as a quantitative indictment of racial oppression in the United States. Other African Americans liked the inflated figures and saw them as fitting revenge on European Americans. Many social scientists also welcomed high numbers as proof that the assimilationist model was as applicable to African Americans as it was to European Americans and would thus provide a solution to "the race problem." The most recent, most careful calculations, made in 1946, estimated that between 2,500 and 2,700 individuals crossed over yearly. These more modest and probably more accurate figures were arrived at by tracking for several decades demographic discrepancies in the census data that showed an increase in the European American population and a decline in the African American population that could not be accounted for by increased immigration and births or emigration and deaths, respectively.[18]

Like discontinuous passing, the continuous sort of crossing over has most often been a means of gaining access to positions of wealth, power, privilege, and prestige normally barred to individuals of African descent. Some people who choose continuous passing may also find it a way of escaping the social stigma and taunts of African Americans who view them as less than black.[19] Individuals of European phenotype who have been socialized as African American rarely make an intellectual decision to pass. Continuous passing is a gradual process in which emotional ties to African Americans are severed as ties to European Americans are achieved.[20] The final break comes when the benefits of becoming white are felt to outweigh the costs of being black. It should not be assumed, however, that continuous passing exacts no price. It is usually extremely difficult for a person to say farewell to family and friends, or to leave without saying anything at all.[21]

Some passers, out of the constant fear of exposure and the feeling of being imposters, adjust to their new identity by overcompensating, at times surpassing even the most rabid white racist in an effort to prove their "white" credentials.[22] This fear of exposure allegedly explained Dinah Shore's refusal to hold Ella Fitzgerald's hand when Fitzgerald appeared as a guest on her weekly variety show in the 1950s, because it was rumored that Dinah Shore was passing.[23] This over-compensatory behavior had tragic consequences for a prominent Philadelphia physician during the same time period. He displayed such strong anti-black prejudice that he refused to allow his son to invite a friend and his African American girlfriend to a social gathering that included many of Philadelphia's white elite. This man was always the first to tell "nigger" jokes and laughed the loudest and hardest whenever anyone else told them. Eventually he developed a serious borderline personality disorder, attributed in part to his passing. During the last weeks of his life he wandered deleriously through the streets of North Philadelphia—the city's predominantly black section—giving away $100 bills to children on the street.[24]

One of the most compelling and fully documented cases of continuous passing is recounted in Gregory Williams's *Life Along the Color Line: The True Story of a White Boy*

Who Discovered He Was Black (1995). Williams—who is now dean of the Ohio State University College of Law—and his younger brother Mike were the children of a European American mother and a father who told them he was white and of Italian descent. When their parents' marriage disintegrated, the boys' mother abandoned them and their father's profitable business deteriorated when he took to drinking. Pursued by debtors and haunted by his racial past, Williams's father took his two sons to live in his hometown of Muncie, Indiana. It was then that he told Gregory and Mike that he was an African American who had been passing as European American. Of course this meant that Gregory and Mike were of African descent as well and thus black. Williams poignantly remembers his father's words on that fateful day: "Life is going to be different from now on. In Virginia you were white boys. In Indiana you're going to be colored boys. I want you to remember that you're the same today that you were yesterday. But people in Indiana will treat you differently."[25]

Williams has remarked that truer words were never spoken. Suddenly he and his brother were faced with the harsh realities of segregation from which they had largely been sheltered and which they were not prepared to handle. In his moving account, William brings into sharp focus the glaring contrast between the white and black worlds, the former marked by wealth, power, privilege, and prestige, the latter by poverty, repression, and struggle. The most startling revelation, and perhaps one of the most touching moments in the book, is Williams's revelation that the woman he and his brother had considered just another employee in his father's tavern was actually their father's mother, their grandmother.

Another intriguing and detailed contemporary account of passing is Shirlee Taylor Haizlip's book, *The Sweeter the Juice: A Family Memoir in Black and White* (1994).[26] Shirlee's mother, Margaret Morris Taylor, was the granddaughter of a mulatto slave named Edward Everett Morris (1849–1903), who was himself the offspring of a mulatto slave named Ruth Morris and a white Virginia federal judge named James Dandridge Halyburton. During the Civil War, Edward Everett Morris, who played the piccolo, put on a union jacket he had found and was able to escape to freedom with the Union band that accompanied troops marching into Virginia near the end of the war. Edward Morris stopped marching when the troops reached Washington, D.C. There he eventually married Margaret Maher (1856–1948), an Irish woman from County Tipperary. Margaret and Edward had several offspring, one of whom was William Morris. William married Rosalind Scott, a woman of African American and European American descent (possibly Italian), who became the parents of Shirlee Taylor Haizlip's mother Margaret and five other siblings.

In 1916, Rosalind died and the family began to unravel. Recently widowed and now alcoholic, William Morris abandoned the children, left Washington, and passed as a white man. A neighbor took in Margaret's younger brother, two-year-old Michael, the baby of the family. Relatives on her mother's side initially took in young Margaret. Eventually she went to live with a seamstress and her husband, who had become foster parents of sorts to homeless and "unable-to-care-for children."[27] In the meantime, several of Margaret's older siblings had crossed the racial divide. Except for one brother, Edward, and his light-skinned wife Minette—who lived in Buffalo and kept in touch with relatives even after they had begun to pass—the other siblings were never heard from again.

In researching *The Sweeter the Juice*, Shirlee Taylor Haizlip was able to track down some of her mother's long-lost relatives, although most of them were deceased by then. Several siblings resided or had resided in the Midwest and on the West Coast. Another sibling, Ruth, and her light-skinned African American husband, had moved to Brazil, where they became members of the white elite. After her husband's death, Ruth is said to have returned to Philadelphia in the 1950s, where her trail ends. But Shirlee was able to reunite her mother Margaret with her sister Grace after almost seventy years of separation. Shirlee also reunited her mother with some of the "European American" descendants of her mother's siblings who had passed as white. These descendants were unaware that they had any African American ancestry.

The Sweeter the Juice not only further underscores the fateful consequences of the one-drop rule but also points out how closely African-descent and European-descent Americans are related genealogically (not to mention culturally), despite the nation's historical amnesia on the subject. Indeed, Shirlee points out that her family history is not an aberration but a typically American story. "Multiply these instances many times over and the foot prints of those who have crossed the color line become infinite and untraceable," she writes.[28]

Blue-vein Societies: The Light Brigade

Passing is necessarily an individual strategy available to a small percentage of African-descent Americans, and probably only a minority of individuals who could pass actually have done so. Those who have been unwilling or unable to pass often have sought collectively to counter systematic subordination through the formation of pluralistic elites within the African American community. Convinced that they suffered from racial stereotypes stemming from the behavior of the "untutored" and "submerged" black masses, who possessed little knowledge of or appreciation for "the laws governing society," the multiracial elites were adamant about holding themselves aloof from the black masses, and vigorously opposed any form of segregation that restricted them to an African American place.[29] Restrained by their pride, however, from mingling in European American society, where they would be rebuffed, the multiracial elites tended to withdraw into their own exclusive social world. The degree of one's acceptance into this social network depended on one's approximation to the dominant European American psychosomatic norm. The multiracial elite valued light skin, straight hair, and sharp features, as well as European culture and thought, and distanced themselves from the image typically held of blacks. Their escape from blackness was illusory, however, for they never achieved social equality with whites.[30]

This multiracial elite, which evolved directly from the antebellum free people of color, was descended from slaves who gained their freedom by enlisting in either the British or American forces during the American Revolution, slaves who had been emancipated by legislation or court decisions, slaves who had gained freedom through self-purchase or whose relatives or friends had purchased their freedom for them, runaway slaves, and others who were born of free parents or at least free mothers.[31] Even more members of this elite descended from parents and grand-parents who were granted preferential emancipation from servitude—both indenture and slavery—which often happened with the offspring of interracial unions, who were "generally freed after a specified term of servitude if the mother was white, or perhaps manumitted by a conscience-stricken white father."[32]

Throughout the antebellum period, most individuals of African descent, multiracial as well as black, were enslaved. In all regions of the United States, however, multiracial individuals were disproportionately represented, compared to blacks, among the free.[33] European Americans successfully prevented antebellum Free Coloreds from integrating into the mainstream of society as their equals, and most of them remained illiterate, propertyless, and poor.[34] Long before the abolition of slavery, however, many had achieved a certain amount of education and economic security and established lifestyles that not only differentiated them from the slave masses but paralleled the social and cultural life of whites.

The multiracial elite was not only culturally and socially but also spatially remote from the black masses, especially from those who were crammed into urban tenements and back-alley dwellings. They lived in relatively comfortable houses in "respectable" and often fashionable neighborhoods, where lifestyle and values more closely resembled those of the "best people" of the dominant European American community. A few of the elite not only owned comfortable urban residences but also "country places" or "summer homes."[35] Others could escape the summer heat by taking cottages in places like Harpers Ferry, Virginia, or at well-known resorts such as Saratoga Springs. Access to certain vacation resorts, like Highland Beach on Chesapeake Bay, were restricted to the phenotypically more European of the elite.[36]

Despite their elitism and attempts to distance themselves from the black masses, the multiracial elite was sympathetic to less fortunate African Americans. They knew that they constituted a privileged class of a stigmatized minority and considered themselves an aristocracy with a legitimate "right to govern socially and a responsibility to serve by example and take action in the cause of racial uplift."[37] If their interest in the moral and intellectual uplift of the black masses was patronizing, the multiracial elite genuinely saw itself as the solution to the race problem. They argued that if they were "given rights as rapidly as they merited them," then they would be inspired and in turn inspire "the fellows of the lower grade."[38] But the multiracial elite often found its efforts at uplift thwarted by the condescension of European Americans on the one hand and criticism from blacks on the other. Few possessed the wealth and leisure to contribute on the scale that their critics seemed to expect of them. And their ambivalence toward the larger African American community was heightened by the numerous problems of the ever-increasing population of unskilled and low-income blacks in American cities. Not even the most civic-minded among the elite could always avoid feeling a sense of futility.[39]

Washington, D.C.'s Colored Elite

The formation of multiracial elites was primarily an urban phenomenon, since rural African American communities lacked the socioeconomic resources for color stratification to develop. This is not to say that color consciousness did not exist in rural areas but that color differences were relatively less important because other factors were absent.[40] In urban areas, by contrast, color combined with cultural and socioeconomic factors to heighten differences between individuals of African descent. Virtually every major urban center in the United States has had a section where predominantly multiracial individuals have resided. In Chicago these elites have historically tended to cluster in Chatham and East Hyde Park; in Los Angeles, they have concentrated in affluent residential enclaves such as Baldwin Hills, Windsor Hills, View Park, and Ladera Heights. In Harlem, the elites have resided primarily in Stivers Row—located between West 138th and West 139th Streets and Seventh and Eight Avenues—as well as in exclusive neighborhoods in and nearby the Sugar Hill section.[41] Cities such as Charleston, Washington, D.C., Philadelphia, Nashville, Louisville, New Orleans, Boston, New York, and Atlanta, to mention only a few, were well known for their "blue-vein" societies, their "Four Hundred," "Talented Tenth," or "Upper Ten."[42]

Washington, D.C., in particular, has historically been described as the "capital" of the multiracial elite. Indeed, Washington's multiracial elite was the envy of "Upper Ten" African Americans throughout the United States and became the standard by which others measured their culture, refinement, and wealth. No other city in the United States possessed such a concentration of old multiracial families. Measured by the standards of the larger African American community, these families were economically well to do and well educated; most were light-skinned and had been free for a generation or more before the Civil War. After the war, they occupied the most important positions in the District's government and educational system. The comparatively more favorable circumstances in Washington for the multiracial elite can be explained by the cultural and educational opportunities available to them, as well as the availability of well-paying white-collar jobs—particularly in government—commensurate with their talents, education, and aspirations. The presence of the prestigious African American college, Howard University, was especially important.

Indeed, a large portion of the elite consisted of public school personnel and university professors primarily serving the African American community.[43]

Their children, often educated in private academies and universities in New England, tended to enter the professions of law, medicine, and education. Where the family was prominent in the business and social life of the African American population before the Civil War, their descendants remained so well into the late nineteenth century. Family continuity was frequently considered an essential prerequisite for admission into the multiracial elite of Washington at the turn of the century. In short, these families constituted an exclusive, self-consciously elite group of individuals who were bound together by shared values, tastes, and self-perceptions emphasizing family background, "good" breeding, occupation, respectability, and color.[44]

Few members of the multiracial elite were more prominent than Washington, D.C.'s Pinckney Benton Stewart Pinchback and his wife Nina. Pinchback, originally from New Orleans, rose rapidly in Republican politics in Louisiana. Elected lieutenant governor in 1871, he served as acting governor for more than a month during the tumultuous Reconstruction era. In 1873, the Louisiana legislature elected him to the U.S. Senate, but after a prolonged and bitter struggle the Senate refused to seat him.

When the Pinchbacks moved to Washington in 1893, they blended quickly and easily into the local multiracial elite. Pinchback's substantial wealth and influence not only earned him and his wife a prominent place at the very peak of light-skinned society in the District but also made it possible for them to entertain lavishly. The Pinchback children—three sons, Pinckney, Walter, and Bismark, and daughter Nina—grew up in a world that Eugene (Jean) Toomer, Nina's son and future writer of the Harlem Renaissance, characterized as existing halfway between the black and white worlds. Pinchback's aspirations for his children were similar to those of most of the ruling-class whites of his time. He sent his daughter to a finishing school in Massachusetts and his sons to Yale, the University of Pennsylvania, and Howard to pursue courses in pharmacy, medicine, and law.[45]

Few members of the multiracial elite in Washington or elsewhere acquired the wealth or attained the prominence of the Pinchbacks. Still, the majority enjoyed a degree of financial security unknown to most African Americans (or to many European Americans, either), which dramatized the economic gulf between themselves and most black Americans. For the day laborer or even the skilled artisan, the economic resources of physicians, public-school teachers, administrators, and attorneys (who largely served the needs of the District's African American population), government employees, certain businessmen, Howard University faculty members, and others constituted wealth almost beyond comprehension. In addition to those who were employed in the professions or in the federal government, the multiracial elite in Washington and elsewhere included families in such service trades as catering, barbering, and tailoring, which brought them into regular contact with elite whites.

Some of the multiracial elite inherited wealth; others accumulated substantial property, especially in real estate; a few were wealthy even by elite white standards.[46]

Even so, many members of the elite struggled to make ends meet while seeking to keep up appearances. The expenses involved in maintaining a residence at a fashionable address and entertaining properly sometimes led them to live beyond their means. And few could be described as wealthy when compared to the enormous fortunes of late-nineteenth- and early-twentieth-century European American families such as the Carnegies, Astors, Guggenheims, Vanderbilts, and Rockefellers. Virtually all of the multiracial elite were part of a "working aristocracy,"[47] despite pretensions, leisurely aspirations, an elevated standard of living, or the educational opportunities they provided their children.

Great financial wealth was not a prerequisite for membership in Washington's colored elite. They surrounded themselves with books, paintings, fine furniture, and musical instruments, but these things did not require great fortunes.[48] More important than money, European ancestry (preferably aristocratic ancestry); a more European phenotype—specifically, skin coloring light enough to show veins—education; industry; thrift; sobriety; fastidiousness in speech habits, manners, and dress; wealth, professional standing, and, sometimes, close social contact with European Americans all combined to qualify one for membership in or marriage into a numerically small and select elite.[49] It is uncertain whether there were actually churches with front doors painted a shade of light brown to discourage entrance by persons of a darker hue. But religious affiliation did frequently follow color, cultural, and class lines. In each city the elite attended two or three high-status churches. Multiracial individuals often gravitated toward Episcopal, Congregational, Presbyterian, and Catholic churches and away from Baptist or Methodist (except Methodist Episcopal), though there were numerous exceptions to the rule, such as the Fifth Street Baptist Church in Louisville, Kentucky.[50]

Disdainful of gaudiness and ostentation, the multiracial elite dressed "tastefully" at social gatherings, where one encountered people who spoke "flawless" English and exhibited all the earmarks of education, sophistication, and wealth. Graduates from Yale, Harvard, Cornell, Oberlin, and other prominent European American institutions of learning were counted at social gatherings among Washington's elite. African American preparatory schools such as the Palmer Institute in North Carolina, M Street High School (later renamed Dunbar) in Washington, D.C., and historically African American colleges such as Howard University, Atlanta University in Georgia, Hampton Institute in Virginia, Morgan University in Baltimore, Spelman Women's College in Atlanta, and Fisk University in Nashville became bastions of the multiracial elite.

Certain Greek fraternities and sororities on these campuses have been accused of partiality to individuals of a comparatively European phenotype. The famous Cotton Club, particularly at its inception, was notorious for excluding all but the most phenotypically European African-descent women from its chorus line, and African Americans, regardless of phenotype, were prohibited from patronizing the establishment.[51] And then there were the infamous paper bag and comb tests that prohibited the entry to social dances and the like of all persons darker than a brown paper bag and whose hair was too curly to allow a comb to pass through smoothly.[52] To this day, elite African American social clubs such as the Links and Jack and Jill—founded in 1938 and 1946, respectively—have a disproportionate number of individuals of "visible" European ancestry, although social and cultural orientation associated with economic affluence now serve as equally if not more important criteria for membership.[53]

The Darkening of the Light

Regional variations notwithstanding, European Americans historically have had little inclination to recognize either legal or informal social distinctions among individuals of African descent. An attempt was made to count blacks and mulattoes among the African American population in each census year from 1850 to 1920 except 1880 and 1900. In 1890, the count was further broken down into quadroon and octoroon. Census enumerators were instructed to be particularly careful to distinguish between blacks, mulattoes, quadroons, and octoroons; "black" was to be used to describe individuals who had three-fourths or more African ancestry; "mulatto" for persons who had three-eighths to five-eighths African ancestry; "quadroon" for individuals of one-fourth African ancestry; and "octoroon" for persons who had one-eighth or less African ancestry. The methods, however, were often sloppy and the definitions of these categories varied. The fact that census takers used visual criteria certainly led to an undercount of the number of African Americans of partial European descent. In 1900 the mulatto, quadroon, and octoroon categories were dropped. Mulatto was reintroduced in 1910 and 1920 but was never used again. Negro, Afro-American, or black became the official census terms.[54] In practice, however, the differences between words describing varying degrees of African American ancestry were always more semantic than social and had little or no significance in the United States beyond their usage in the creation of a pecking order among individuals of African descent.[55]

The preoccupation with classifying African-descent Americans in the 1890 census represented an attempt to measure the extent of miscegenation and reflected white concern about the decline of Anglo-American civilization. This concern reached new heights in the eugenics movement of the early twentieth century, which held that mental and other qualities, including "frailties" and "debilitating propensities," were for the most part inherited. Eugenicists advocated preserving (and "improving") Anglo-North American "racial stock" as a "master" or "super" race by encouraging reproduction only of people of exceptional intelligence. They also advocated ridding the population of inferior elements through sterilization and other means. Ultimately the eugenics movement succeeded in getting Congress to pass national-origins quota legislation, notably the Immigration Act of 1924, which restricted immigration to the United States from everywhere except Northern and Western Europe and the Western Hemisphere.[56]

The preoccupation with degrees of blackness must also be seen against the prevailing racial politics, which sought to prevent multiracial individuals from crossing the racial divide and taking advantage of white privilege. This was particularly true in the southern states, where the emancipation of slaves meant that African Americans were no longer as easily counted as in pre–Civil War censuses that divided the population into free people and slaves.[57] Southern whites' fear of miscegenation led to the consolidation of the one-drop rule in the early part of the twentieth century.

Whatever success the multiracial elites may have had in dissociating themselves from the surrounding African American community, they were unable to escape the disabilities and proscriptions imposed on all African-descent Americans by a racist society that believed that one-drop of African blood was enough to place an individual in the "inferior caste."[58]

From 1896 to 1904, the U.S. Supreme Court upheld southern strategies to deprive African Americans of the right to vote, which they had been granted by the Fifteenth Amendment during Reconstruction. The Court also upheld southern laws mandating the racial segregation of all public facilities (although it insisted that they be equally maintained, in keeping with the Equal Protection Clause of the Fourteenth Amendment, passed during Reconstruction), including schools and housing. In the North, theaters, restaurants, hotels, housing, and schools were also segregated in practice, even where the law forbade it.[59]

The climate of the military branches also reflected these trends. During World War I, segregated African American military troops did not receive the same support as did European American troops. And after returning from this "war to save democracy," many patriotic African American soldiers were lynched in their uniforms during the urban race riots of the early 1920s.[60] The number of African American lynchings by white mobs had declined from 150 a year in the 1890s to 75 per year after 1905, but in the 1920s race riots erupted in southern cities, as well as in New York, Tulsa, Oklahoma, and Springfield, Illinois. White mobs went on a rampage, indiscriminately murdering African Americans and wantonly destroying their property. In 1919, at the end of the war, a wave of race riots swept through twenty cities, to the indifference (or with the encouragement) of local police. By this time many African Americans had armed themselves and fired back at white mobs.[61]

White racism was not limited to the judicial and legislative branches of the U.S. government and the military but was reflected in the attitudes and policies of the executive branch as well. President Theodore Roosevelt initially praised African

American troops for their bravery during the Battle of San Juan Hill during the Spanish American War in 1898. Later he called them cowards, while publicly praising former Confederate leaders. In 1906 Roosevelt dealt harshly with black troops involved in the Brownsville race riots and falsely stated to Congress that lynchings were precipitated by the sexual assault of white women by black men. President William Howard Taft endorsed restrictions on African American suffrage and began the segregation of federal offices in Washington, D.C., a policy that was expanded during President Woodrow Wilson's administration; and President Warren G. Harding denounced racial amalgamation.[62]

The loss of the few privileges enjoyed by free people of color during the antebellum period dashed the multiracial elite's hopes of being integrated into the European American mainstream. Many sought to resist their loss of status by withdrawing ever more self-consciously into themselves.[63] Others held out hope that African Americans would ultimately achieve equality, even as they witnessed the hardening of racist practices and the erosion of civil rights. Most still expected to be in the vanguard of racial progress, which led to a marked shift in political consciousness, as the multiracial elite moved toward greater alliance with blacks. They provided a significant number of leaders in the early fight for civil rights, in part because these elite individuals continued to benefit from the advantages bestowed on them over generations.[64] Although a disproportionate number of the elite remained considerably European American in appearance and culture, the changing political climate diminished somewhat the emphasis that had previously been placed on skin color.[65]

This shift was demonstrated in the experience of Roscoe Bruce, the son of one of Washington's elite Mississippi senators, John Bruce. In his relations with European Americans, Senator Bruce tended to think of himself in class rather than racial terms, much as did others of the multiracial elite. But Bruce received a rude awakening when Harvard President A. Lawrence Lowell personally denied his son Roscoe a room in the freshman dormitory. Bruce expressed disappointment and dismay that his alma mater had adopted such a discriminatory policy, which diverged so sharply from the racial climate during his own tenure as a Harvard undergraduate. Bruce informed Lowell, "No son of mine will ever deny his name or his blood or his tradition in order to enter Harvard."[66]

Bruce had rarely confronted such overt racial discrimination. As a man who took great pride in his Harvard education, Bruce, like others of his class, viewed himself as a cultural broker who could speak both to African Americans and for African Americans to European Americans. Intimately acquainted with the culture of both racial groups, he had for most of his career functioned as a carrier of European American culture into the African American community. The refusal of his alma mater to extend to his son the same privileges that he had enjoyed twenty years earlier undoubtedly prompted him to reassess his place in American society, as similar incidents prompted other members of the multiracial elite to reexamine theirs. As a result, many began to attach greater significance to their African American ancestry and display a closer identification with African American society and culture.[67]

As European Americans became more obsessed with the delusions of their own racial purity, exclusivity, and superiority over individuals they designated as "Negroes," African Americans embraced the identifier "Negro"—as well as the one-drop rule—as part of what they considered a mutually beneficial process of "democratization" among black and multiracial individuals. Publicly the multiracial elite assumed positions of cultural and political leadership within the larger African American community, which now increasingly combined both blacks and mulattoes. Socially they removed the formal barriers against marriage with darker-skinned African Americans; they retained these barriers only as matters of personal preference, snobbery, and what was later defined as "colorism."

In addition, the cumulative effects of enforced endogamy and "internal miscegenation" between multiracial individuals and blacks reached such a point by the 1920s that the majority of African Americans were well on their way to becoming more or less multiracial in terms of ancestry; and census takers ceased to enumerate African Americans as "multiracial" and "black."[68] Official state policies reflected these changes. Fourteen southern states found it necessary to define legal blackness. Seven of them adopted the one-drop rule as the official definition. In 1910 Virginia abandoned its one-fourth rule and settled for one-sixteenth, on the assumption that lesser amounts could not be detected. Not until 1930 did Virginia explicitly resort to the one-drop rule. Early in the century seven states adopted the one-eighth rule. This allowed some persons to be classified as white who appeared to be partly black or had at least some African American forebears. Yet legislators were fully aware that the one-drop rule would prevail in cases where there was any serious question.[69]

These seismic sociocultural shifts of the late nineteenth and early twentieth centuries eclipsed the relatively privileged status maintained by the multiracial elite for almost three hundred years. By 1925, African Americans of all phenotypes were more equally scattered throughout the African American social structure. Wealth and cultural attributes had become more important than color in determining social status. Both formally and informally, as more African Americans became multiracial in terms of ancestry, individuals of a more European phenotype gradually came to regard themselves, and were regarded, less as multiracial and more as light-skinned blacks.[70]

The Harlem Renaissance—Rebirth or Still Birth?

Nowhere was this shift more clearly demonstrated than among the vanguard of the Harlem Renaissance of the 1920s. Although the Harlem Renaissance attracted both black and multiracial individuals, the descendants of the mulatto elite led the way.

Largely a product of the Talented Tenth, which itself was disproportionately made up of the multiracial elite, the Harlem Renaissance vanguard assumed a leadership role in defining and describing African Americans to themselves and the larger society. The term "Talented Tenth" was coined in 1896 by Henry L. Morehouse—a patron of liberal arts study for African Americans—to refer to a class of highly educated and morally upright African Americans he hoped would act as the vanguard for the black masses. In 1905, W.E.B. Du Bois, the most prominent African American in the country and founder in 1910 of *The Crisis*—the monthly publication of the National Association for the Advancement of Colored People (NAACP)—appropriated Morehouse's term when he called for a cadre of African Americans to be "leaders of thought and missionaries of culture among their people."[71]

Fully conscious that this cadre of exceptional men and women constituted a privileged class of a despised minority, Du Bois saw the Talented Tenth as spokespeople for less privileged African Americans. He genuinely believed that they held the key to the solution of the race problem in the United States. If this elite were given rights as rapidly as they merited them, the argument went, they would be inspired and in turn would inspire ordinary black people. Although the concept of the Talented Tenth was inherently elitist, Du Bois did not believe that membership was premised on color and would in fact have rejected such a notion as racist.

Light skin color was nevertheless an implicit attribute of this vanguard, and Du Bois later rejected the notion of the Talented Tenth as a misguided form of elitist assimilationism. But the concept must be examined in historical context. Despite its elitism and even its preference for light-skinned African Americans, the concept of the Talented Tenth may be viewed as one of the tactics African Americans have deployed in the struggle for equality.

The emergence of this "New Negro" in Harlem is closely tied to the fact that in the first two decades of the twentieth century New York had become the new land of opportunity for African Americans, just as Washington, D.C., had been during and after Reconstruction. Between 1914 and 1930, there was a significant migration of African Americans of all colors and classes from the South to the North, due to an economic depression, the ravages of the cotton boll weevil, which caused massive crop failures, and terrible flooding. During World War I, the conscription of many white males to the military draft and the reduction in European immigration created a labor shortage in the North that accelerated this migration. Plentiful jobs that paid relatively well—along with the disincentives of Jim Crow laws and virulent racism in the South—drew many African Americans to northern cities.[72]

African Americans thus were no longer merely a southern rural people but became part of the growing metropolitan areas that formed the twentieth century's urban ghettos—most famously Chicago's South Side, and, especially, Harlem, the upper part of Manhattan island first established as a Dutch village early in the seventeenth century. The same job opportunities that attracted African Americans to the North attracted African-descent populations from Latin America and the Caribbean as well.[73] Thanks to this deluge of black migrants and immigrants, the African American population in New York City increased by 250 percent between 1914 and 1930, when it reached 327,706; virtually all African American New Yorkers lived in Harlem. But this African American mecca was a segregated ghetto and slum. Thirty percent of all dwellings lacked bathing facilities; the death rate from tuberculosis was five times greater than for whites in Manhattan; and schools were segregated—education for blacks reflected their predominant employment in domestic service and unskilled labor and their exclusion from skilled blue-collar, clerical, and professional work.[74]

Scholar of philosophy Naomi Zack points out that it is indeed impressive, if not miraculous, that the leaders of the Harlem Renaissance forged a positive sense of cultural identity and awareness in such abject circumstances, as well as in the face of the hostilities of the larger racial ecology of the United States.[75] Although it began in New York, Harlem's Renaissance extended to Chicago, Washington, Atlanta, and every other city with a large African American population. As part of the "New Negro Movement," the Harlem Renaissance also attracted the attention of European Americans and reflected a mutually beneficial, egalitarian integration of many whites and blacks. Some individuals, such as Carl Van Vechten, were genuine patrons of the arts who sought to expose the white world to the tremendous outpouring of talent involved in the Harlem Renaissance.[76] The Harlem Renaissance also influenced the thinking of many white European and American intellectuals, who espoused different forms of pragmatism and cultural nationalism, and these thinkers in turn helped shape the Harlem movement. For example, anthropologist Franz Boas challenged the scientific racism on which the eugenics movement and other racist projects were premised, while sociologist Robert Park supported, among other things, the endeavors of African Americans to build their own institutions and culture in the manner of egalitarian pluralism.[77]

Other European Americans were racial voyeurs who looked to Harlem as a place where they could "let down their own hair," or liberate themselves from the constraints of Protestant American values and morality by "releasing themselves" in what they considered the "carefree" and "uninhibited" lifestyle of African Americans.[78] Their appropriation of blackness, which they saw as chic, exotic, or risqué, often bordered on cultural grand larceny, and it should not be confused with a willingness to exchange white privilege for the hipness or "cool" they associated with black life. And it certainly did not translate into the extension of white privilege to African Americans.[79]

By denying African-descent Americans equality with European Americans, the changing circumstances in the first quarter of the twentieth century, including enforcement of the one-drop rule, furthered the process of "intraracial democratization" between black and multiracial individuals. Ultimately, these circumstances would serve as the basis for mass mobilization and collective action in the twentieth-century struggle for civil rights—a struggle in which the multiracial elite was able to provide much-needed leadership. Even given the heightened racial consciousness, the racial attitudes of the Harlem Renaissance vanguard were very much different from the eugenics movement, at one extreme, and Black Nationalism, at the other. Many of the Harlem Renaissance artists and thinkers had close personal and professional relationships with European Americans. Some married interracially, and a few even explored the multiracial experience in their writing. But the message that comes through loud and clear in Harlem Renaissance writings on multiracialism is that the only meaningful future for multiracial individuals involved a full and joyful embrace of black identity. If, therefore, the Harlem Renaissance was a "rebirth" of African American identity, and at the same time an important "interracial moment," it was also a "still birth." The protagonists of the Harlem Renaissance sacrificed the concept of multiracial identity as an "intellectual weapon" and "theoretical wedge" against the essentialized conceptualization of biological race and racial categories, as well as white racism and the dichotomization and hierarchical valuation of blackness and whiteness that originated in Eurocentric dynamics.[80]

The "pan-African Americanism" forged by Harlem Renaissance leaders such as W.E.B. Du Bois, Jean Toomer, Countee Cullen, Langston Hughes, Zora Neale Hurston, and James Weldon Johnson is therefore somewhat paradoxical. This vanguard turned for inspiration to the black experience—to African American culture and the vitality of African American art, music, and social relations—and was directly engaged with the question of what it meant to be an African American. They sought to achieve this identity through a new appreciation of southern rural African American life, the human dignity of African American slaves, and early-twentieth-century African American urban poverty. Yet at the same time they fused this vision with their own essentially European American sociocultural tradition.[81]

This "double consciousness" was best captured by W.E.B. Du Bois, although this duality was not seen as an actual racial "twoness." Rather, blacks viewed themselves as products of two warring cultural identities and nations—one American and the other African American. By forging what was essentially a hybridized "Afro-Saxon" tradition within an African American cultural framework, the Harlem Renaissance vanguard were perhaps able to act out symbolically their own multiple backgrounds without daring to confront them fully. Multiple racial ancestries, therefore, were overridden by a single racial identity and a bicultural experience forged in the American context. The Harlem Renaissance leaders could not, or would not, even so much as conceptualize a multiracial identity intermediate to black and white that was constructed on egalitarian premises.[82]

Naomi Zack points out that any critique of the Harlem Renaissance's rejection of multiracial identity as a neutral position between black and white must consider the limitations of the contemporary racial order and can be meaningful only in light of the alternative choices that were available later.[83] The one-drop rule was not a neutral theoretical demarcation but an expression of the virulent racist sentiment that pervaded white society in the early twentieth century. The one-drop rule reinforced the low regard in which European Americans held African Americans and the stigma they attached to African ancestry.

Although the elite of the Harlem Renaissance fully embraced the one-drop rule and set themselves up as the spokespeople of ordinary blacks, this role would in fact fall to Marcus Garvey, the more militant pan-Africanist from Jamaica, who declared that he spoke for the "untalented ninetieth" of the black masses. The leaders of the Harlem Renaissance were representatives of the Talented Tenth and maintained an elite class position in the African American community, no matter how they may have sought to deny or transcend that fact. They were also numerically few, and actually touched relatively few people. Yet they were a dynamic vanguard that sought to challenge the racial elitism of the past, and as harbingers of the future, they signaled the winds of social change.

CHAPTER FOUR

Black by Law: Multiracial Identity and the Ternary Racial Project

Triracial Isolates: Runaways and Refusniks

Scattered throughout the eastern United States, particularly in the southeast, there are some two hundred communities of varying combinations and degrees of European American, Native American, and African American descent, commonly called triracial isolates. They are pluralistic in nature, like the blue-vein societies, yet whereas the latter formed an urban elite within the African American community, the former live apart from both blacks and whites, in communities on the fringes of villages and towns or in isolated rural enclaves. Many individuals have remained in these rural communities as unskilled laborers or as impoverished tillers of the soil. Others have migrated to the cities and become prosperous farmers, college graduates, and professionals.[1] Among the prominent individuals descended from these communities is actress Heather Locklear, whose mother's lineage is predominantly Scottish, and whose father's side of the family includes distant antecedents who were Lumbees, which is a community located in Robeson County, North Carolina.[2]

Although these communities have much in common and have been collectively designated by social scientists as triracial isolates, many of their members vehemently reject such labeling, and they are not a single identifiable group.[3] While most are small and located in hilly, swampy, or densely wooded areas not accessible to the general public, the Lumbees, for example, have had as many as forty thousand members.[4] The common attributes of these communities have less to do with cultural bonds than with similarities in experience and in living conditions that unite them in their refusal to accept the United States binary racial project.[5]

Because documentary evidence is scanty, the exact origins of these groups and their names are unknown. This uncertainty is compounded by the fact that at different times in the antebellum period, depending on the determination of the census enumerator, the same families were sometimes listed as white, mulatto, and free people of color.[6] To complicate matters further, it was not until the mid-nineteenth century that the last term came to be more or less interchangeable with the categories of free mulatto and free black. Up to that time, the term free people of color had included Native American reservations; Native American rural communities; multiracial populations of Native American, European American, and African American descent; multiracial populations of European American and African American descent; and free blacks. In all probability, the triracial isolate communities evolved from frontier settlements that became magnets for runaway slaves, trappers, homesteaders, adventurers, deserters, outlaws, outcasts, and nonconformists of all racial backgrounds, but "internal miscegenation," fostered by self-imposed isolation, led to a generalized blending over time.

The triracial isolates are known by a wide variety of names. New York is the home of the Van Guilders, the Clappers, the Shinnecock, the Poospatuck, the Montauk, the Mantinecock, and the Jackson Whites. In Pennsylvania, they are called Pools; in Delaware, Nanticokes; in Rhode Island, Narragansetts; in Massachusetts, Gay Heads and Mashpees; in Ohio, Carmelites. Maryland has its Wesorts; West Virginia its Guineas; and Tennessee its Melungeons. There are the Ramps, Issues, and Chickahominy in Virginia; the Lumbees, Haliwas, Waccamaws, and Smilings in North Carolina; Chavises, Creels, Brass Ankles, Redbones, Redlegs, Buckheads, and Yellowhammers, all in South Carolina. Louisiana is the home of a host of triracial communities.[7]

Appellations such as Chavis and Creel are family names, although many others, such as Brass Ankle and Redbone, are externally imposed and are clearly meant to be disparaging epithets. As such, they are anathema to those who bear them. Names such as Chickahominy and Nanticoke, which suggest Native American derivation, are borne proudly. Some individuals in these communities would in fact readily be taken as Native American. Others are indistinguishable from whites, and a good many show varying degrees of African ancestry in combination with European or Native American descent. Enclaves in St. Landry Parish, Louisiana, in Gouldtown, New Jersey, and in Darke County, Ohio, have always acknowledged their African ancestry, although they have isolated themselves somewhat from mainstream society and have drawn a line between themselves and other locals of African descent.[8]

In the southeast, any term describing a racially blended background generally has included African American ancestry, been equated with mulatto, and been translated into black. Most of these communities have thus affirmed only two components historically—Native American and European American—if they acknowledge their multiracial ancestry at all.[9] In this sense, the triracial isolate quest for identity appears to be more reactionary than revolutionary. Yet these communities have manipulated the United States binary racial project to their advantage, and have variously forged a ternary racial project, which has destabilized binary racial thinking in the process.[10]

The Case of Allen Platt

This dynamic was most clearly demonstrated in the celebrated case of *Allen Platt et al. v. The Board of Public Instruction of Lake County, Florida*. The Platt family had remained apart from African Americans in Holly Hill, South Carolina, for generations, but they had never been part of the European American community either. In the fall of 1954, Allen Platt decided to leave his home near Holly Hill and move to Florida in order to make a better life for himself and his family. His brother, who had earlier moved to Florida, experienced a significant improvement in his financial situation, and he and his family were readily accepted as whites. Allen Platt left Holly Hill with similar expectations.[11]

The Platt family moved to Florida and eventually settled in Mount Dora, a small town in the center of the state. Allen Platt soon secured employment as a fruit picker and rented a cottage. The move to Florida seemed to be paying off until five of the Platt children started school. A few classmates noticed their tan skin coloring and told their parents. Rumors about the racial background of the Platts reached the sheriff of Lake County, in which Mount Dora was located. The sheriff, an avowed white supremacist, gathered two armed deputies and a photographer and paid the Platt family a visit. Upon arriving, the sheriff had the terrified children line up to have their photographs taken. Pointing to one of the male children the sheriff said, "You know, he favors a nigger." Squinting at one of the female siblings he said, "I don't like the shape of that one's nose."[12] On the basis of this "evidence," the sheriff concluded that the Platts were African American and advised them to stay out of school until he could investigate the matter further. The principal, the superintendent, and the school board agreed that the Platt children should not return until the matter was settled.[13]

Allen Platt tried to present "evidence" that he and his family were not African American. When his words fell on deaf ears, he considered moving to another county, especially after the family began to be harassed. For example, an unidentified man notified the Platts' landlord that their house might burn down if they were not evicted, and the landlord promptly insisted that they move. Although the Platts had difficulty persuading anyone else to rent to them, they eventually found another home in nearby Orange County, where they were at least safe from the sheriff.[14]

The entire matter might have ended at that point had it not been for the editor of Mount Dora's weekly newspaper, the *Topic*, who gave Allen Platt an opportunity to publish his side of the story. Platt insisted that he was a blend of Irish and Native American descent and had absolutely no African American ancestry. "If the children never see the inside of another school, they will not go to a Negro school," he said.[15] The article infuriated Mount Dora's white residents, and many of them joined a campaign of terror against both the editor of the *Topic* and the Platts. Others supported Allen Platt and contributed to a legal fund established in his name. Several white lawyers volun-

teered to defend his case and filed a suit in circuit court asking for a declaratory judg-
ment fixing the rights of the Platt children to attend a white school. The defendants'
attorneys filed a motion to dismiss the case on technical grounds but the court refused,
so they took their motion to the Supreme Court, which denied the appeal.

The case dragged on for several months. Witnesses were heard, depositions were
taken, evidence pro and con was amassed, and experts were consulted. There was
plenty of "evidence" to support the Platts' claims that they were not African American, to wit:

1. They never associated with African Americans.
2. They never attended African American churches.
3. Their relatives were buried in cemeteries that excluded African Americans.
4. Allen Platt's grandfather had served in the Confederate army and had subse-
   quently drawn a pension from the state of South Carolina.
5. Allen Platt's wife Laura's grandfather was a Confederate veteran, and received
   a pension.
6. They had attended schools that were classified as white.
7. Allen Platt's older sons had served as whites in the National Guard and had
   received honorable discharges.
8. Allen Platt was registered as white by the Selective Service in World War II.
9. Allen and Laura Platt's marriage license listed them as white.
10. They had always voted in the all-white Democratic primaries.[16]

Attorneys for the defendants were unable to find any loopholes in this formidable
evidence and had nothing with which to refute it. Their case rested on the flimsy argument that the Platts were called Croatian Native Americans on some records, and Webster's dictionary defined Croatians as people of blended Native American, European
American, and African American ancestry.[17] The sheriff also produced photocopies of
birth records of a number of South Carolinians by the name of Platt, all of them
African American. But the defense collapsed because it was unable to show any ancestral relationship between those individuals and the Platt family involved in the case.
Finally, on October 8, 1955—one year after the children had been expelled from the
Mount Dora School (and one year after the landmark *Brown v. Board of Education* decision that legally desegregated the public schools)—the court handed down its decision declaring that the Platts were legally white. Local residents nevertheless staunchly
defended their belief that the Platts were African American. A few nights after the decision, a mob set their home on fire. The sheriff declared to the local Lions' Club, "In
my book they're still mulattoes," and received a standing ovation.[18]

Triracial isolate communities have historically tended to deny African ancestry
and hold on to aboriginal descent as a prized possession, despite the fact that they
typically retain little or nothing of Native American culture, have no memory of
their tribal affiliations, and are culturally indistinguishable from local whites.[19] This

positive bias toward aboriginal ancestry is explained in part by the fact that although both Native Americans and African Americans were enslaved by European Americans and still experience oppression in one form or another, aboriginal ancestry has never carried the stigma that has consistently been attached to African descent.[20] In addition, the smallest amount of Native American ancestry has qualified individuals for federal assistance, voting rights, and land claims—meager privileges that have not always been available to blacks. Moreover, by the twentieth century, the Native American threat to white territorial expansion had been sufficiently neutralized by extermination and relocation. Hence the romanticization of Native Americans and the phenomenon of white pride in any trace of aboriginal ancestry.[21] This romanticization, like any other cultural or psychological fact, has changed over time, depending on prevailing attitudes and policies. This is ironic, and tragic, given that it is usually far more difficult for Native Americans today to achieve political, economic, and educational equity than it is for African Americans.[22]

Moreover, if racial composition and ancestry have always determined who is African American, there is by contrast no universally accepted definition of Native American.[23] The definitions of the U.S. Census Bureau and the Bureau of Indian Affairs have often been at odds with each other, and both have shifted over time. The Bureau of Indian Affairs includes on its rolls only those individuals entitled to bureau services. Acceptance by a tribe, however it may be defined, in conjunction with proof of at least one-quarter degree of aboriginal ancestry, is generally required. For census purposes, self-definition has been the prevailing policy for all racial and ethnic groups since 1970. In the past, however, enumerators were instructed to record as Native American only those individuals enrolled on reservations or listed on agency rolls, persons of one-fourth or more aboriginal ancestry, or individuals regarded as Native Americans by their communities.[24]

Although these regulations were applied primarily to multiracial individuals of Native American and European descent, or to individuals who were perceived to be completely aboriginal in ancestry, the censuses of 1930 and 1940 and some state codes have applied the same criteria to multiracial individuals of Native American and African descent and to those of Native American, African, and European descent. For the most part, however, such individuals have been classified as black. Thus prevented by society from affirming all that they are without also being classified as African American, yet unable to claim residence on a reservation or prove that they meet the ancestry requirements, various triracial communities have nevertheless used the flexibility in the definition of Native American to their advantage.[25]

The Lumbees of North Carolina

The experience of the Lumbees of southeastern North Carolina is one of the best-documented cases studies of this dynamic. Historical accounts and oral traditions reveal that the indigenous ancestors of the contemporary Lumbees were composed largely of Cheraw and related Siouan-speaking people who were known to have inhabited the area in present-day Robeson County. They were first observed on Drowning Creek (known today as the Lumber River), when the first European settlers arrived in the area in 1724. The Lumbees' name is thus a neologism, coined in the 1950s from the manner in which the older generation pronounced the name of the Lumber River, which flows through their homeland.[26]

The Lumbees have been known as a "prickly and cantankerous" people who drove off Confederate tax collectors during the Civil War and, perhaps unique in the South, forced the Ku Klux Klan to flee Robeson County after their much-publicized attack on Klansmen in a pitched battle in 1958. They have been recognized by the state of North Carolina as a Native American tribe since 1885. With this recognition came educational assistance and other services. In 1887 the state established a Native American teacher training school for the Lumbees, which grew into the first state-supported school in the country to provide higher education for Native Americans. Today it is known as the University of North Carolina at Pembroke and boasts an enrollment of approximately three thousand students. The school is one of the sixteen institutions that make up the University of North Carolina system, and it may explain Lumbee assertions that they have produced more doctors, lawyers, and Ph.D.s than any other Native American community in the United States.[27]

According to the 1990 census, 48,444 Native Americans identified their tribe as Lumbee. This makes the Lumbees the second-largest tribe east of the Mississippi River and the ninth-largest in the country. The Lumbees are also the largest non-reservation and non-federally recognized tribe in the United States. In addition, they make up roughly half of North Carolina's Native American population of 84,000.[28] It was not until 1956, however, that the U.S. Congress passed the Lumbee Act, which officially recognized the Lumbees of Robeson and adjoining counties as the Lumbee Indians of North Carolina. Unfortunately for the Lumbees, the bill contained language that made them ineligible for financial aid and program services administered by the Bureau of Indian Affairs, partly because the bill was passed at a time when federal assistance to Native Americans was being cut back substantially. Although recognized as Native Americans by North Carolina and the federal government—and thus eligible for some federal services and assistance from the Department of Labor, Office of Indian Education, and the Administration for Native Americans—the Lumbees are nevertheless excluded from most services provided by the Bureau of Indian Affairs.[29]

Many Lumbees have held local elective office, and a Lumbee has represented Robeson County in the North Carolina legislature. Lumbee tribal members are active in American Indian affairs at the state and national levels and are still fighting, with the aid of the Lumbee Regional Development Association (LRDA), for federal recognition as a tribe. North Carolina Senator Jesse Helms is largely responsible for the fact that, in 1992, the Lumbees' federal recognition petition failed by only two votes in the U.S. Senate. Helms said funds for such things as education and health care for the Lumbees would just be too expensive. Some say that even other Native American tribes did not want recognition of the Lumbees because this would decrease their share of government funds. Other critics point out that the Lumbees do not live on a reservation, have never signed a treaty with the United States, and cannot prove they are all members of the same tribe.[30] To the Lumbees, Native American identity has nothing to with such arbitrary criteria. It is a matter of how they are perceived and whether they are respected. The Lumbees continue to work through the current federal channels for the establishment of an independent commission to evaluate Native American applications for recognition.[31] Such a bill has failed in the past, and the prospects continue to look unfavorable.[32] Neither the Congress nor the Bureau of Indian Affairs has yet granted recognition.

By 1980 the Nanticokes of Delaware, the Houma of western Louisiana, and the Poospatuck of Long Island, New York, following in the footsteps of the Lumbees and after a prolonged struggle, succeeded in officially changing their earlier classification as mulattoes to non-treaty Native Americans. Although this status excludes such groups as the Lumbees, the Nanticokes, the Houma, and the Poospatuck from government benefits, it does place them squarely on the aboriginal side of the racial divide. Many Lumbees, however, have become active in Native American affairs, only to have their claims to aboriginal status opposed by treaty or reservation groups such as the Cherokee, the Comanche, and the Choctaw, who do qualify for federal subsidies.[33]

Although some African Americans have accused the triracial isolate communities of donning feathers in order to escape the stigma of being black, various triracial groups have cast their lot with African Americans (communities in Darke County, Ohio, Gouldtown, New Jersey, and Cumberland County, Kentucky), and some individuals have committed the "unforgivable sin" of marrying blacks. Most have historically maintained a strong anti-black prejudice that has helped bolster white support for their Native American identity. The clearest example of this came during the era of segregation. Denied entry into white schools, numerous triracial isolate communities refused to attend the schools or use the public facilities designated for African Americans, and gained support for establishing their own public restrooms and education facilities, as well as their own separate sections in churches and theaters.[34]

Groups such as the Jackson Whites and the Issues have succeeded in negotiating alternative identities as "other non-whites."[35] Although some triracial individuals have always passed for white, groups such as the Brass Ankles and the Melungeons, who have persistently fought for legal status as white, have succeeded in their local communities if not with the government.[36] Other communities enjoy a status just below that of whites; elsewhere their status is hardly distinguishable from that of blacks. Overall, they seem to have a status intermediate to both. The price for all this has been the denial of African ancestry, sometimes the casting off of darker relatives, and the avoidance of every suspicion of association with blacks.[37]

Louisiana Creoles of Color: The French Resistance

The history of multiracial individuals in Louisiana and the Gulf ports after annexation by the United States is in many ways a synthesis of other strategies of resistance to the rule of hypodescent. In this region multiracial individuals sought to contest constructions of black and white racial categories and identities and at the same time sought to maintain their own racial privilege. The region has unique features that stem largely from the fact that the early patterns of French, Spanish, and English settlement in the lower South—the lower Mississippi Valley, the Gulf Coast, and South Carolina—followed the Latin American model. White settlers in "Latin" North America were small in number and primarily single males, who formed liaisons initially with Native American women and, after the introduction of slavery, with women of African descent. As in the rest of the Americas, there were formidable barriers to intermarriage. Informal unions, however, were more or less approved, if not encouraged, by the prevailing moral code.[38]

In fact, despite these legal restrictions, interracial unions became such an accepted social practice in Louisiana that they developed into a well-established institution called *plaçage*. This involved relationships, sometimes lasting for life, contracted between white men and women of color. The white male provided financial support for his multiracial offspring according to an agreement negotiated with the young woman's parents (usually her mother). But he could maintain his interracial family on one side of town while at the same time maintaining his life in white society in every respect, including, if he desired, marriage to a white woman.[39] This arrangement of institutional, if not legal, concubinage, along with the Quadroon Balls that emerged at the turn of the nineteenth century, made it possible for wealthy white men to maintain romantic and sexual liaisons with women of African descent, specifically multiracial women. Because most women of African descent were brutalized, auctioned, and enslaved, the *plaçage* system gave them the illusion of relative equality despite its patent classism, sexism, racism, and colorism.[40]

Compared to "Anglo" North America, the more socially sanctioned miscegenation in "Latin" North America—and Latin America generally speaking—coupled with the preferential liberation of slave mistresses and their multiracial offspring, made it possible for multiracial individuals early in colonial French Louisiana to enter the free classes. A similar pattern evolved in Spanish Alabama and Florida, particularly in the area surrounding Mobile, Pensacola, and St. Augustine.[41] Free people of color filled interstitial economic roles—particularly in the artisanal, manual, and skilled trades—and became an integral part of the economy by virtue of insufficient numbers of whites. Since whites and most Free Coloreds shared bonds of ancestry and culture, whites viewed Free Coloreds as natural and valuable allies against the black slave majority. This alliance often entailed the suppression of slave uprisings, as well as the capture and return of fugitive slaves.

The region's comparatively favorable situation for multiracial persons was enhanced by the fact that during the colonial period the distant European monarchs saw Free Coloreds as a military "balance-wheel" against independence-minded whites and necessarily provided some protection of their rights.[42] By granting multiracial individuals an intermediate status and privileges superior to those of blacks but inferior to those of whites, both the Crown and the colonists in "Latin" North America won the loyalty of the free people of color while maintaining white domination and control. In fact, many of Louisiana's multiracial citizens were slave-holding planters in parishes such as St. Landry, Iberville, and Plaquemines. Wealth not only made it possible for some to live in luxury and receive an education in Europe but, most important, gave them the means "to maintain themselves with poise and dignity in a white-dominated world."[43]

One of the most prosperous of these communities was inhabited by descendants of an African woman and a Frenchman named Metoyer who resided in Nachitoches Parish along the Cane River. Initially the Metoyers often found it necessary to marry among themselves because of the shortage of other free people of color in the immediate vicinity, the legal restrictions against marriages between whites and individuals of African descent, and the taint of slavery that would be attached to marrying blacks. With successive generations, however, the Cane River colony sought multiracial spouses either from families newly arrived in the area or from New Orleans, through a process of careful selection in which a more European phenotype and French cultural orientation were highly esteemed.[44]

The hostilities with Native Americans in the region, as well as the inhospitable climate and the difficulty of maintaining social and civic order, made the colony a source of greater trouble than profit for France. The French Crown welcomed the opportunity to rid itself of such an economic burden in the secret Treaty of Fontainebleau, signed on November 3, 1762, and in the public Treaty of Paris that ended the Seven Years' War (also known as the French and Indian War) in 1763. Canada and the eastern bank of the Mississippi River, excluding New Orleans, were ceded to Britain; New Orleans and the west bank of the Mississippi, to Spain. Britain returned Havana to Spain in exchange for Florida. Consequently, Louisiana became part of the well-established and wealthy Spanish empire in the Americas.[45]

By 1769 the Spanish had fully reestablished rule of Louisiana. Under the Spanish regime free people of color expanded rapidly, both by natural increase and because of the comparatively lenient manumission policies. In particular, Spanish law codified a customary practice known as *coartación*, which gave slaves the right to self-purchase based on a price stipulated by the master or arbitrated by the court.[46] At the same time, Spanish authorities—in part at the behest of the growing number of white women who saw free colored women as rivals—attempted to curb their activities in both the public and private spheres. In 1785 they passed legislation forbidding free women of color from wearing jewels and feathers and forcing them to wear their hair bound in a kerchief.[47] Officials eventually sought to outlaw the Quadroon Balls through similar legislation. Nevertheless, the *plaçage* system continued unabated. In addition, some legalized unions were contracted between European American men and women of African descent when Spanish authorities granted dispensation in individual cases. Both types of relationship were important sources for the continued growth in the numbers and wealth of Free Coloreds, particularly because mistresses of color and their mulatto offspring often received sizeable inheritances from wealthy white progenitors. These relationships also furthered the "mulattoization" and Europeanization of Louisiana's free people of color.[48]

By the end of the 1790s, Napoleon Bonaparte had reconsidered Louisiana's strategic location and New Orleans's importance as a port that could help him achieve his imperialist goals. On November 30, 1803, France regained control of the colony through negotiations with Spain (in fact Spain secretly transferred the colony to France on October 1, 1800, in exchange for an Italian kingdom for the Duke of Parma). A mere twenty days later France in turn transferred Louisiana to the United States.[49] By the time of the annexation of Louisiana by Anglo North America in 1803, free people of color had increased fourfold to number almost eight thousand, largely as a result of the influx of émigrés fleeing the revolution in Saint-Domingue.[50] Whites in Louisiana sought to prevent the entry of West Indian refugees through legislation but found such restrictions difficult to enforce because of lax administration of the laws or humane attitudes on the part of government officials.[51]

Whites feared the growth of the ranks of Free Coloreds by these West Indian émigrés, but even more worrisome was the black slave majority that surrounded them. They therefore tended to see the prosperity of multiracial individuals as a convenient hindrance to any potential alliance between Free Coloreds and black slaves. Acutely aware of their rights and interests, as well as of their fragile position, Free Coloreds thus tended to act with a high degree of cohesiveness. This enhanced their socioeconomic status and made Louisiana home to the most numerically significant and economically integrated population of Free Coloreds in the southeast. These same factors also heightened the distinction between multiracial and black, and thus ultimately helped to bolster the dominant position of whites.[52] Despite the generally oppressive conditions throughout North America, Free Coloreds in Louisiana were able not only to secure a relatively favorable status but also enjoyed the most secure position of any free people of color in the South.[53]

The Anglo-Americanization of "Latin" North America

The comparatively favorable circumstances in the lower South changed when the composite Creole population, including Spanish- and French-speaking whites as well as people of color in Louisiana and the Gulf ports of Mobile and Pensacola, came under U.S. control with the annexation of Louisiana (1803) and the Floridas (1810, 1819). Overwhelmed by an English-speaking majority, Creoles of all racial backgrounds remained aloof from the new arrivals, which they correctly perceived as a threat to their cultural and political survival.[54] They fought to maintain French (or Spanish) civil law, their unique cultural traditions, the teaching of French (or Spanish) in public schools, and Creole dominance over local and regional governments.[55] With Anglo-North Americanization, Creoles of color began the long quest to preserve their intermediate status, as they watched Louisiana's ternary racial order polarize into black and white.[56]

The U.S. occupation of Louisiana, along with the gradual though informal implementation of the one-drop rule in that region over the course of the nineteenth century, dismantled the intermediate status Creoles had maintained under the French and Spanish regimes. Ultimately, multiracial individuals were relegated to the subordinate status of blacks, deprived of citizenship, politically disenfranchised, and eventually segregated from European Americans.[57]

As part of their strategy for achieving this goal, Anglo-North Americans concentrated on securing economic, political, and social dominance by building a united ethno-racial white front against all individuals of African descent. By the time of the Civil War, the ethno-cultural tension between Anglo-Americans and Creoles of European descent abated, as whites rallied in support of "racial purity" and redefined Creoles on the basis of their Spanish and French ancestry.[58] Abandoned by their white brethren, many Creoles of color nevertheless had a vested social and economic interest in the southern way of life (close to one in every three Creole families owned slaves), and thus supported the Confederacy in a desperate attempt to arrest further erosion of their status.[59] With the Union capture of New Orleans, most switched their loyalties, hoping that with emancipation racial prejudice also would fall.

However, Union victory not only deprived them of wealth and property but dealt another blow to the status of Creoles, since all people of African descent were now free. Although the Louisiana Supreme Court as late as 1910 continued to distinguish between the terms "negro" and "person of color," which respectively designated black and multiracial individuals, the so-called "mystic letters" F.M.C. (free man of color) obviously no longer had the same significance as they had had in antebellum Louisiana.[60] Many Creoles of color resisted this decline by denying any similarity or community of interests with the sea of ex-slaves and English-speaking African Americans. Others, benefiting from the social, cultural, and intellectual advantages vested in them over generations, provided much of the political leadership of the freed slaves, serving as state senators and representatives in the Reconstruction government imposed by a victorious North on an embittered and hostile South.[61]

Plessy v. Ferguson and the Judicial Precedent

The withdrawal of federal troops brought the winds of change to post-Reconstruction Louisiana. A backlash by southern whites against the idea of racial democracy thwarted attempts by Creoles of color to hold on to the hard-won franchise and arrest the segregationist tide. Yet, given the relatively fluid racial and cultural relations in Louisiana, and the assertiveness and self-confidence of the Louisiana Creoles of color, a number of prominent Creoles continued to hope that something could be done to rescind the new and unjust laws.[62] In 1891, Creoles Louis A. Martinet, Caeser C. Antoine, Rodolphe Desdunes, and Artur Estèves, with the financial assistance of a venerable and radical Reconstruction Creole of color named Aristide Mary, founded the Comité des Citoyens (Citizens Committee) with the goal of mobilizing Creole resistance to state-imposed segregation.[63]

One of the Committee's first acts was to test the constitutionality of a railroad segregation statute—the 1890 Louisiana Separate Car Law—that required individuals of African descent to ride in special streetcars and railway carriages.[64] The Committee chose Homère A. Plessy, a young Creole artisan and community activist—who was of one-eighth African descent and thus indistinguishable from European Americans—as the perfect candidate to challenge the absurdity of this type of segregation. The newly created Citizens' Committtee, in cooperation with the *Crusader* newspaper, was the vehicle for negotiation on behalf of New Orleans's Creoles of color. On June 7, 1892, the Committee set its plan in motion when Plessy boarded the East Louisiana Railway in New Orleans and took a seat in the segregated white coach of the train. When approached by the conductor for his fare, Plessy declared himself to be an individual of African descent. He was asked to move to the car reserved for coloreds but refused. He was arrested, removed from the train, and fined.[65]

Plessy was bound over to the criminal court of the parish of New Orleans, where a plea was presented by his attorney, James C. Walker, but probably written by another attorney, Albion W. Tourgée. The plea contained fourteen specific objections to the segregation statute. Among these was the argument that "the Statute impairs the right of passengers of the class to which Relator [Plessy] belongs, to wit: Octoroons, to be classed among white persons, although color be not discernible in the complexion, and makes penal their refusal to abide by the decision of a Railroad conductor in this respect."[66] With Plessy's arrest, the Committee's legal counsel denounced the separate-car law for establishing "an insidious distinction and discrimination between Citizens of the United States based on race which is obnoxious to the fundamental principles of National Citizenship."[67] The segregation statute perpetrated "involuntary servitude as regards Citizens of the Colored Race under the merest pretense of promoting the comfort of passengers on railway trains."[68]

In these and other respects, the Committee asserted, the separate-car law abridged "the privileges and immunities of the Citizens of the United States and the rights secured by the 13th and 14th Amendments to the Federal Constitution."[69] Plessy and his supporters on the Committee took his case to the local court. They won their first suit against the separate-car law for trains that crossed state borders, but their opponents appealed to a higher court, which upheld the law. When state courts denied their arguments against the 1890 law, the Committee proceeded to the nation's highest court.[70] In light of the changing racial climate in Louisiana and earlier Supreme Court decisions, the prospect for a favorable outcome was not good. Nonetheless, when a despairing supporter of the Citizens' Committee complained that New Orleans Creoles of color were engaged in "a battle which is forlorn," Creole leader Rodolphe Desdunes insisted upon a militant strategy: "Liberty is won by continued resistance to tyranny. . . . [It is] more noble and dignified to fight, no matter what, than to show a passive attitude of resignation. Absolute submission augments the oppressor's power and creates doubts about the feelings of the oppressed."[71] On May 19, 1896, the Supreme Court did in fact uphold the lower court's decision and articulated the notorious "separate but equal" doctrine. It also denied that segregation was oppressive as long as facilities were equally maintained.

Plessy appeared before the New Orleans Criminal District Court in January 1897, pleaded guilty, paid a fine of twenty-five dollars, and was discharged. Before disbanding, the Citizens' Committee issued a final statement: "The Majority of Judges of the highest tribunal of this American government have cast their voice against our just appeal in demanding the nullification of a State law which is in direct conflict with the American Declaration of Independence, which declares that 'all men are created free and equal.' Notwithstanding this decision, which was rendered contrary to our expectations, we, as freemen, still believe that we were right, and our cause was sacred. . . . In defending the cause of liberty, we met with defeat, but not with ignominy."[72]

It was no surprise that part of Plessy's case rested on the question of racial definition. In the "brief for Homère Plessy" prepared by Tourgeé, the issue was raised to point out the arbitrary nature of the racial classification and to challenge the state's authority to define blackness.

Is not the question of race, scientifically considered, very often impossible of determination?

Is not the question of race, legally considered, one impossible to be determined, in the absence of statutory definition? . . .

The Court will take notice of the fact that, in all parts of the country, race-mixture has proceeded to such an extent that there are great numbers of citizens in whom the preponderance of blood of one race or another, is impossible of ascertainment, except by careful scrutiny of the pedigree. . . .

But even if it were possible to determine preponderance of blood and so determine racial character in certain cases, what should be said of those cases in which the race admixture is equal. Are they white or colored?

There is no law of the United States, or of the State of Louisiana defining the limits of race—who are white and who are "colored." By what rule then shall any tribunal be guided in determining racial character? It may be said that all those should be classified as colored in whom appears a visible admixture of colored blood. By what law? With what justice? Why not count every one as white in whom is visible any trace of white blood? There is but one reason, to wit, the domination of the white race.[73]

Plessy and his counsel were indicting the legality of enforced segregation. The brief implicitly points out that racial apartheid was based on the patently absurd notion that a trace of African blood could disqualify a person from the rights of equal citizenship. Although the Supreme Court conceded that the legal definition of blackness varied from state to state and was thus beyond its jurisdiction, it nevertheless took what is called "judicial notice" of what it assumed to be racial commonsense: An African American was anyone with any amount of African American traceable descent.[74]

The Plessy decision not only set a judicial precedent for future court rulings on legal definitions of blackness but also enforced the legality of segregation, so long as separate facilities were equally maintained. *Plessy's* disingenuous affirmation of de jure equality was meaningless, given the de facto inequality endorsed by the decision.[75] In Louisiana, as elsewhere in the South, state-mandated segregation was thus established in public transportation and, shortly thereafter, in public facilities and schools. Jim Crow laws were extended to nearly every public arena, including libraries, restaurants, prisons, playgrounds, hospitals, restrooms, drinking fountains, and even cemeteries. Finally, in 1898, a new state constitution stripped African-descent Americans in Louisiana of the right to vote. Thus was Reconstruction's promise of freedom, opportunity, and equal citizenship broken. What was actually reconstructed was African American servitude.[76]

African Creole and African American

Creoles of color, who prior to the 1890s had enjoyed a status separate from blacks, were dealt a final blow by state-mandated segregation and suddenly found themselves pushed into the larger African American community. One of the paradoxical consequences of this development was that Creoles began collaborating with African Americans, not only in the fight for civil rights but also in the creation of one of the United States' most vibrant art forms: jazz. Creoles contributed a valuable formal knowledge of musical structure. Although they favored French classical musical forms—particularly French opera—Creole music, like other aspects of Creole culture, displayed significant African and West Indian influences. The Creole classical musical forms, traditional French love songs in particular, converged with the emotional content of African American blues songs,[77] and with the spontaneity and freedom of a musical form that had always been passed on informally.[78]

Other Creoles, who did not welcome the changes taking place in post-Recon-struction Louisiana, left for Mexico and the Caribbean, where racial lines were more fluid and where color rather than ancestry was the primary criterion for defining race, in a manner that was reminiscent of Louisiana's antebellum past. Other Cre-oles moved to Florida, Kansas, and especially California, where they crossed the racial divide or congregated to form residential enclaves. Large numbers went north, where they passed for white. A smaller number passed for white in Louisiana by destroying the birth records that were the only legal proof of their ancestry. It has been estimated that in Louisiana one hundred to five hundred African-descent Americans crossed the racial divide every year from 1875 to the 1890s. In a des-perate search for solace and seclusion, still others refused to learn English, remained staunchly Catholic, and sought refuge within the narrow confines of their own world in the downtown section of New Orleans north of Canal Street, particularly in the Seventh Ward.[79] Over time, the multiracial clan of Metoyers on Cane River emerged as a pluralistic enclave similar to the triracial isolates.[80] In both cases, racial seclusion was often accompanied by a refusal to associate with either whites or blacks, and by a denial of African ancestry.

The Culture of Racial Resistance: White Domination and a "War of Maneuver"

Even during the most oppressive periods of American race relations, multiracial indi-viduals have countered with their own forms of organization and identity. Histor-ically they have tended to move both outward, to the margins of society, and inward, to the relative safety of their own exclusive (and excluded) communities. While this isolation has in many ways provided them with relative comfort and security, it has also deprived multiracial individuals of a significant power base upon which to mount opposition or make inroads into the mainstream political process.

Following Gramsci, Omi and Winant have described this process as a *war of maneuver:* a conflict between disenfranchised and systematically subordinated groups and a dictatorial and comprehensively dominant power. In a war of maneu-ver, multiracial individuals, like other subordinated "Others," have devoted them-selves principally to racial projects aimed at self-preservation.[81] This has included everyday, small-scale, or individual forms of opposition, such as passing. It has also included larger-scale collective challenges such as those mounted by the blue-vein societies, which have allowed multiracial individuals to develop an internal soci-ety as an alternative to the repressive racial order.

Generated by racist pressure that has rewarded whiteness and punished black-ness, the tactics of resistance devised by multiracial individuals have been less a reac-tion to the forced denial of their European American ancestry than to the subordination and the denial of privileges that such ancestry is supposed to guarantee. Despite their tacit acceptance of the hierarchical values assigned to blackness and whiteness, the tactics of passing and the formation of blue-vein societies should be seen as legitimate tactics in the struggle against racial oppression.[82]

Racial Theft, Fraud, and Trespassing

The goal of racial passing, as reflected in its political initiative, has been primarily utilitarian, that is, pursued in order to gain access to social and economic opportunities of the dominant European American culture. The cultural initiative of passing is perhaps the phenomenon's most subversive aspect. It has been associated primarily with the adoption of a "fraudulent" white racial identity by an individual who is defined as African American according to customary social and legal definitions of blackness based on the rule of hypodescent. Passing as white has necessarily involved movement away from one's previous life as African American both in terms of space (geographically) and time (one's experiential past). If it can be argued that European Americans have historically maintained a possessive investment in "whiteness as property," then passers have crossed the racial divide—and indeed "trespassed"—to become "racial thieves" of a sort.[83] They have pirated an identity that allows them to escape racial subordination and gain privileges and status that are not "rightfully" theirs.[84]

The phenomenon of racial passing also questions several problematical assumptions. One of these is that identity categories such as race are inherent and unalterable essences. Indeed, the cultural logic of racial passing by its very nature is posited on an essential and supposedly more "authentic" and "true" African American identity that existed prior to one's assuming a "false" or "fictive" white identity. But passing not only exposes racial difference as a continually emerging distinction devoid of any essential content but also reduces whiteness to the realm of histrionics. It attests to the fact that whiteness can be performed or enacted, donned, or even discredited if not convincingly performed.[85] Ultimately this brings into sharp focus the anxieties about racial status and hierarchy created by the potential of boundary trespassing on the part of someone who has mastered the art of racial cross-dressing and disguise.[86]

In addition, the discursive dimension of passing challenges the "race-as-objective-reality position," which presupposes that race is absolutely fixed in biological fact. Race is supposedly visible in phenotypical features such as skin and hair color— "epidermal schema" of racial difference. Both difference and visibility (or "Otherness") are linked by the necessity of the dominant cultural imagery to see difference in order to interpret it and guard against a difference that might call one's own identity into question. The discursive initiative of passing therefore forces reconsideration of the cultural associations of the physical body with race, and of the assumed visibility of this identity category, and also reveals that racial identities are not singularly true or false but rather "multiple and contingent."[87]

Racial Discretion, Denial, and the Genteel Performance

Collective racial projects such as the formation of blue-vein societies were characterized by a cultural initiative that sought to rescue multiracial identities from distortion and erasure by the dominant society. Their political initiative sought to counter systematic subordination and the arbitrary line between white and black through the formation of pluralistic elites within the African American community. By emphasizing light skin, straight hair, and narrow features, as well as European culture and thought—including gentility and social discretion—multiracial individuals were able to distance themselves from the image typically held of blacks. Moreover, this "genteel performance" allowed them to achieve vicarious, if not actual, parity with whites.[88]

The politics of blue-vein societies was specifically aimed at resource mobilization and redistribution (economic gain, enfranchisement, etc.) along particular racial lines. Even as they became champions in the struggle for the rights of the black masses, the multiracial elites maintained at least an implicit bias toward the dominant psychosomatic norm image in support of their own self-interest.[89] The multiracial elites argued that their sociocultural and physical whiteness entitled them to special privileges and made them more deserving than blacks of full integration into the mainstream of life in the United States. They had so internalized Eurocentrism and the oppression embedded in the American racial order that they had become perpetrators of a divisive and pernicious "colorism" among individuals of African descent,[90] which had significant socioeconomic implications.[91] Yet by re-creating the dominant psychosomatic norm image within the subordinate African American group, the blue-vein societies did bring into sharp focus the "illogical logic" in the rule of hypodescent, which deemed as inferior, and as "black," individuals who were culturally, and in many cases phenotypically (and often genotypically), different from whites in name only.[92]

The multiracial elite, though small and lacking wealth or power, lived largely in a state of racial denial. They convinced themselves that they were achieving acceptance among European Americans and could make similar gains for the black masses.[93] The multiracial elite never abandoned its mission of service to and racial uplift of less privileged African Americans. This enduring legacy, in spite of its significant value, is diminished by the negative consequences of the colorism that they also bequeathed to subsequent generations of African Americans.

The phenomenon of passing and the formation of blue-vein societies challenged the binary racial project, but neither racial project actually broke the rule of hypodescent.[94]

Racial Retreat and Regrouping

Other collective racial projects, such as the triracial isolates and the Louisiana Creoles of color, implemented more extreme tactics than the blue-vein societies as they developed alternative communities. The blue-vein societies used their racial and cultural whiteness to challenge the legal liabilities attached to the social designation of blackness. Regarding themselves, however tenuously, as part of the larger African American community, they sought to maximize their legal rights, and the rights of the black masses by extension, without necessarily seeking to overturn official racial classifications that buttressed social inequities.

The triracial isolates and the Louisiana Creoles of color, by contrast, challenged these social inequities through the formation of communities "outside" the social and cultural parameters of the African American community. Triracial isolate appeals for changes in official racial classification have been supported by a political initiative specifically aimed at resource mobilization and redistribution along particular racial lines (e.g., separate schools, enfranchisement, government benefits, etc.). Triracial isolates have often called upon the state to play a significant role in the pursuit of these goals, considering its historical importance in the politics of racial exclusion, particularly in enforcing racial definition.

The Louisiana Creoles of color have not historically pursued changes in official racial classification that would place them outside the parameters of legally defined blackness, as was the case with the triracial isolates. At their most extreme, the Louisiana Creoles sought collectively to counter systematic subordination and to compensate for the arbitrary racial divide perpetuated by the rule of hypodescent, through the formation of communities that operated on the periphery of both the black and white communities. Accordingly, they have viewed themselves, and sometimes others have viewed them, as a racially intermediate group separate from blacks and whites in a manner similar to the triracial isolates.

In 1910 the Louisiana Supreme Court distinguished between the terms "negro" and "person of color" to designate black and multiracial individuals,[95] although these official distinctions had few legal implications and do not appear to have made any significant difference in the everyday treatment of these persons. Indeed, for the better part of the twentieth century the Louisiana Creoles of color have been considered legally black. They have accordingly been subjected to the indignities of blackness even when they have considered themselves and been considered by others an elite stratum or French cultural variant within a larger "pan-African American" community.[96]

This trend has been mirrored in the census, where, for example, in 1970 "Creole" write-in entries in the race question were reassigned to the "black" category if the respondent resided in Louisiana. Outside this region the entry remained in the "other" category. In 1980, this write-in entry was recoded as black, regardless of location.[97]

Yet, by emphasizing their light skin, straight hair, and narrow features, as well as Catholicism and French culture and thought, Louisiana Creoles of color have historically been able to cushion the impact of their legal blackness, and to achieve in this way vicarious parity with whites by distancing themselves from the image typically held of African Americans.[98]

Yet radical Creoles of color argued neither for white status nor for an intermediate status that carried with it some of the legal rights and privileges of whiteness. Despite the elitism that has historically characterized the self-identity of Louisiana Creoles of color, these radicals focused on issues of racial composition to point out the arbitrary nature of racial classification and to challenge anyone's authority to define blackness.[99]

The formation of the Louisiana Creoles of color and triracial isolates, much like passing and blue-vein societies, was motivated by the segregation that sought to control the potential African American threat to white dominance. These tactics of resistance have accordingly had an inegalitarian dynamic and have tended to be hierarchical and Eurocentric. The phenomenon of passing (see Figure 1b) and the phenomenon of the Louisiana Creoles of Color, triracial isolates, and blue-vein societies (Figure 1g) are responses to Figure 1f. In both cases the relationship between the circles is not only vertical (inegalitarian) and thus hierarchical, but the gray and black circles are also bracketed into one category. Also, both circles are separated and excluded by virtue of their differences, despite a somewhat higher positioning of the subdominant gray circle in relationship to the black circle. Integration through passing (Figure 1b) and the formation of pluralistic urban elites and rural enclaves (Figure 1g) disconnect the bracketing between the two subdominant circles in Figure 1f. The difference is that in Figure 1b (passing), the gray circle is linked to the white circle, whereas in Figure 1g (Louisiana Creoles of Color, triracial isolates, blue-vein societies), no such linkage occurs. In both cases, however, the hierarchy remains intact.

Racial Resurgence and Rearticulation

After more than a century and a half of resistance to Anglo-North Americanization, most Creoles no longer speak French or the Louisiana variant commonly called "patois."[100] Although a few French words remain in their vocabulary, they have incorporated a number of "African Americanisms" into their speech. Younger Creoles have felt the heightened pride and black consciousness that has affected nearly all individuals of African descent since the 1960s. Like others before them, many have begun to realize that it is advantageous to join forces with blacks in the fight for civil rights, where unity is essential if gains for Creoles as well as for blacks are to be made.

As a consequence of these influences, traditional attitudes toward the color line have softened.[101] These changes have affected Creoles in both rural and urban

Louisiana but have been particularly evident in New Orleans. The change in attitude has been even more evident in diasporic Creole communities in California, especially Los Angeles. Creoles seeking refuge from the segregation and racial oppression of the Jim Crow South found that Los Angeles was not the racial paradise they had expected. Los Angeles's own brand of racial segregation brought Creoles of color and African Americans into intimate contact beginning with the arrival of the first migrants in the early twentieth century, and especially since the great Creole migration during and after World War II.[102]

But if Creole identity is changing, it is no less intact. It still involves a sense of solidarity, belonging, and pride based on a shared sense of the past, pride in ancestry, the religious and cultural traditions of Catholicism, linguistic heritage, distinctive cuisine, and an interconnected social network of family and friends.[103] In the 1990s, there were signs of a Creole revitalization movement, as indicated by such groups such Creole, Inc., an organization that publishes a monthly magazine for Creole communities in Louisiana. There has also been a revival of Creole dance clubs featuring Creole musicians. The national attention recently given to Zydeco (the most popular Creole musical form) has inspired a celebration of Creole culture in general, as has the immense popularity of the annual Creole festivals that are attended by thousands of people in California, Texas, and Louisiana.

These festivals have drawn on the large number of Creoles who reside in those states as well as thousands who live elsewhere.[104] The Louisiana to Los Angeles Festival (LaLa), inaugurated in 1988 and frequently held in February during Black History Month around the time of Mardi Gras, has brought together young and old, Creole and non-Creole, New Orleanians, Louisianians, and Los Angelenos. The festival, sponsored by the Los Angeles Cultural Affairs Department and the LaLa Festival Planning Committee, has become a generalized street fair, yet it still reflects the influence of basic elements of Creole culture. Catholic clergy, Creole social clubs, parades, jazz bands, and Louisiana cuisine all play an integral part of the day's activities, which are open to the public.[105]

These changes indicate that growing numbers of Creoles have begun to display a greater openness to inclusion in a larger "Pan-African American" identity. The new Creole identity relinquishes the legacy of racial and cultural isolation and exclusivity without discarding other beliefs, values, and customs from their French and Spanish heritage. *Inside the Creole Mafia* is an outstanding performance piece by Los Angeles musician and vocalist Mark Broyard and actor Roger Guenveur Smith that perhaps best captures the complexities of this process.

Other individuals seek to maintain a Creole identity distinct from African American culture, much as many Puerto Ricans and Cuban Americans do. For the most part, Puerto Rican and Cuban Americans acknowledge multiple racial and cultural backgrounds, including African ancestry. Even when they consider themselves white, black, or multiracial in their own communities, the majority identify themselves primarily as Latinos or Hispanics.[106] Another variant of this new Creole identity might be described as a "multiracial" identity, although many of these individuals will still identify themselves primarily as "Creole," and only secondarily as "multiracial." These new Creole identity configurations arise not from a desire for special privileges; nor do they suggest the psychosocial pathology of colorism traditionally associated with Creole identity. They resist both the dichotomization and hierarchical valuation of African American and European American cultural and racial differences.[107] This shift in attitude has revitalized Creole identity and, more importantly, has allowed Creoles to "rearticulate" their political interests and racial identities by recombining familiar ideas and values in new ways.[108] The contrast between the "old" and "new" Creole identities is captured in Figures 1g and 1d respectively. The pluralistic relationship is indicated by the circles' being separated rather than linked, as they are in the integrationist half of the chart (Figure 1a and 1b). The dynamics in 1g, which represent the "old" Creole identity, are not only vertical (inegalitarian) and thus hierarchical but also sever the bracketing between the two subdominant gray and black circles in 1f. Although both circles are separated and excluded by virtue of their differences, the gray circle is in a somewhat higher position than the black circle. The dynamics in 1d, which characterize the "new" Creole identity, are horizontal (egalitarian) and thus equal in value to the white, gray, and black circles.

A similar change in attitude has taken place among some triracial isolate communities, such as the Melungeons on the Cumberland Plateau of Virginia, Kentucky, North Carolina, West Virginia, and Tennessee. This about-face is best expressed in Mike McGlothlen's *Melungeons and Other Mestee Groups* (1994) and Brent Kennedy's *The Melungeons: The Resurrection of a Proud People—An Untold Story of Ethnic Cleansing in America* (1997). Both authors are of Melungeon descent and have sought to recover the Melungeon history in order to acknowledge and affirm all of the ancestries found in their background.

In his introduction, Kennedy, who was born in the 1950s, describes the Melungeons and other triracial communities as "a people ravaged, and nearly destroyed, by the senseless excesses of racial prejudice and ethnic cleansing."[109] Kennedy acknowledges that the injustices suffered by triracial isolates do not surpass those suffered by their "Native American and African American cousins."[110] Indeed, Kennedy argues that in some ways the Melungeon experience may have been less traumatic. But unlike African and Native Americans, "the Melungeons were dealt the additional insult of being robbed of their identity by the violent onslaught of Anglo-North American jingoism" that denied multiracial individuals full acknowledgment of their background.[111]

In conclusion Kennedy muses over family reunions and how he now sees in the faces of his living relatives a panorama of all of those who have gone before:

When I watch my own summer skin turn with lightning speed too reddish-brown for a blue-eyed Scotsman, and struggle to tame the steel-like waves in my graying black hair, I smile at the living traces of unknown Mediterranean, African, and Native American ancestors whose ancient precious lives still express themselves in my countenance. . . . And in my mind's eye, I can see those ancestors smiling back, wondering why it took the children of their children's children so long to rediscover the truth. But, I also hope they can acknowledge that after all these years their descendants have done just that—rediscovered the truth.[112]

Part III

More Than Black

CHAPTER FIVE

The New Multiracial Identity:
Both Black and White

The Road Less Traveled: Days of Future Past

Alongside the phenomenon of passing and the formation of pluralistic blue-vein elites, triracial isolate communities, and the Louisiana Creoles of color, there were other, more egalitarian racial projects that sought to resist the rule of hypodescent. Although most individual experiences of the past remain unknown and unreported, there have been a few notable cases, such as those of Jean Toomer, Harlem Renaissance author, and Philippa Schuyler, who took the road less traveled by embracing both their African American and European American backgrounds. Several groups for interracial families that emerged between the 1890s and 1940s (such as the Manasseh Societies, Penguin Clubs, and Club Miscegenation), also sought to help multiracial individuals affirm their black and white backgrounds by assisting couples who married interracially.[1]

The identity configuration exemplified by Jean Toomer, Philippa Schuyler, and the members of these early organizations also prefigured the contemporary "new" multiracial identity that was embraced by growing numbers of individuals in the 1990s and supported by more than thirty present-day organizations for interracial couples and multiracial-identified individuals (e.g., Interracial/Intercultural Pride, the Biracial Family Network, Multiracial Americans of Southern California). These support groups have come into existence since the dismantling of Jim Crow segregation—including the removal of the last antimiscegenation laws in 1967—though most of them were established within the past decade.[2] They are composed primarily of black and white couples and of "first-generation" offspring of these unions, such as Philippa Schuyler. Many organizations also include a smaller number of otherwise interracially married couples and also "multigenerational" individuals. The latter share backgrounds made up of African American, European American, and other ancestries. They are viewed by mainstream society as black but have resisted identifying solely with the African American community.[3]

Jean Toomer

Nathan Eugene "Jean" Toomer (1894–1967) was a prominent writer of the Harlem Renaissance. Toomer's masterpiece *Cane* (1923) weaves together contrasting portraits of the love lives and sensibilities of African Americans in the rural South and urban North. The middle section of the book explores the psychological conflict of the multiracial elite. Although *Cane* is generally considered a novel, at times the work is more like poetry than prose. The author often slips from one form into the other almost imperceptibly.[4] *Cane* reflects Toomer's "deepening appreciation" of his African American background and his immersion in the African American community in a way that he had not previously experienced and perhaps could never feel for his European American background or the white community.[5] The irony is that Toomer does not appear to have been singularly African American in his identity. That *Cane* is a structural and stylistic hybrid reflects the author's more general challenge to the arbitrary nature of categories and boundaries—racial or otherwise—that influenced his personal identity.[6]

In the summer of 1922 Toomer sent a collection of his writings to Max Eastman and his assistant Claude McKay, the editors of the *Liberator*. They accepted some of the pieces enthusiastically and requested biographical material from the author. Toomer responded with the following:

> Racially, I seem to have (who knows for sure) seven blood mixtures: French, Dutch, Welsh, Negro, German, Jewish, and Indian. Because of these, my position in America has been a curious one. I have lived equally amid the two race groups. Now white, now colored. From my own point of view I am naturally and inevitably an American. I have strived for a spiritual fusion analogous to the fact of racial intermingling. Without denying a single element in me, with no desire to subsume one to the other, I have tried to let them function as complements. I have tried to let them live in harmony. . . .[7] Human blood is human blood. Human beings are human beings. . . . No racial or social factors can adequately account for the uniqueness of each—or for the individual differences which people display concurrently with basic commonality.[8]

Toomer's problematization of blackness cannot be framed as "passing," at least not in the sense in which this concept has traditionally been defined (although he allegedly did pass as white at various times in his life). Rather, the underlying premise of Toomer's identity and his immersion in the mysticism of George Gurdjieff's metaphysics reflects a desire to transcend racial categories altogether. Toomer's goal was to embrace an identity that sought a spiritual union and blending analogous to multiracialism without the partisanship of race. He embraced this identity privately and did not publicly engage the social forces arrayed against the idea of multiracial identification.[9]

Philippa Schuyler

Philippa Duke Schuyler (1931–1967) was the daughter of George Schuyler, the renowned and controversial African American journalist of the Harlem Renaissance, and Josephine Cogdell, a European American dancer, artist, heiress of a Texas rancher, and granddaughter of slave owners. The Schuylers were prominent in African American intellectual, political, and cultural circles, and entertained dignitaries from all over the African diasporic world. Their daughter Philippa, who was reading and writing at the age of two-and-a-half, playing the piano at four, and composing music at five, was often compared to Mozart. Philippa was exposed to African culture and history as well as to the classical music tradition of Western Europe, and she studied with some of the finest piano teachers in New York. She also became acquainted with many prominent intellectual, cultural, and political figures of African descent from the United States and abroad.[10]

Suffering the double oppression of racism and sexism, Philippa was largely rejected by the European American elite classical music milieu. She found audiences abroad, however, where she flourished as a performer and composer. She traveled throughout seventy countries in South America, Africa, Asia, and Europe, performing before royalty and heads of state. Eventually Philippa added a second career as an author and foreign correspondent reporting on events around the globe, from Albert Schweitzer's leper colony in Lamberéné, Gabon, to the upheavals in the Belgian Congo. She spent her final days reporting on the turbulent conflict in Vietnam. While in Vietnam, Philippa co-founded an organization called the Amerasian Foundation, which provided relief to the multiracial offspring of U.S. servicemen and Vietnamese women. On May 9, 1967, Philippa's life was cut short tragically in a helicopter crash while she was on a mission of mercy to evacuate children to Da Nang from a Catholic orphanage in Hue.[11]

Philippa experienced many of the ambiguities, strains, and conflicts that naturally surround multiracial identity in a society that views black and white as mutually exclusive and hierarchical categories of experience. In fact, during Phillipa's lifetime, social forces were significantly more hostile than they are today to an egalitarian multiracial identity that values both black and white backgrounds. In retrospect, the Schuylers seem hopelessly naive, and perhaps somewhat narcissistic, in hoping that Philippa would replace popular images of "hybrid degeneracy" with notions of "hybrid vigor," while also proving that multiracial children represented the solution to the American race problem. Nevertheless, their struggle to integrate African American and European American backgrounds in their daughter's identity, along with Philippa's own struggle to be both black and white, yet neither, were significant departures from the norm. Despite the sometimes disturbing twists and turns, their endeavors may be legitimately viewed as prefiguring the contemporary quest of individuals who resist the one-drop rule and navigate the uncharted waters of multiracial identity.

The Manasseh Societies

Several groups—the Manasseh Societies (named after the biblical Joseph's half-Egyptian son) in Milwaukee, Chicago, and Des Moines, between 1892 and 1932; the Penguin Club in New York during the 1930s; Club Miscegenation in Los Angeles; and groups in Washington, D.C., and Detroit during the 1940s—also sought, with the support they provided interracial couples, to help multiracial individuals affirm both their black and white backgrounds.[12] The best documented of these groups is the Chicago chapter of the Manasseh Society, which was already in operation by 1892 (though Milwaukee is thought to be the home of the original organization). It disintegrated in the late 1920s, but the surviving members retained a measure of informal solidarity well into the 1950s.[13]

The Society was formed as a mutual benefit organization and is said to have had as many as seven hundred members in its heyday. It owned a cemetery plot, had elaborate burial rituals, and engaged in many social activities, including an annual picnic and dance. Its annual ball, held at the Eighth Regiment Armory, was one of the high points of the social season.[14] The club's motto was "Equal Rights for All" and it elevated intermarriage to a social good. In this it was similar to the Bahá'í faith, its more religious contemporary, which provided a very supportive environment for interracial families.

Manasseh Society members, who generally were stable working-class couples, performed elaborate initiation ceremonies for the induction of new members. They carefully scrutinized all new candidates for membership and barred common-law unions and individuals of "questionable" moral character. The Chicago chapter was especially sensitive about its reputation during the period of the Great Migration, during which a wave of "illicit" interracial relationships swept the city and made all interracial couples suspect.[15] Reverdy Ransom, a well-known A.M.E. clergyman in Chicago who performed services for many interracial couples who belonged to the Manasseh Society, claimed that contrary to popular opinion, European Americans involved in such marriages were not representative of the "lowest stratum" of white society. Moreover, many of their children, whose education was a parental priority, often became attorneys, physicians, and teachers.[16]

The mere existence of such organizations as the Manasseh Society demonstrates that interracial couples felt themselves to be sufficiently anomalous to need psychological and social support from other intermarried couples. Although the Manasseh Society had become an established part of the associational complex of the

African American community in Chicago by 1910, European Americans largely rejected the organization. African Americans, if they did not ostracize these interracial couples outright, did not necessarily receive them with great warmth. For the most part the interracially married were outcasts who had to make substantial provision for their personal security and comfort.[17]

Black and White Together: Contemporary Trends in Interracial Marriage

The dismantling of Jim Crow segregation and the implementation of civil rights legislation during the 1950s and 1960s dissolved the formal mechanism barring individuals of African descent from contact with whites as equals. When whites and blacks began living in the same neighborhoods, working in the same offices, and attending the same educational institutions, interracial friendships, dating, and intermarriage naturally increased.[18] By 1967 the number of marriages between African Americans and European Americans was increasing in the North and the West, and by January of that year legal prohibitions against interracial black-white marriages remained on the books of only the seventeen southern and border states. In March 1967 Maryland repealed its antimiscegenation law and on June 12 of that year the U.S. Supreme Court ruled unanimously that the Virginia statute prohibiting interracial marriage was unconstitutional and a violation of the Equal Protection Clause of the Fourteenth Amendment in *Loving v. Commonwealth of Virginia*, which involved interracial couple Mildred Jeter (an African-descent American) and Richard Perry Loving (a European American).[19]

The *Loving* decision ended several centuries of legal barriers to interracial marriage not only in Virginia but in other southern and border states. Along with the Fair Housing Act of 1968, *Loving* helped dismantle apartheid in the United States. This process began with the *Brown* decision in 1954, which reversed *Plessy v. Ferguson,* and culminated in the passage of the Civil Rights Act of 1964 and the Voting Rights Act of 1965. Unlike either the *Brown* decision or the Voting Rights Act, the *Loving* decision did not meet with massive resistance or violence in the South. Nevertheless, several states were slow to nullify their statutes, and federal and state courts found it necessary to direct defiant clerks and registrars to issue marriage licenses to interracial couples.[20]

If there was no massive backlash in the South against removal of the last antimiscegenation laws, data collected by Robert E. T. Roberts show that neither was there an immediate upsurge in black-white marriages.[21] Roberts did find that outmarriage patterns and the percentage of blacks and black marriages in a given state are fairly closely correlated. Roberts found that states with the lowest percentages of African American marriage partners have the highest percentages of African American grooms and brides who outmarry, but very low percentages of white brides and grooms who marry African Americans. In states with high numbers of blacks and of black marriage partners, the intermarriage rates of black grooms and brides are much lower. Only the District of Columbia has a black majority of total marriages, as well as the highest proportion of black-white marriages.[22]

In the years 1980–1987, the five states (South Carolina, Virginia, Delaware, Florida, and Illinois) with 11.5 to 23.2 percent black partners in all marriages had intermarriage rates of.2 to.7 percent for white grooms;.6 to 1.6 percent for white brides; 2.2 to 7.7 percent for black grooms, and.9 to 3.6 percent for black brides. The five states (Alaska, Hawaii, Rhode Island, Nebraska, and New Hampshire) with 2.1 to 5.4 percent black partners in all marriages had, for the same years, inter-marriage rates of.1 to.6 for white grooms;.4 to 1.9 percent for white brides; 15.9 to 46.5 percent for black grooms, and 2.7 to 17.0 percent for black brides. The five states with the fewest blacks, with.3 to 1.3 percent black partners in all marriages (South Dakota, Wyoming, Montana, Maine, Vermont) had for these years inter-marriage rates of.01 to.2 for white grooms;.2 to.7 percent for white brides; 27.6 to 91.3 percent for black grooms, and 6.5 to 71.4 percent for black brides.

The southern and border states, which prohibited interracial marriage until 1967, showed the greatest proportional increase in black-white marriages from the 1970s to 1985. In fact, by 1985 Virginia, Missouri, Florida, and Delaware had intermar-riage rates comparable to those of Illinois and other northern states with high pro-portions of blacks. Nebraska, South Dakota, Wyoming, Montana, and other west-ern states that prohibited interracial marriages until the 1950s and early 1960s and which had small black populations, now had high proportions of black-white mar-riages.[23] The 1960 census counted 51,000 black-white couples in the United States; in the 1970 census, there were about 65,000 black-white unions among the nation's 321,000 interracial couples.

By the 1980s, the number of interracial couples approached 1 million, includ-ing 599,000 white-other race unions and some 167,000 black-white unions. The number of interracial couples continued to increase steadily until by the 1990s there were approximately 1.5 million interracial unions, of which 883,000 were white-other race unions and 246,000 black-white unions.[24] Despite this substan-tial overall increase during the past three decades, and despite the fact that the total number of interracial couples did not vary significantly by region, the percentage of interracial marriages between African Americans and European Americans was far lower in the South than in other geographic regions, by virtue of the heavy con-centration of African Americans in that section of the country.[25]

According to 1970, 1980, and 1990 census data, the proportion of white hus-bands with black wives increased slightly, while the percentage of black husbands with white wives more than doubled. In addition to changes over time, there have been regional variations. In New England during the late nineteenth century, the marriages between black men and white women far exceeded marriages between white men and black women. In the South, by contrast, in the 1870s and 1880s (during and after Reconstruction, when intermarriage was permitted in the South), most interracial marriages were between white men and black women. This pattern prevailed in the District of Columbia up until 1940 but has since been reversed.[26]

In recent years, in states where more than 8 percent of all marriages included black partners, 65 to 75 percent of black-white marriages were of black men to white women. In states where fewer than 1.2 percent of marriages included a black partner, black male-white female unions totaled from 80 to well above 90 percent.[27] Since 1967, black male-white female marriage has predominated in the South, but to a lesser extent than in the West and northeast. Urban centers on the West Coast, such as Seattle, San Francisco, and Los Angeles, appear to have the highest rates of interracial marriage in the continental United States for blacks and whites, as well as other racial and ethnic groups.[28] The 1990 census indicates that California, Florida, Oklahoma, Texas, and Washington state have the highest rates of racial intermarriage. (Hawaii has the highest proportion of intermarriages due to the state's small size, but the actual number of intermarriages is smaller.)[29]

Census data collected over the last three decades indicate that outmarriage rates increase with more years of education and are highest among the middle and upper classes. Although most individuals marry within their socioeconomic class, higher levels of education and income increase the incidence of racial intermarriage, presumably because better-educated people are less racially biased and more open to racial diversity. A 1980 sample of marriage data from seventeen states revealed that both black and white partners in interracial marriages have more years of education than those who marry within their race. Black men and women who married whites had more years of education than those who married other blacks. While only 9 percent of black men who married black women had completed college, 13 percent of black men who married white women held college degrees. Twenty-four percent of white men who married black women had college degrees, whereas only 18 percent of white men who married white women had completed college.[30]

Artists and entertainers have traditionally been more likely to marry interracially by virtue of their relatively "liberal" or countercultural values. This is not the case, however, for the top level of the white elite, whose very existence has historically been predicated on preserving its wealth, power, privilege, and prestige through racially endogamous marriage patterns, in spite of high levels of education.[31]

Although outmarriage rates tend to increase with more years of education and intermarriages between European Americans and African Americans are increasing, approximately 94 to 98 percent of blacks and whites still marry within their respective races. Individuals from comparatively smaller racial and ethnic groups (Native Americans, Asian and Pacific Islanders, Latinos) have higher rates of outmarriage than either European Americans or African Americans. In addition, about 92 percent of intact interracial marriages or consensual unions in the United States involve one white spouse (or unmarried partner), simply because European Americans make up such a large proportion of the total national population.

With the exception of African Americans, women of color are more likely to outmarry, generally to European American men, although the number of black women who outmarry is on the rise.[32] Increased interracial contact, in both the public and private spheres, has contributed to this trend, just as it has contributed to the general increase in intermarriage. The rising number of African American women who outmarry is also related to the shortage of marriageable African American males, however. This shortage can be attributed to the ravages of poverty, drugs, high mortality, and incarceration, which have removed a disproportionate number of African American males from the pool of potential marriage partners. In addition, declining university enrollments and graduation of black men relative to black women has led to a drop in the number of college-educated African American males. Since most individuals marry within their socioeconomic class even when they outmarry racially, college-educated African American women are necessarily seeking partners outside the African American population, usually white men, since they are most numerous in the class settings in which educated black women are most likely to find themselves.[33]

It is among Native Americans and Japanese Americans, however, that intermarriage with European Americans has become normative. According to 1990 census data, the non-white partner in 22 percent of all interracial couples was Native American or Alaska Native; in 31 percent, Asian or Pacific Islander; 14 percent, African American; and 25 percent, "other race" (most of whom were of Latino origin).

Trends among Latinos are somewhat difficult to gauge because the official census category ("Hispanic") is considered an "ethnic" rather than a racial category. "Hispanics" may therefore belong to any of the various populations the census classifies as racial groups (e.g., white, black, Native American, Asian American, Pacific Islander American). However, 1990 census data confirm a trend among Latinos similar to the larger trend in intermarriage. Approximately 26 percent of Latinos were married to partners who were not of Latino origin, but the actual breakdown varied depending on whether Latinos were of Cuban, Puerto Rican, or Mexican descent, and so on.[34]

Biracial and Multiracial: The First-Generation and Multigenerational Experiences

Although statistical surveys historically do not provide reliable figures on the offspring of interracial unions, census data indicate that the number of children born to interracial couples grew from less than half a million in 1970 to about 2 million in 1990, and that the majority of these children have one European American parent. In about 34 percent of these cases, the other parent was Native American, in 45 percent, Asian American, and in 20 percent, African American. In California and the Southwest the majority of multiracial offspring born in the past decade have one white and one Latino parent (24.4 percent white mother-Latino father; 22.9 percent Latina mother-white father). In other words, a Latino parent was involved in nearly three-fourths of all "multiracial/multiethnic births" in this region. It is still unclear, however, what percentage of these offspring actually identify as "multiracial/multiethnic" as compared to those who identify as either "Latino" or "European American."[35]

Data on birth certificates indicate that intermarriage has increased significantly over the past three decades. In 1968, only 28 percent of all children born to at least one Native American or Alaska Native parent listed the second parent as European American (6,900); in 1994, this percentage had increased to 45 percent (23,000), so that for every 100 children born to two Native American parents, 140 have one parent who is European American and one who is Native American.[36] Among births to couples in which at least one partner was Asian or Pacific Islander American, the percentage in which the second parent was European American was 28 percent in 1968, approximately 32 percent between 1971 and 1979, and 26 percent in 1994. The most significant increase is found among Japanese Americans; 139 children are now born to one Japanese American parent and one European American parent for every 100 children born to two Japanese American parents.[37]

In 1968, the birth certificates of 2 percent of infants with at least one African American parent (8,800) reported the second parent as white. Between 1968 and 1988, there was little change in the number of children born to two European American or two African American parents. There was, however, a marked increase in children born to black-white couples, from 8,758 in 1968 to 41,301 in 1988, reaching 1.23 percent of all live births in which the race of both parents was reported. There was a slight increase in the proportion of white fathers and black mothers after 1980. Between 1968 and 1988 children born to white fathers and black mothers increased from .05 to.31 percent of all live births, while children of black fathers and white mothers increased from .21 to .92 percent of all live births in which the race of both parents was reported. In 1994, the total percentage of children born to one black parent and one white parent had increased to 9 percent (63,000).[38] Despite statistical limitations, the total population of children of black-white parentage, ranging in age from infants to young adults, is believed to number from 600,000 to several million.[39]

This growing population received limited attention from educators, researchers, sociologists, and mental health professionals prior to the 1980s. Previous research is outdated, contradictory, or based on small-scale case studies of children who were experiencing "problems" with personal identity and had been referred for psychological counseling.[40] In the case of children of black-white parentage, most professionals stressed that they learn to cope as African Americans on the grounds that that is how they would be viewed by society. These children's mental health was defined in terms of how successfully or unsuccessfully they achieved an African American identity. Among black-white couples, however, there is a considerable range of opinion as to how children's identity should be developed and supported. Some parents believe that race is irrelevant. Others raise their children as black and teach them African American survival skills. A significant number of intermarried couples, however, seek to give their children an appreciation of both their black and white backgrounds. They describe their children as "rainbow," "brown," "melange," "blended," "mixed," "mixed-race," "biracial," "interracial," and "multiracial."[41] All of these terms challenge social attitudes that rest, albeit less consistently than in the past, on the one-drop rule.

The primary carriers of this new multiracial identity are these "first-generation" offspring of interracial marriages (although a significant number of first-generation individuals embrace an African American identity or, less frequently, a European American identity). This first-generation identity is derived from having one parent who is socially designated, and self-identified, as black, and one who is socially designated, and self-identified, as white, regardless of the multiple racial and cultural backgrounds in their parents' genealogy.[42]

The experience of Allegra Larsen (this name and the names of other individuals below have been changed unless otherwise indicated) is typical of first-generation individuals.[43] Allegra's mother is European American and her father is African American. She has had intimate contact with aunts, uncles, and cousins on both her mother's and father's sides of the family and has visited both sets of grandparents during summer vacations. Both of her parents' families have hosted holiday and other social gatherings attended by African American and European American relatives. The first-generation identity typified by Allegra's experience generally involves intimate contact with both parents' extended family. These first-generation individuals often identify themselves as "biracial," irrespective of the multiplicity of actual backgrounds in their lineage. When asked to describe themselves, they may also respond, "I'm black and white," "I'm part white and part black," "I'm mixed," or "I'm multiracial" or "interracial."[44]

A smaller number of "multigenerational" individuals identify themselves in similar terms. The multigenerational identity may encompass the experience of individuals who are socially designated as black but have two biracial-identified parents; one parent who is biracial-identified and one whose social designation and means of personal identification is African American; or a biracial-identified parent and one whose social designation and means of personal identification is European American (or another single-racial/cultural reference group). Specifically, this identity applies to individuals who have parents, or ancestors, who have been designated socially as black but who actually have multiple racial/cultural backgrounds and may have resisted embracing single-racial/cultural identities as African American.[45]

Ashley Fisher exhibits an identity that is representative of this multigenerational experience. His mother is of African American, Native American (Choctaw), and Irish American descent, and his father is of African American, Native American, East Indian, and German American descent, although both parents identify as African American. Ashley was socialized in the African American community and identified as African American until he went to college. At that time he began to explore and embrace an identity that included the other parts of his background.[46]

Specific backgrounds are not typically delineated in the home or by extended family, however. The multigenerational identity is based primarily on having more than one racial/cultural reference group in the more distant genealogical past. Multigenerational individuals more commonly refer to themselves as "multiracial" than as "biracial," because this more accurately describes their true ancestry. However, both first-generation and multigenerational individuals often described themselves as "mixed."[47]

Both first-generation and multigenerational individuals must develop constructive strategies for resisting the one-drop rule, which categorizes them in a way that contradicts both the facts of their ancestry and their self-identity.[48] One of the most poignant examples of this contradiction is found in the experience of Chelsi Smith, winner of the 1995 Miss USA pageant. When asked how it felt to be the crowned the first black Miss USA, she responded that she was both black and white. Although many people saw this as a victory for multiracial-identified individuals, Smith's comments set off a firestorm of controversy, particularly in the black press.[49]

The lack of a formally recognized multiracial community in the United States, and an accompanying sense of community identification, affects both first-generation and multigenerational individuals. This is gradually changing, however, as first-generation individuals, particularly teenagers and young adults, now form a significant cohort of peers in both public and private interactions.

In contrast to the experience of youths, first-generation and particularly multigenerational adults have often experienced a sense of racial isolation. As a way of coping with this sense of isolation, many of them have identified vicariously with multiracial populations in South Africa or Latin America that have been an acknowledged part of social reality for centuries. Others have identified with multiracial communities in the United States (such as the Louisiana Creoles), although they have no known genealogical ties, personal experience, or contact with these communities. Multigenerational individuals with ancestors from triracial isolate communities or Louisiana Creoles of color prove the exception to the rule. Yet many of them tend to identify themselves primarily as "Creole" or as members of their respective triracial communities (e.g., Melungeons, Jackson Whites) and only secondarily as "multiracial" if at all.[50] These new identity configurations affirm what might be described as an egalitarian triracial isolate or Creole identity, one based not on the desire for special privileges or on the psychosocial pathology of colorism traditionally associated with Louisiana Creoles and triracial isolate communities. This new identity resists both the dichotomization and the hierarchical valuation of cultural and racial difference.

The sense of isolation experienced by multigenerational people generally abates when they meet other multiracial-identified individuals. We see this happen in support groups such as Multiracial Americans of Southern California (MASC). Rachel Parker, a multigenerational woman in her late forties, spoke of the great joy she felt when she was first able to use the word "brother" in reference to a person of the same racial identity. She had heard African Americans use this term and had in fact used it herself with the rise of black consciousness in the 1960s. But she always felt somewhat awkward about it because she did not feel the same intimate sense of racial kinship with African Americans that she would have felt with other multiracial-identified individuals, had she known any.[51]

Nina Gordon (real name) is a multigenerational individual of West Indian descent whose experience reflects a similar awkwardness and ambivalence. Like most multigenerational individuals, Nina was socialized in the African American community. At an early age she became frustrated at not being able to identify with her Chinese, Asian Indian, and European ancestry, even while she embraced a black identity. She always felt like an imposter when she denied her other backgrounds. African American children taunted her because of her light skin, and she strongly embraced an African American identity so as to fit in. Her frustration increased when she attended a historically black college during the height of the civil rights and black consciousness movements in the late 1960s and early 1970s. Only in the 1990s, when Nina joined a support group for multiracial-identified individuals, did she finally feel she had found a home and begin fully to assert her multiracial identity.[52]

The contrast between the multigenerational and first-generation experiences is further underscored by the fact that the latter is frequently viewed as a more legitimate basis for multiracial identity. The reasons for this are related to the repeal of antimiscegenation laws in 1967 and the liberalization of social attitudes on race over the past three decades. Moreover, the first-generation experience originates in the context of interracial marriage and thus includes an element of choice. Marriages confer equal legal status on both parties and, by extension, equal legitimacy on both parents' identities. The one-drop rule, therefore, has been less consistently enforced, both in theory and in practice, in the case of their offspring. This is particularly true of policies at the National Center for Health Statistics (NCHS) and to a lesser extent of the Census Bureau. Before the 1980s, the NCHS classified racially blended children in terms of the "minority" parent, while the Census Bureau classified them in terms of the father's racial or ethnic identity. Since the 1980s both agencies have based the children's race on the racial identity of the mother. Many multiracial children of European American mothers have therefore been designated as "white" rather than as "biracial." Since the mid-1960s, however, adoption agencies have tended to describe blended children as "racially mixed" or "biracial" in order to attract white adoptive parents by appealing to their Eurocentric bias.[53]

Such flexibility has not been extended so readily to multigenerational individuals. Their experience carries with it the implicit stigma of concubinage, rape, and illegitimacy; and the parents and families of these individuals have typically been seen as African American. Attitudes toward Native Americans and Latinos—two other populations that have experienced significant miscegenation with European Americans— provide a point of contrast. The European American, as well as the Native American and Latino communities, have more openly acknowledged multiple racial and cultural backgrounds in the discourse on identity. In these populations as well, however, the same divisive and pernicious "colorism" that has infected African-descent Americans has arisen, with the result that lighter-skinned and otherwise more European-appearing Latinos and Native Americans are often treated preferentially within and outside their communities. Nevertheless, the greater openness among these groups to multiracialism has mitigated the generational differences as the primary factor determining the legitimacy of multiracial identity. Multigenerational individuals of European American and African American descent, therefore, find themselves at odds not only with the larger society and the African American community, but often with first-generation individuals as well. Since most African-descent Americans have some European American ancestry in their genealogy but identify themselves as black, blacks often accuse multigenerational individuals of trying to escape the stigma attached to "blackness." Some first-generation individuals contend that their own biracial experience is the legitimate starting point for a blended identity.[54]

For Levonne Gaddy (real name), a multigenerational woman in her late thirties, contact with first-generation individuals has been especially frustrating. Levonne is a professional social worker, and in 1987–1988 she founded and directed the Center for Interracial Counseling and Therapy in Los Angeles, before moving to Canada in 1989. She is now an adjunct professor at Arizona State University at Tucson, a former president of the Association of Multiethnic Americans (AMEA), and co-founder of Multiethnics of Southern Arizona in Celebration (MOSAIC) in Tucson. First-generation individuals have frequently questioned the legitimacy of Levonne's multiracial identity because her parents identify themselves as African American, even though they themselves are first-generation individuals. They raised Levonne as African American and told her nothing of their own biracial parentage until she reached adulthood. Levonne, like the majority of other multiracial adults, came of age during the civil rights and black consciousness movements, and embraced a black identity. She began to identify as multiracial in her late twenties and early thirties when she, along with other multiracial-identified individuals and interracial couples, founded MASC.

Levonne was irritated and disappointed to find that after all the years of struggle to express her multiracial identity she was now told that she was not legitimate by the very individuals with whom she felt a sense of kinship.[55] It makes no sense, therefore, to confine the new multiracial identity to the experience of first-generation individuals born since 1967, for this would ignore and invalidate the experience of earlier generations of first-generation individuals and their offspring, who have struggled and still struggle to liberate themselves from the shackles of hypodescent.[56]

Betwixt and Between: Playing the Middle by Embracing Both Ends

The new multiracial identity differs from that of African Americans—who for the most part have multiple racial/cultural backgrounds but a single-racial/cultural identity as black—in that it constructs a more multidimensional configuration.[57] According to Los Angeles psychologist Patricia Johnson, the psychic development of multiracial-identified individuals is different from that of single-race identified individuals.[58] Nor does the new multiracial identity correspond to Ramirez's multicultural identity model.[59] Ramirez's model is applicable to any individual who, regardless of genealogy or ancestry, displays a general openness and sensitivity to racial and cultural differences, has an affinity with the beliefs, values, customs, and artifacts of more than one racial/cultural context, or blends aspects of these contexts into a new personal synthesis. This is not to say that there are no similarities between the behavior of individuals who display Ramirez's multicultural identity and those who exhibit the new multiracial identity. Nevertheless, there are considerable differences in the subjective motivations of the two groups.

The new multiracial identity belongs to individuals who feel a sense of kinship with both the black and white communities as a result of their multiple backgrounds. Their identity is not grounded in a biological notion of race but on ancestry. Exposure to ancestral backgrounds enhances and makes real their feeling of kinship.[60] Simple awareness of those backgrounds, however, can catalyze this sentiment, and lack of contact does not preclude its presence.

Individuals who claim the new multiracial identity are neither totally dependent on nor completely free of the cultural predispositions of any given racial group in their backgrounds.[61] Their style of self-consciousness shapes their identity through "incorporating here, discarding there, responding situationally."[62] They maintain no rigid boundaries between themselves and the various communities in which they operate. They are liminal individuals whose identity has no fixed or predictable parameters. It has multiple points of reference but no circumference because it manifests itself *on* the boundary.[63]

Such individuals do not experience this liminality, this sense of being "betwixt and between," in such a way as to make them feel marginal in the negative sense in which "marginality" is conventionally associated with multiracial individuals.[64]

Social science frameworks (particularly misinterpretations of sociologist Robert E. Park's theories) formulated prior to the 1970s regarded marginality as necessarily pathological. Because they viewed black and white racial identities as mutually exclusive, they predicted lifelong personal conflict characterized by divided loyalties, ambivalence, and hypersensitivity for multiracial individuals.[65] Emerging at a time when the United States was far less tolerant of multiracial identity, these theories supported the prevailing ideology, which prohibited or discouraged miscegenation and ignored the sociological forces that put multiracial individuals at risk psychologically.[66]

These theories thus distorted Park's actual theory of marginality and overshadowed other theories that marginality could give individuals a broader vision and wider range of sympathies.[67] The theories on "negative" marginality have been further refuted by sociology since the 1970s[68] and by data collected since the 1980s.[69] The concept of "positive" marginality has gained greater acceptance among health professionals and in the larger society as well. There is a growing consensus that multiracial-identified individuals, in their journey to racial and cultural wholeness, may experience some of the ambiguities, strains, and conflicts that come from living in a society that views black and white identities as mutually exclusive. Those feelings can be significantly counterbalanced, however, by increased sensitivity to commonalities and an appreciation of the differences in interpersonal and intergroup situations, as an extension of their feelings of kinship with both blacks and whites.

Chiaroscuro: Various Shades of Gray[70]

Although multiracial-identified individuals tend to be at home in both black and white settings, they may feel a stronger affinity for one or the other. Data show that this affinity is determined less by the phenotypical traits than by the influence of family, peers, and society in general.[71]

Most multiracial-identified individuals manifest an identity of some shade of gray on the integrative-pluralistic continuum, as illustrated in Figure 1a and d.[72] The spectrum can be broken down into three trends that are similar to Ramirez's multicultural identity model but differ in their subjective motivations: (1) synthesized identity, (2) functional identity/European American orientation, and (3) functional identity/African American orientation.[73]

The Synthesized Identity

Individuals displaying a *synthesized integrative identity* reference themselves in the black and white communities in fairly equal measure. They feel comfortable in European American social settings, but are committed to issues that concern African

Americans. They are able to function competently and maintain credibility among African Americans and European Americans as well as "shuttle" between both groups (Figure 1a). Individuals displaying a *synthesized pluralistic identity* reference themselves in both the black and white communities, as well as in multiracial settings, in roughly equal measure. Although they feel comfortable in European American social settings, they also maintain a strong commitment to issues concerning multiracial individuals and African Americans. They are able to function competently and maintain credibility in the company of people from all three groups, as well as shuttle between all three (Figure 1d).

Both synthesized types exhibit an identity that seeks to transcend questions of racial or cultural specificity without denying their value and significance.[74] An apparent "racelessness" (or "culturelessness") often seems to emerge in this process, as indicated by the absence of attitudinal and behavioral markers that "specifically" and "clearly" affirm their affinity with normative constructions and understandings of "blackness." The synthesized identity does not, however, suggest a desire to embrace a white identity through deracination or deculturation (the distortion or loss of black "Otherness"). It is not so much that whiteness is an unmarked racial category but that racially unmarked phenomena are often assumed to be white by default. This is a reflection of the pervasive and universal status that whiteness enjoys in mainstream American culture as the standard against which all difference is measured. Wealth, power, purity, cleanliness, intelligence, diligence, ambition, and many other positive qualities are typically associated with whiteness. Poverty, powerlessness, filthiness, stupidity, and laziness often become associated with blackness, however implicit or unspoken the association may be. The racial and cultural litmus tests for authentic blackness and whiteness thus emerge from the prevailing socially and culturally constructed notions of African Americans and European Americans at any given historical moment.[75]

This is not to suggest that synthesized individuals and individuals who embrace whiteness for its privileges share no similarities in attitude or behavior. Indeed, both display a notable absence of the attitudinal and behavioral markers that "specifically" and "clearly" affirm their affinity with black "Otherness." But these two identity configurations differ significantly in terms of motive.[76]

The identity configuration of Alexis Reed displays traits characteristic of the synthesized identity. Alexis was raised in Los Angeles by an African American father and European American mother. She maintained friendships with her African American, European American, Latino, and Asian American peers, and with a few multiracial-identified peers. She is a freelance flutist and has studied music in the United States, Europe, and Latin America. In high school Alexis developed an interest in chamber music as a means of enhancing intercultural communication. In college she furthered that goal by organizing a woodwind quintet that reflected the campus's racial and cultural diversity, both in the makeup of the musicians and in its repertoire. Alexis found support for her identity in Eastern philosophy, particularly in Taoism and in the principles of yin and yang expressed in the Tai Chi. These systems of thought support the belief that opposites are not absolutely different but are relative and complementary categories of experience in which each extreme contains some aspect of the other. The metaphysical world is viewed as the domain of the "real" self, whereas the world of physical matter, of which race is a part, is considered an illusion.[77]

Marcus Bradford is another individual who displays synthesized identity traits. His father was an African American serviceman stationed in Germany and his mother was a German national. Marcus was born in Germany but came to the United States at age three to live with his family in Washington, D.C. He established close friendships with peers from the different countries and cities in which he lived; he could speak both German and English fluently. In his last two years of high school he excelled in soccer, was a member of the debate team, and was an active member in the Model United Nations. In college African American and European American peers, as well as those in other racial and ethnic groups, viewed him as a leader. He wants to pursue a degree in International Law and would eventually like to work at the United Nations or in the diplomatic service. He would like to see the United Nations (or some other international body) move beyond its limited character and serve as a genuinely "democratic universalist" governing body. This would not only provide a forum where national, regional, and local conflicts and disputes could be negotiated but would also serve the interests of the global community rather than the narrow interests of a few powerful nations.[78]

Alexis Reed sees herself as "neither black nor white." She expresses a pluralistic identity and identifies primarily as multiracial. Marcus Bradford sees himself primarily as "both black and white" and displays an integrative identity. But both consider themselves racially multiple and also as carriers of a synthesized identity. They view their racial identity as merely one of the many factors they share with various groups of people. Their primary identity is the one they share with the largest number of people (a more universal and inclusive self) and that is at the same time grounded in those things that are unique to themselves individually—beyond questions of racial, cultural, or any other characteristic.[79]

The Functional Identity

Individuals who display a functional integrative identity may identify with and function in both the black and white communities. *Functional integrative/European American orientation* individuals feel greater acceptance from European Americans and are more comfortable in European American social settings (Figure 1a, with greater emphasis on the white circle). *Functional integrative/African American orientation* individuals feel greater acceptance from African Americans, are more comfortable in

African American social settings, and are more committed to issues concerning the black community (Figure 1a with greater emphasis on the black circle).[80]

Individuals displaying a *functional pluralistic identity* variously identify with blacks, whites, and other multiracial individuals (Figure 1d). *Functional pluralistic/European American orientation* individuals feel more comfortable in the company of other multiracial individuals and in European American social settings. They also feel more accepted by European Americans (Figure 1d, with greater emphasis on the white circle). *Functional pluralistic/African American orientation* individuals are more comfortable in the company of other multiracial individuals and in African American social settings. They also feel more accepted by African Americans and have a greater commitment to issues that concern the African American community (Figure 1d, with greater emphasis on the black circle).

One of the most apparent differences between individuals who display a synthesized identity and those who exhibit a functional identity—whether pluralistic or integrative, or African American or European American in orientation—is that race is a more important part of the latter's identity. Functional identity individuals tend to view the world through the lens of race in a much more immediate sense, such that everyday encounters are somewhat more racialized.

Patricia Landry, a college senior, fits the functional integrative/European American orientation type. She spent most of her formative years in a predominately European American suburb in northern California among affluent whites. Most of her early childhood associates were European American and her tastes in music, clothing, and so on followed along the lines of her European American friends. It was not until she went to college that she had much contact with African Americans. Because her exposure to black vernacular culture had been limited, she initially felt awkward in African American social settings, and she felt some discomfort with the highly politicized nature of black identity. Yet her interest in black history grew, and in time she developed close friendships with African Americans. She admitted, however, that she still felt much more "at home" in European American social settings similar to those she had experienced growing up.[81]

In the case of Rodney Barrett, an individual with a functional integrative/African American orientation, the situation was almost the reverse. He grew up in integrated neighborhoods and went to integrated public schools but gravitated socially toward African American students and was very much involved in the Black Students' Alliance in high school. In college he joined an African American fraternity and tended to socialize largely with African American students. He listens to various types of music but is particularly committed to rap and reggae because of their politically engaged stance.

The most salient difference between the functional integrative and functional pluralistic identities—regardless of whether individuals display an African American or European American cultural and social orientation—is that individuals exhibiting the pluralistic identity see themselves primarily as part of a newly emerging "third culture," or collective subjectivity, made up of multiracial identified individuals. Meloney Parks, a functional pluralistic/European American orientation individual, grew up in a diverse environment on the East Coast. Although she generally feels more accepted by European Americans than by African Americans, she always sought out other biracial students in high school and was instrumental in organizing a biracial student support group on her college campus, as well as several national collegiate biracial conferences. Meloney also helped publish an anthology of poems and essays written by biracial college students. She is pursuing an M.A. in education and eventually would like to organize a school to support the healthy identity development of biracial youth.

Chris Owens, a functional pluralistic/African American orientation individual, seeks to build better communication between African Americans and multiracial individuals in order to combat the divisiveness and colorism that has historically plagued both groups. He was instrumental in getting his campus's African Students Union to hold a forum on these issues. His goal is to pursue graduate study in social welfare in order to work with biracial and African American youth in juvenile facilities.[82]

It should be pointed out, however, that racial considerations are not the only factor motivating the behavior and activities of multiracial-identified individuals. They lead everyday lives that for the most part differ very little from those of other individuals. These examples show that the configuration of the new multiracial identity is not based on the desire to gain special privileges usually denied to blacks. Nor does it reflect the psychosocial pathology of colorism, as was the case with previous racial projects such as passing, the blue-vein societies, the triracial isolates, and Louisiana Creoles of color. This is not to suggest that some multiracial-identified individuals do not display problematic attitudes and behavior associated with those previous projects. Whether it operates as an integrative identity, with both the black and white communities as reference groups, as a pluralistic and intermediate identity that blends aspects of both black and white but is neither, or as an identity that operates from both of these trends, the new multiracial identity is not synonymous with those other projects. It resists both the dichotomization and hierarchical valuation of African American and European American cultural and racial differences.[83]

CHAPTER SIX

The New Multiracial Identity: Neither Black nor White

The Formation of a Multiracial Collective Subjectivity: A Constructivist Perspective

Multiracial consciousness is both an explanation of racial dynamics and an effort to reorganize the social structure along racial lines. It involves both an interpretation of racial dynamics and a political initiative that seeks to bring about changes in official racial classifications. The inclusion of a multiracial identification in official racial classifications would have consequences for the distribution of resources, such as the enforcement of civil rights legislation, the tracking of historical and contemporary patterns of discrimination, and the pursuit of social and economic equity.

To date, interracial couples and multiracial-identified individuals have not mobilized on the basis of multiracial consciousness to achieve gains in these areas. Their immediate goal over the past ten years has been to rescue multiracial identities from distortion and erasure by the operation of the one-drop rule. The new multiracial identity politics demands that both dominant and subordinate groups make major changes in the definitions of self and community, difference and hierarchy, which go well beyond gaining political and economic advantages.

Traditional explanations of social movements that rely on deprivation, resource mobilization, and responses to political opportunities, while useful, have limited applicability to collective action by interracial couples and multiracial-identified individuals. They do not analyze the related process of identity formation. Self-conscious identity has little power to shape group members' actions until it involves more than simple awareness of membership in a particular group—although this self-consciousness is a necessary prerequisite for collective action. Once established, racial or ethnic identity becomes a lens through which individuals make sense of the world, and a starting point for action. Identity shapes the way in which other issues and interests are perceived and can be acted upon in the formation of a social movement.[1]

Sociologists Cornell and Hartmann argue that racial and ethnic groups and identities are formed by the interaction between "assignment" (what others say individuals are) and "assertion" (who or what individuals claim to be). Groups as collective subjectivities do not simply respond to circumstantial factors or build their identities within the constraints imposed by external forces. The interaction between identity and external circumstances is intrinsic to the process of group formation.[2] According to sociologists Fenstermaker and West, race and racial identity are therefore much more than individual characteristics or some vaguely defined set of role expectations. They are shaped through interaction with others and must be situated in social situations and structure. The accomplishment of race portrays the social dynamics based on race as normal and natural; that is, it legitimizes ways of organizing social life, which in turn reaffirms institutional practice, the racial order, and the respective power relations associated with them.[3]

Individual accountability to race categories is the key to understanding this process. Situated social action contributes to the reproduction of racialized social structure and systems of domination by extension, whose entrenched ideas, practices, and procedures construct dichotomous racial hierarchies that exclude, control, and constrain human agency.[4] Individuals are nevertheless active agents in constructing, maintaining, reproducing, transforming, reconstructing, and deconstructing their own identities. Moreover, those identities are capable of reconstructing circumstances via the actions they set in motion. Identities change over time as the forces that shape them change, and as the claims made by both group members and others change.[5] The American racial order is continually constructed in everyday life, and individuals acting as singular agents or as collective subjectivities may and do resist pressures to conform to those social forces. The new multiracial identity represents just such a form of resistance to the U.S. binary racial project. Multiracial-identified individuals who attach equal value to their European American and African American backgrounds are implicitly, and often explicitly, challenging the racial status quo.[6]

The Multiracial Experience

Resistance to the binary racial project, which originates in identification with more than one racial group, is what binds multiracial-identified individuals together most powerfully. This racial liminality, or sense of being "betwixt and between," becomes a fundamental part of the self-conception of multiracial individuals and a defining component of the multiracial experience.[7] This is not to suggest that interracial couples, or families involved in transracial adoption—who also form part of the multiracial consciousness—do not experience liminality. Indeed, they are both "insiders" and "outsiders" who seek to combine their different backgrounds in their interracial and transracial relationships.[8]

The experiences of families who adopt children across the racial divide originate in their exposure to different backgrounds, irrespective of their own genealogy. Their experience differs from the "multiracial" experience, which is based on identification with two or more different backgrounds in an individual's genealogy. Yet the similarities between transracial adoptees, interracial couples, and multiracial individuals have often led to serious conflict and confusion related to the definition and usage of the term "multiracial." For example, the parents of biracial children often consider themselves "multiracial" rather than "interracial." Similarly, individuals of color (particularly "monoracial" individuals), who have been adopted by European American families, often refer to themselves as multiracial, when the more appropriate term would be "transracial."

Because there are as many different types of multiracial identification and experience as there are multiracial backgrounds, there has been some debate as to whether multiracial-identified individuals actually form a group. Some have questioned whether the experience of liminality in and of itself can be a valid defining characteristic for group formation, particularly since it is not unique to multiracial-identified individuals. It has even been argued that individuals with similar backgrounds (e.g., black-white, white-Asian) have more in common with individuals of the same background than with other multiracial-identified individuals. This view argues against a "pan-multiracial" experience and identity, which, this camp maintains, is a necessary prerequisite for multiracial group identity.[9]

Despite the many differences in background, experience, and identity, and the fact that the experience of being multiracial is refracted through the lenses of sex/gender, class, and a host of other social categories, the common denominator among multiracial-identified individuals is the direct experience of liminality originating in identification with multiple backgrounds. It is this shared experience that has been instrumental in the formation of a multiracial collective subjectivity, irrespective of the specific backgrounds that give rise to and define various multiracial experiences and identities. Most multiracial-identified individuals will never know, meet, or even hear of each other. Yet they hold in their minds a vision of their communion, or imagined community, which provides connections across social and geographical space and time.[10]

Interest, Institutions, and Culture

According to Cornell and Hartmann, individuals negotiate boundaries, assert meaning, interpret their own pasts, resist imposition of the present, and claim the future as these relate to five key elements: interests, institutions, culture, experience, and inertia. Interests, institutions, and organizations each offer a different potential basis for group attachment and formation, but they are not mutually exclusive. The potency of each kind of bond in the formation of a multiracial identity, therefore, varies from individual to individual and is almost certain to change over time. Indeed, a single identity might fit several hypothetical patterns at different times.

Bonds of interest, which are generally of a utilitarian nature, tend to be somewhat more volatile than institutional bonds and significantly more volatile than more elaborate cultural bonds. For example, interests such as the attempt to change official racial classifications are the most mutable of the three because they are the most dependent on external factors. Bonds of interest may be strong, but circumstances change, and the shared interests that once bound individuals together disappear.[11] In contrast, identities grounded in institutions (e.g., support groups) gain an inertial force that may endure because they are embedded in social relations over which the group has some influence. They not only offer a reason to act but also facilitate action, which further strengthens them. Shared culture tends to be even stronger because it can provide a conceptual scheme of beliefs, ideals, meanings, values, and customs that help individuals make sense of the world. It binds group members together as a community through the perception that they think alike, or at least view aspects of their own lives and certain critical features of the world similarly. If a common culture can be said to exist among multiracial-identified individuals, it is nevertheless in an embryonic state.

There is, however, evidence that a common linguistic culture exists among multiracial individuals, and it reflects the importance of self-ascription in the face of a socially assigned black identity. The very word "multiracial" is evidence of this. The evolution of the word as it relates to multiracial identification is unclear and has caused some confusion because of its original, more comprehensive definition, which originated in the discourse on racial difference and diversity. In that discourse it referred to the acknowledgment or valuing of racial difference, much as the term "multicultural" suggests the validation of cultural difference. The term "multiracial" first appeared in 1980 in Christine Hall's groundbreaking doctoral dissertation on black-Japanese identity and came into widespread use in the late 1980s.[12]

Activists chose "multiracial" because it was in keeping with the discourse on diversity and thus conveyed a more "progressive" tone than "mixed" "mixed-race," or, even worse, "mulatto." These terms were considered vestiges of the colonial past and also suggested that a person so designated was "mixed up" or psychologically confused about his or her identity. However, Hapa Issues Forum and other groups of multiracial individuals of Asian descent (including those of Asian-African American descent), often prefer the term "mixed-race" to "multiracial."[13]

The term "multiracial" has gained greater currency over other contemporary designators such as "interracial" or "biracial," though it has not actually replaced these terms. It was embraced formally in 1987 with the founding of Multiracial

Americans of Southern California (MASC). The term seems to have spread from there due to the extensive coverage of MASC, along with increased attention to the issues of intermarriage and multiracial identity in California generally and Los Angeles specifically.[14]

The "multiracial lexicon" also includes the term "monoracial," which refers to single racial-identified individuals. The term "monoracial" was previously used in psychology—particularly in black identity studies—to refer to the presence of an "in-group" or same-race reference group orientation, preference, or attitudinal pattern, as compared to an "out-group" ("mainstream" or European American) or multiple reference group orientation.[15] The term "monoracial" is widely used to distinguish individuals with a single-racial identity from those with a multiracial identity.[16]

Ritualistic practices within the multiracial community include the reading of Maria Root's "Bill of Rights for Racially Mixed People" at support group meetings and conferences, the evocation of the Lovings as the progenitors of the new interracial family and the new multiracial identity, and the hailing of the *Loving* decision itself as a historical marker in the formation of multiracial consciousness.[17] There have also been efforts to "recover" individuals from the past, as well as to cite those in the present, who have identified themselves as multiracial. While these "recovery" operations may enhance the self-esteem of those doing the recovering, they have sometimes singled out individuals who do not identify with their multiple racial backgrounds,[18] which has understandably drawn criticism from some sectors—particularly African Americans—as a form of appropriation or revisionism.[19]

The process of racial identity formation is also influenced by how "thick" (more comprehensive) or how "thin" (less comprehensive) identity boundaries and centers are, and the degree to which they have gained sufficient inertial force to organize the social and cultural life of the group. The diversity of racial identities within a single racial group is important in terms of these dynamics.[20] Multiracial individuals variously experience their identity as "thick" or "thin." As a collective subjectivity, their sense of group boundaries and centers is much closer to the thin end of the spectrum, which can be attributed to the diffuse and multidimensional nature of the multiracial identity configuration. In addition, multiracial identification as the basis for the formation of a collective subjectivity is very much an emerging phenomenon.[21] Identities do thicken and gain inertial force as these various kinds of bonds are combined.[22] If a significant number of institutions, cultural practices, or new interests crystallize around a multiracial identity, it may thicken, the boundaries may solidify, and the centers may consolidate into a collective "third racial experience." This in turn may be catalytic in the solidification of a "third culture" (or plurality) that is neither black nor white but displays unique characteristics of its own.[23]

The Culture of Racial Resistance:
White Domination and a "War of Position"

As we have seen, interracial couples and multiracial individuals in the past coun-
terpoised their own forms of organization and identity in a "war of maneuver"
against the dehumanization and enforced invisibility imposed by the white power
structure. They lacked the power to mount a *war of position* that would achieve
strategic incursions into the mainstream political process. The multiracial consciousness movement has a natural affinity with previous multiracial identity projects. For example, there is a historical parallel between triracial isolates and the
appeals of the new multiracial consciousness movement for changes in official
racial classification.

The historical circumstances that gave rise to the Manasseh societies parallel
those that have nourished multiracial support groups since the 1967 *Loving* decision. Both the late nineteenth and the late twentieth centuries were characterized
by both an opening up of opportunities for increased interracial marriage and, at
the same time, social isolation due to the unsupportive racial climate of the larger
society. Multiracial organizations of the 1940s and 1950s in Los Angeles, Washington, D.C., and Detroit did not arise in response to an increase in the number of
interracial marriages per se. But interracial military families returning from abroad
after World War II, particularly from Europe, where many had experienced comparatively greater acceptance, formed these organizations in order to provide mutual
support, just as the Manasseh Societies and other groups had done.[24]

For the most part, however, the founders of contemporary support groups have
not drawn inspiration from previous groups. They have generally been unaware of
the existence of such groups.[25] In addition, the motivation behind triracial isolate
appeals for changes in racial classification differs significantly from that of the multiracial consciousness movement. The former originated in the desire to escape the
social stigma of blackness, whereas the latter originates in the desire to embrace an
identity that reflects the various backgrounds in one's genealogy.[26] Consequently,
the new multiracial consciousness cannot be viewed as part of a continuous collective tradition of racial resistance, as has been the case with the long struggle of
African Americans for racial equality.[27]

From Civil Rights to Black Consciousness

After World War II, African Americans and other subordinated racial groups made
sustained strategic incursions into the mainstream political process.[28] Given the dictatorial white power structure, the struggles for voting rights, the sit-ins and boycotts to desegregate public facilities in the 1950s, the urban uprisings of the mid-
1960s, and the political mobilizations of Latinos, Native Americans, Asian

Americans, and Pacific Islander Americans were prepared in large measure by tactics deployed in wars of maneuver. Consequently, individuals devoted themselves principally to the formation of racial projects aimed at self-preservation.[29] This included everyday, small-scale, or individual forms of opposition as well as larger-scale collective challenges, which allowed individuals to develop an internal society as an alternative to the repressive racial order. The racial movements of the 1950s and 1960s achieved limited but real reforms that dramatically transformed the political and cultural landscape of the United States. These gains provided the basis for other oppositional political projects, and made possible a war of position rather than of maneuver. New conceptions of racial identity and the social meaning of race, new modes of political organization and confrontation, and new definitions of the state's role in promoting and achieving "equality" were explored, debated, and contested on the political battleground.[30]

The civil rights movement that began in the 1950s had integration as its goal. The early movement organizations—the NAACP, National Urban League, and Southern Christian Leadership Conference (SCLC)—and leaders such as Dr. Martin Luther King, Jr. sought to assure the integration of each individual under the American creed of equality for all. The movement initially focused its energies on the South, where integration was most viciously opposed by whites.[31] Racial injustice and inequality were generally understood to be a matter of prejudice and bigotry. In the liberal tradition of Myrdal, the solution to the "American dilemma" was believed to reside in the abolition of discriminatory practices in public accommodations, jobs, education, housing, and so on. The early civil rights movement explicitly reflected these views. In its quest for integration and a "beloved community," the movement sought to overcome racial prejudice by appealing to the moral conscience of the nation.[32]

The limitations of the integrationist vision were revealed during the wave of uprisings in cities outside the South, like Los Angeles, Detroit, Newark, and Washington, D.C. from 1964 to 1968. These uprisings did more than expose the underlying inegalitarian pluralism that existed throughout the United States. They also led to a tactical shift in the African American struggle for equality and the establishment of radical Black Power groups such as the Student Nonviolent Coordinating Committee (SNCC) and the Black Panthers. The leaders of these more militant organizations rejected the integrationism of Martin Luther King and advocated Black Nationalism, black separatism, and black power (other communities of color followed this lead and began talking in terms of "brown power," "red power," and "yellow power"). The radical groups argued that racism excluded African Americans, and people of color generally, from the protections guaranteed by the nation's founding documents. Communities of color, they maintained, were doomed to perpetual dehumanization and exploitation as subordinated and excluded racial groups.[33]

This ideology drew parallels between Africans Americans (and other U.S. minorities) and colonized people of the Third World. This "colonial analogy" emerged in the 1960s as the rallying cry for Malcolm X, Kwame Touré (formerly Stokely Carmichael), and the Black Panther Party. The analogy also caught the attention of scholars Robert Blauner, Robert L. Allen, William K. Tabb, and others. They sought to reexamine the experience of African Americans, and people of color generally in the United States, by reframing that experience as a form of "internal colonialism." In this way the colonial analogy gained respectability and a scholarly pedigree.[34]

From the racial turbulence of the late 1960s emerged an alternative perspective on the historical experience of African Americans and other groups of color in American society. This perspective recognized that racial inequality and injustice were not simply products of prejudice and that discriminatory behavior was more than a matter of intentionally informed action. Prejudice and discrimination had deeper roots and were embedded in the very structure of society. Racial prejudice and discrimination were the products of centuries of systematic exclusion, exploitation, and disregard of racially defined minorities, and were thus the unavoidable outcome of patterns of socialization that affected whites as well as racial minorities themselves. Although the term "racism" had surfaced occasionally in the past, it did not become part of the common lexicon until the 1960s.[35]

By the late 1960s, the ambiguous success of the civil rights movement had led to a redefinition of the basis and meaning of racial inequality and to a sharp break with the integrationist vision of leaders like Dr. King. The concept of integration had become identified with the problematic concept of "the melting pot" and was too close, in the view of more radical thinkers, to assimilation—that is, inegalitarian integration. The melting-pot ideology, by which immigrants were expected to assimilate themselves into the dominant Anglo-Protestant culture, worked well enough for Germans, Irish, Italians, and other European immigrants, but it effectively excluded Americans of color. In practice the melting pot meant assimilation for European-descent individuals and apartheid for groups perceived as racially different. And of course assimilation, even for white ethnics, was largely a patronizing device that created an illusion of power sharing without requiring white Anglo-Protestants to actually give up control.

Individuals who advocated pluralism argued that integration would inevitably lead to assimilation, that is, to inegalitarian integration. Consequently, pluralists were very suspicious of any notion of integration without hierarchy, that is, of egalitarian integration. If egalitarian integration was to become a reality it could not be achieved until the long and arduous struggle to achieve equality of difference had been won.

Many felt that the best way for any oppressed group to achieve equality was to recover its own sense of itself and become more effective as a collective force in the world. They envisioned a process of dissimilation that would create intergroup accommodation, or a mosaic of mutually respectful, separate racial and ethnic pluralities with equal status both in law and in fact.[36] In this scenario, the selective pattern would be voluntary, rather than mandated and enforced by European Americans, as has been the case with the apartheid paradigm. More importantly, if and when people of color chose to integrate, they would do so with the bargaining power of equals. These ideas are illustrated in Figures 1c and 1d. The relationship is horizontal (egalitarian) and therefore differs significantly from the dynamics in Figure 1f and 1b, which are hierarchical and inegalitarian. In Figure 1c the black and gray circles are bracketed by virtue of their shared dissimilarities to the white, but the intention is neither to diminish the uniqueness of the gray circle nor to exclude the white circle. Rather, the goal is to establish a horizontal (as opposed to hierarchical) and thus egalitarian relationship that valorizes the two gray and black circles. This would be a necessary prerequisite to achieving the egalitarian dynamics in Figure 1a, as well as guarding against the inegalitarian dynamics in Figures 1b and 1f.

Egalitarian pluralism was seen as necessary to right a wrong in which difference had been the vehicle for perpetuating inequality. This wrong could be righted in part through compensatory programs such as affirmative action. Those who promoted such compensatory strategies did not argue that all African Americans have experienced the disadvantages of blackness equally, or that individual African Americans have not succeeded in achieving the "American Dream" based on merit and excellence. They argued, rather, that African Americans as a racial plurality were at a structural disadvantage in their pursuit of the "American Dream," quite apart from questions of individual merit and excellence.

Integrationists, in contrast to pluralists, sought to redefine (or reaffirm) their premise of a universal humanism that could support the democratic principles of individual free association. They sought to acknowledge the legacy of racism without perpetuating the Manichean distinction between "white guilt" and "black victimization." Nevertheless, integrationists often predicated their vision on a myopic understanding of egalitarian pluralism. Many believed that merely focusing on epidermal differences reinforced a divisive us/them dynamic that undermined the basic democratic principles of individual free association. Consequently, they frequently misunderstood much of the admittedly abrasive and often chauvinistic rhetoric of many radical pluralists. They interpreted what was actually a defensive pro–people of color stance (aimed at forging an oppositional egalitarian plurality as a means of mobilizing against racial oppression), as an offensive anti-white stance (that sought to replace European American domination with a new domination by people of color).[37] This idea is illustrated in Figure 1e. The relationship is vertical (inegalitarian) and the positions of the previously subdominant black and dominant white circles in Figure 1f are reversed. Accordingly, the goal is to establish a hierarchical (as opposed to horizontal) and thus inegalitarian relationship that valorizes the two gray and black circles and excludes the white circle.

Some integrationists also erroneously believed that the repudiation of white supremacy and the elimination of legal impediments to equality had caused race to decline in significance. Many were coming to view government enforcement of anti-discrimination regulations as actually detrimental rather than helpful. Some even argued that government programs were contrary to the American creed and had gone so far in "balancing" that they now amounted to reverse discrimination against whites.[38]

From Civil Rights to Multiracial Consciousness

By the 1970s, the racial movements of the late 1960s had lost their vitality and coherence as the result of repression, cooptation, and fragmentation. The economic, political, and cultural crises of the 1970s eroded the clarity of the terms "racism" and "racial discrimination" and also led to a backlash by right-wing conservative forces, who attempted to dismantle the moderate gains that had been achieved. Despite such setbacks, the race-based movements of the 1950s and 1960s expanded the political terrain, set the stage for the general reorganization of U.S. politics, and created "the great transformation" of racial awareness.[39] Race was henceforth considered a preeminently social phenomenon, something that not only penetrated state institutions and market relationships but suffused individual identity, family, and community.[40] Race came to be understood as a matter not only of politics, economics, or culture, but of each of these "levels" of lived experience simultaneously. The racial movements of the period, therefore, were the first "new social movements," the first to expand the concerns of politics to the terrain of everyday life. Their goals, particularly those formed around identity politics, did not seek merely to resist the oppressive racial order, or change the rules of the game, or bring about greater material rewards. They sought a wholesale transformation of racial identities in order to dismantle the oppression and marginality embedded in them.[41]

The forging of new collective racial identities during the 1960s and 1970s has been the enduring legacy of the racial "minority" movements of the late twentieth century. Racial identity, the state, and the very nature of racial politics were radically transformed. This new social-movement politics would later prove "contagious," leading to the mobilization of other groups—students, feminists, gays, and, eventually, interracial couples and multiracial-identified individuals—who have drawn upon the African American struggle "as a central organizational fact or as a defining political metaphor and inspiration."[42] Indeed, many interracial couples and multiracial-identified adults came of age in the 1960s and were actively involved in the civil rights movement.[43]

Although the war of maneuver of the civil rights movement ended legalized segregation in the public sphere and led to the removal of restrictions against interracial marriage, the one-drop rule continued to operate throughout the 1960s and

1970s. The one-drop rule is the lifeblood of the American binary racial project. It is what sociologist Pierre Bourdieu calls the *doxa*, a sacred or unquestioned social concept or dogma that has acquired the force of nature.[44] Robert E. T. Roberts's interviews with individuals in Chicago echo the national trend. His data reveal that from the 1930s through the 1960s the majority of offspring of interracial marriage identified themselves as African American, although by the 1950s about a third identified as both black and white.[45] The 1980 census data show that roughly 70 percent of such offspring were also identified as African American, irrespective of whether the mother or father in the marriage was black or white.[46] The 1970 and 1980 census data, which were the first to allow self-identification, indicate continuing high levels of black identity for the parents' designations for their offspring.[47] Because the only alternative was the "other" box, it is possible that many couples selected "black" in the tradition of the one-drop rule but were actually raising their children as biracial. These data also say more about the parents' than the children's choice in identities. Whatever the case may be, most black-white interracial couples continued to identify their offspring as black as late as 1980, and so did the larger society.

Dismantling the One-Drop Rule

Paradoxically, the one-drop rule sowed the seeds of its own demise. By drawing boundaries that solidified blackness, this mechanism had the unintended consequence of forging a black group identity that provided a basis for the mass mobilization and collective action that generated the civil rights movement. This in turn led to the dismantling of Jim Crow segregation and ultimately prepared the way for the removal of the last laws against intermarriage in the 1967 *Loving* decision. The *Loving* decision, and the relatively fluid social relations that followed, led to a growth not only in the number of interracial marriages but also the births of "first-generation" biracial offspring. And finally, many interracial couples began challenging the one-drop rule by instilling in their children pride in both their black and white ancestries.

In 1979 interracial couples in Berkeley, California, founded I-Pride (Interracial/Intercultural Pride) in order to provide general support for interracial families, as had the Manasseh Societies and similar organizations. Their more specific purpose was to petition the Berkeley Public Schools to reflect the identity of their offspring accurately by including a multiracial designator on school forms. During 1979–80 the Berkeley Public Schools adopted "interracial" as a new identifier on school forms, making it the first such designator in U.S. history. In 1980–81, however, California state education officials restricted the use of this designator to internal district uses only, citing federal reporting requirements that do not permit such a category.[48]

With the exception of I-Pride, there was no organized collective mobilization against enforcement of the one-drop rule. By the 1990s, however, what had begun a decade earlier as a racial project organized by and largely limited to the membership of I-Pride expanded to include a critical mass of similar grassroots support groups and educational organizations and forums. This network began pressuring the state to change procedures for collecting official data on race—particularly on the decennial census—so that multiracial-identified individuals could be statistically enumerated. This not only provided the cultural terrain upon which other oppositional political projects could be mounted but also made possible inroads into the institutional process through which the state could be confronted in a war of position. This in turn escalated and expanded informal resistance to the one-drop rule to include a formal dismantling of this device at the municipal, state, and national levels.[49] In addition, new conceptions of racial identity and confrontation, as well as new definitions of the state's role in promoting this process, were explored, debated, and contested on the battlefield of racial politics.

The organizations behind this new multiracial consciousness include thirty to forty support groups with names such as Multiracial Americans of Southern California in Los Angeles (MASC), the Biracial Family Network in Chicago (BFN), the Interracial Family Alliance in Atlanta (IFA), the Interracial Family Circle in Washington, D.C. (IFC), and a national umbrella organization called the Association of Multiethnic Americans (AMEA), that have come into existence over the past decade.[50] Other organizations are A Place for Us/National, a national, non-denominational religious support network for interracial families, and Project RACE (Reclassify All Children Equally), an informational and educational organization. There are also several national popular magazines that address the concerns of the interracial/multiracial community, including *Interrace, New People,* and *Mavin,* as well as *Interracial Voice* and *The Multiracial Activist,* advocacy journals on the internet. These publications provide a public forum for the discussion of issues of interest to multiracial-identified and transracially adopted individuals, as well as to individuals in interracial relationships.[51]

Although black-white couples make up only a small percentage of the national population of interracial families, they have spearheaded the formation of BFN, MASC, I-Pride, Project RACE, and other support groups, and have taken the lead in the effort to change the way racial and ethnic data are classified. The complexities of multiracial identity are not limited to the experience of individuals of partial African descent but encompass a wide variety of backgrounds. Indeed, there are more Asian American–European American, Native American–European American, and European American-Latino intermarriages and offspring than there are African American–European American ones. The rule of hypodescent nonetheless presents unique challenges for black-white couples and for multiracial-identified individuals of partial African descent. The new multiracial consciousness as a racial project has thus attracted a disproportionate number of these individuals.[52]

Like other social movements, the multiracial consciousness movement contains a small core of leaders. Interracial couples—particularly those involving white women and black men—disproportionately make up the membership of support and grassroots advocacy groups and educational organizations. Yet the key leadership of the movement is disproportionately made up of multiracial adults, a majority of them first-generation offspring and a smaller number of multigenerational individuals. Several organizations and forums independent of the support groups have formed specifically to address multigenerational concerns (e.g., the Melungeon Society, Tan American Community Forum, the Amerigroid Society of America, the Tirah Society, Famlee, Mis-ce-ge-NATION, etc.).[53]

Beyond the leadership and membership of the educational and support groups, there is a wider circle of people who have played a part in the movement; further beyond that there is a general constituency of potential supporters who are vaguely sympathetic to the movement's objectives. This larger membership of the multiracial consciousness movement includes individuals from various class backgrounds, but movement leaders come predominantly from the professional class. Indeed, the leadership and advisory boards of two organizations, MASC and I-Pride, consist of a disproportionate number of individuals with M.A. and Ph.D. degrees and has a cadre of academics—the largest of all of the support groups. Most of these scholars have been in the vanguard of new research on interracial relationships and multiracial identity. They not only help formulate strategy but also enhanced the credibility of the movement by testifying at congressional subcommittee hearings on official racial classification held between 1993 and 1997.

The multiracial consciousness movement's primary political focus in terms of action campaigns has been changing bureaucratic procedures in the collection of data on race and ethnicity. There has been some lobbying—particularly at the state level—for legislative change, but greater emphasis has been put on letter writing, phone calls, public appearances in the media, and testimony at hearings. The relatively "quiet" nature of the multiracial consciousness movement differentiates it significantly from the boycotts, demonstrations, sit-ins, and uprisings of the civil rights era. Yet the advocates of the new multiracial identity have benefited, as have other individuals of African descent, from the comparatively fluid intergroup relations and the socioeconomic gains of the civil rights era. The identity movement represents a logical next step in the progression of civil rights, the expansion of strategies, and the achievement of both socioeconomic equity and a "holocentric" racial self.

This new multiracial identity recognizes the commonalities among blacks and whites and at the same time appreciates the differences between them. It views these categories of experience as relative, not as absolutes, on a continuum of grays. Accordingly, the new multiracial identity builds on the egalitarian pluralist tenets of the racial movements of the late 1960s, which sought to achieve the equality of difference, but also resuscitates the integrationist goals of the 1950s by seeking to replace hierarchical integration with a more egalitarian dynamic.

CHAPTER SEVEN

Black by Popular Demand: Multiracial Identity and the Decennial Census

The Racial State: Public Policy and the Quest for Equality

The new multiracial identity is a form of resistance to "commonsense" notions of race based on the one-drop rule. This resistance has taken the form of microlevel racial projects in which singular actors are the agents of resistance. It has also been manifest in collective action that calls on the state to play a significant role, particularly in amending the federal standards for collecting data on race and ethnicity to make possible a multiracial identification.[1] In the 1990s, this initiative was pursued most vigorously with respect to the decennial census;[2] and activists succeeded in getting census officials to accept and code write-in responses of "biracial," "multiracial," and similar designations in the "other" category on the 1990 census. This was a departure from previous censuses and marked the beginning of a shift in the policies of the racial state.

The Racial State

From the beginning, the state (which includes not only state and federal governments but other institutions and their policies and rules), has been concerned with the politics of race and has linked its system of political rule to the racial classification of individuals and groups. Historically the state has practiced a politics of racial exclusion (and inclusion), particularly by enforcing racial definition and classification on the basis of the one-drop rule. Indeed, for much of its history, the racial state in America has been characterized by racial despotism and tyranny. Its main objective, whether formal or informal, has been repression and exclusion in the manner of inegalitarian pluralism, or patronizing inclusion in the manner of inegalitarian integration. Under normal conditions, state institutions have effectively enforced the racial status quo. The political space necessary to forge an oppositional racial ideology and a certain minimal conceptual flexibility about race have been extremely limited. Consequently, the racial status quo has gone undisturbed for centuries. Indeed, the use of political channels for the expression of racial opposition and reform is a relatively recent phenomenon. Opposition has been achieved primarily by individuals and groups that have been excluded, on the basis of race, from the body politic and from the democratic process itself.[3]

Both the racial policies of the state and opposition to them alternate between virtual stasis and rapid change, between eras of relative passivity and of massive mobilization, and periods of change and disruption tend to be followed by restoration of the racial order. Although state institutions organize and enforce the racial politics of everyday life, race occupies a central place in state institutions and policies at different historical moments. It becomes a political issue only when state institutions are thought by a significant number of people to enforce a racially unjust social order. State institutions also acquire their racial orientation from the processes of conflict with and accommodation to racially based opposition, which involves a process of clash and compromise.[4] The state intervenes in racial conflict, but not in a coherent or unified manner.[5] Various state institutions often act in a contradictory manner and do not serve one coordinated racial objective; indeed, they often work at cross-purposes. The state's ability to manage and manipulate conflicting demands is thus unstable and unreliable. The American racial order, although equilibrated by the state, is therefore an "unstable equilibrium" by virtue of the many conflicting interests that bear on it at any given time.

Counting by Race

For much of its history, the U.S. government has gathered data on race and ethnicity through censuses, surveys, and administrative records in order to monitor changes in the social, demographic, health, and economic characteristics of various population groups. These data collections have provided a historical record of population diversity and of changing social attitudes, health status, and policy concerns. In the 1960s, federal agencies began to rely heavily on compatible, non-duplicative data in monitoring and enforcing civil rights legislation covering areas of education, employment, housing and mortgage lending, health care, and the administering of justice for population groups that historically have been the targets of discrimination on the basis of race or ethnicity. This legislation includes the Home

Mortgage Disclosure Act, the Fair Housing Act, the Equal Credit Opportunity Act, public school desegregation plans, and minority business development programs.[6] The collection of data on race and ethnicity is also used in the enforcement of legislation affecting redistribution of the 435 seats in the U.S. House of Representatives through congressional reapportionment and determining the counts of voter-eligible "minorities," as well as the ability of such groups to mount successful voter dilution claims in order to draw a district with a voter-eligible "minority" population in the majority, according to statutes in the Voting Rights Act.[7]

In order to meet these legislative demands and administrative priorities, including the requirements of Public Law 94-311 of June 16, 1976, mandating the collection, analysis, and publication of economic and social statistics on "individuals of Spanish origin or descent," the Office of Management and Budget (OMB)—the agency responsible for implementing changes in federal statistical surveys—issued Directive No. 15 in May 1977 as the federal standard for collecting and presenting data on race and ethnicity. Directive No. 15 provides a minimum set of racial categories: American Indian or Alaskan Native, Asian or Pacific Islander, black, and white, as well as two ethnic categories ("Hispanic origin" and "not of Hispanic origin"), when racial and ethnic data are collected separately. If a combined format is used, the minimum categories are: (1) American Indian or Alaskan Native; (2) Asian or Pacific Islander; (3) black, not of Hispanic origin; (4) Hispanic; and (5) white, not of Hispanic origin.[8]

The goal was to develop consistent terms and definitions for a wide variety of data on race and ethnicity to be collected by federal agencies on a compatible and non-duplicative basis. This would make it possible to aggregate, disaggregate, or otherwise utilize and combine data collected by one agency in conjunction with data collected by another agency.[9] In order to maintain comparability, agency officials recommended that data from one major racial or ethnic category should never be combined with data from another category. Yet the basic racial and ethnic categories could be divided into more detailed subgroups to meet users' needs. These categories do not, however, designate certain populations as "minority groups," and are not to be used in determining the eligibility of population groups for participation in federal programs. Furthermore, the racial and ethnic categories were not interpreted as scientific or anthropological in nature. Rather, they were developed primarily on the basis of geography and represented a sociopolitical construct designed for the collection of data on major broad population groups in the United States. In addition, Directive No. 15 neither establishes criteria (such as "blood quantum") for individuals' classification in terms of these broad population groups, nor specifies how individuals should classify themselves. Self-identification is the preferred means of obtaining information about an individual's race and ethnicity, except in instances where this is impossible (e.g., in the case of death certificates).[10]

The 1990 Census: Encountering the Racial State

The national furor over the issue of multiracial identity first arose in response to a January 20, 1988, OMB *Federal Register* notice soliciting public comment on revisions of Directive No. 15. These revisions would permit individuals to identify themselves as "other," if they believed they did not fall into one of the four basic official racial categories (black; white; Asian/Pacific Islander; American Indian and Alaska Native—and, in the "ethnic" category, Hispanic or not of Hispanic origin). (Although a residual "other" category has been provided on each census since 1910 to increase the response rate to the race question, it has not been used as a standard category on all statistical surveys.) Henceforth, the OMB advised, the category that best reflected individuals' identity within their communities should be used in cases where there was any uncertainty.[11] Under the requirements of Directive No. 15, however, alternative write-in entries in the "other" category were to be "retrofitted" into the four basic racial categories. Yet these data do not appear in any publicly available Census Bureau reports.[12]

The census question on ancestry (question no. 14), which appears only on the long form, does allow for the acknowledgment of multiple backgrounds, but the Census Bureau accepts only two entries for this question. In 1980 "Hispanic" was added to the official categories but appeared as part of the question on ethnicity (question no. 7)—"Hispanic or not of Hispanic origin." Although "Hispanic" does appear as a separate racial category on some official forms (e.g., affirmative action, employment, university admissions), it usually appears in a combined format—"white (not of Hispanic origin); black (not of Hispanic origin); Asian/Pacific Islander; Hispanic; American Indian and Alaska Native." Technically speaking, indigenous individuals (including Asian/Pacific Islanders or any other individuals, for that matter), who originate in Latin America could also be identified as "Hispanic" to distinguish them from individuals identified as "Native American (not of Hispanic origin)," who originate in the continental United States; but this option is not given.

Public Response to the *Federal Register* Notice

In response to the OMB notice, members of several support groups for interracial couples and multiracial-identified individuals requested that the category "multiracial" or "biracial" be added to the five official categories.[13] Public comment was to end on April 19 but was extended through July 15 to enable the OMB to evaluate the large number of comments. While many multiracial individuals and interracial couples supported the addition of a "biracial" or "multiracial" identifier, the public response to these changes was overwhelmingly negative. According to a spokesperson for the OMB, of the ninety-five letters and 675 signatures received in response to the circular, approximately three-fourths opposed the addition of a multiracial designator. Among the opponents were several federal agencies, including the Civil Rights Division of the Department of Justice, the Department of Health and Human Services, the Equal Employment Opportunity Commission (EEOC), and the Office of Personnel Management, as well as several large corporations.[14]

Some of this opposition was based on logistical and financial concerns about the increase in paperwork, changes in the format of forms and computer programs for data analysis, and data burden on respondents. Various African American leaders, such as Senator Diane Watson and Representative Augustus Hawkins, and some black organizations, were particularly vocal in their opposition to any change that would make it possible for individuals to report a multiracial identification. Aware that most African-descent Americans have some European, and in many cases Native American, ancestry they also feared the defection of a significant number of individuals who for reasons of self-esteem or pragmatism would designate themselves as "multiracial" rather than black if given the option.

In actuality, however, most African-descent Americans (approximately 95 percent) claimed only black ancestry on the 1980 and 1990 censuses, thus reaffirming their African American identity.[15] In addition, field testing conducted from 1993 to 1997 for the 2000 census showed that only about 1 percent of the U.S. population identified itself as multiracial. This tiny figure may have aided the multiracial consciousness movement by allaying fears of a massive defection from the black category. Even taking into account a dramatic increase in the rate of interracial marriages and births of multiracial offspring, this population remains relatively small and is likely to remain so for some time. It seems likely that African American opponents of the census change were less concerned about multiracial-identified individuals (who are primarily the first-generation offspring of interracial marriages), than about the potential number of multigenerational individuals who might choose the multiracial check-off option.[16]

A March 29, 1988, bill in the Rhode Island legislature, which would have required application forms for state employment to include a check-off for "multiracial," was likewise opposed by the same groups. Senator Walton, an African American legislator, shot down the bill on the grounds that racial categories were demeaning to begin with and that the preoccupation with racial classification smacked of South African apartheid.[17]

There is a historical irony, however, in African American opposition to multiracial identity. In the 1950s and 1960s the integrationist leadership in the African American community, along with white liberal (and radical) supporters, sought to dismantle barriers to social equality for blacks. Their efforts led eventually to the repeal of laws against interracial marriage and the subsequent growth in the number of interracial couples and multiracial offspring. In light of their previous integrationist platform, African Americans' resistance to the legitimization of multiracial identity—a logical step in the progression of civil rights—appears somewhat paradoxical when compared to the concerns of both their black nationalist and white segregationist foes.[18]

Opponents of multiracial identity contend that, statistically speaking, the one-drop rule is a means of preventing erosion in the number of individuals who under the current system are counted as black. Such erosion, they argue, would harm the case for civil rights enforcement and diminish the number of valid claims of the patterns of discrimination that result, under federal law, in compensatory programs such as affirmative action.[19] In response to such opposition, the OMB retracted its proposal to revise Directive No. 15.[20]

The Association of Multiethnic Americans

In April 1986 Carlos Fernández, who is of European American and Mexican American descent and was then president of I-Pride in Berkeley, California, joined John Brown, an interracially married African-descent American who was then a member of the Interracial Family Alliance (IFA) in Atlanta, Georgia, to discuss starting a nationwide umbrella organization for the various independent advocacy and support groups of interracial couples and multiracial-identified individuals. The Association of Multiethnic Americans (AMEA), founded on November 12, 1988, would serve as a national agent to coordinate strategies for gaining official recognition of multiracial-identified individuals. Carlos Fernández was elected president, and Ramona Douglass, who is of Italian American, African American, and Native American descent and was then a representative of the Biracial Family Network, was elected vice president.[21]

Ideologically, the AMEA sought to transform the dominant ideology by redefining political interests and identities. One of its goals was to challenge dysfunctional and pathological images of interracial couples and multiracial-identified individuals as race traitors, misfits, and the like. The AMEA sought to promote images that depicted these individuals not only as stable and "normal" but also as potential "racial bridges" in the balkanized landscape of American race relations. The organization also sought to increase public awareness of the prejudice and discrimination directed at these individuals. More specifically, it aimed to galvanize people's consciousness about the need for a multiracial identifier on official forms.[22]

At the founding meeting and in subsequent discussions, much attention was focused on concerns—particularly in the African American community—about the effect a multiracial identifier would have on affirmative action programs and other race-based government initiatives.[23] There was no general agreement on how the organization should deal with these issues—nor could consensus be reached on how to characterize multiracial individuals for that purpose. Members voiced differing opinions as to whether a multiracial designator was applicable to everyone who identified as multiracial or whether the term should be restricted to first-generation individuals. One thing that was generally agreed was that multiracial identity should not be defined on the basis of biological notions of race, that is, on some DNA percentage in an individual's genetic makeup. There was general support for a definition based on ancestral backgrounds. Even then, participants generally rejected any notion of ancestral quantum as the basis for the definition of multiracial.

In the 1990s the AMEA, along with other activists in the multiracial consciousness movement, came close to supporting biological notions of race in the context of health research, where comprehensive data on racial background is important. A federal standard permitting the reporting of multiracial responses, they argued, could improve the identification of individuals at high risk for certain medical conditions (e.g., sickle cell anemia, tay sacks), as well as of donor matches for organ transplants. The motive behind this recommendation, however, was to use medical concerns to gain the support of health officials, and then to appeal to recalcitrant federal officials—and ultimately the general public—for changes in official racial designations. Unfortunately this strategy had the disadvantage of reifying biological notions of race and came under criticism from some quarters.[24]

The organization's name was the subject of vigorous debate at the AMEA's founding meeting. Carlos Fernández considered the concept of race to be very problematic and argued that any organization representing the interests of interracial families and multiracial individuals should question the whole concept of race. He advocated that the group call itself "multiethnic" rather than "multiracial."[25] Despite initial resistance, Fernández prevailed, and the organization was christened the Association of Multiethnic Americans (AMEA).

Others felt that "ethnicity" had taken on a confusing array of meanings and tended to suggest cultural factors rather than racial ones.[26] They argued that the overriding structural wedge in the United States has been ethno-racial difference and only secondarily ethno-cultural difference. Since the immediate goal was to make it possible to collect data on individuals who identified with more than one of the current official racial categories in Directive No. 15,[27] use of "ethnicity" would only confuse matters, they argued.[28]

The formats that might be used to collect data were also discussed. These included a separate multiracial identifier (the "pluralistic format"); checking more than one box (the "integrative format"); a separate multiracial identifier in conjunction with some means of acknowledging more than one of the other groups either through write-ins, fill-in blanks, or actually checking the various other boxes that were applicable (the "combined format").[29] Although there was no national consensus as to format, the AMEA leadership recommended the combined format. The general public and the media, however, typically framed discussion in terms of "multiracial classification" or "multiracial category," as if a stand-alone multiracial identifier or "box" (the pluralistic format) was the only proposal supported by the multiracial consciousness movement. In fact, that format has always been only one of the various possibilities.

Part of the struggle over the next ten years would involve arriving at an acceptable format for data collection and defining the multiracial phenomenon in a manner that was acceptable and intelligible to both the movement's constituents and the larger public. This was a daunting task at times, given the illusive nature of identity and the limits of language to describe it—especially the language of race in the United States. The academics and the grassroots activists of the movement often talked past each other—compelling evidence in itself of the difficulties involved in pinning down a mutually acceptable terminology. Although both camps played a critical role in refining terminology, the language of the academics often struck the grassroots activists as too abstract. And since the activists were frequently the first to be contacted by the media, they often unwittingly misrepresented the movement's goals and premises by failing to grasp or convey the subtleties and complexities involved.

From "Black" to "Other"

Prior to the founding of the AMEA there was no national agent working to gain official recognition of multiracial-identified individuals. From the standpoint of the federal government, multiracial identity politics was a marginal project located outside the normal arena of governmental activity. However, the disparity between the existing racial order, organized and enforced by the state, and the growing oppositional ideology, whose proponents were the real and potential adherents of a movement comprised of multiracial-identified individuals and intermarried couples, eventually led to a crisis.

In the months after the founding of the AMEA, support groups held public education forums to discuss the complexities and controversy surrounding multiracial identity, particularly as these related to the upcoming 1990 census.[30] In addition, members of some advocacy groups, particularly the Interracial Family Circle (IFC) in Washington D.C., began to express frustration with the AMEA's slow progress in this area. Many individuals had received delayed or no response to phone calls. Some of the AMEA's administrative inefficiency was the result of financial constraints and shortage of personnel, as the AMEA, like most of the local support groups, is a nonprofit organization relying entirely on volunteer staff. However, the AMEA's leadership was also very cautious about involvement in political activities that might conflict with the organization's goal of securing and maintaining its official status as a 501(c)(3) nonprofit organization, which would have been jeopardized had a substantial part of its activities been devoted to influencing the U.S. Congress or other elected officials.[31]

In any case, in November 1989 several members of the IFC formed a splinter group that circumvented the AMEA leadership and communicated directly with officials at the OMB, the Bureau of the Census, and the congressional subcommittee on the census. A flurry of phone calls and correspondence between the OMB, the Census

Bureau, the leadership of the AMEA, the IFC, and various individuals and support groups affiliated with the AMEA ultimately led to a small but significant reform in official policy. Federal officials representing government institutions (the OMB and the Census Bureau) realized that the demand for recognition of multiracial-identified individuals could become an irritant (or potential "threat") to the racial order if they were not addressed in some form. In December the Census Bureau announced that there would be no multiracial identifier on the 1990 census; but at the same time they developed a policy of "insulation" that confined demands for the official recognition of multiracial-identified individuals to largely symbolic terrain.

The support groups were quietly notified that the government would accept "biracial," "multiracial," or some other designation clearly indicating a blended identity as a write-in response to the "other" category. These write-in responses would be coded in order to determine roughly the actual number of people who identified themselves in this manner. This would give the OMB a clearer indication of what, if any, changes should be made to the 2000 census.[32] The OMB did not, however, make this announcement to the general public, and the various support groups therefore had to pass the word to their membership through their newsletters and other channels. Some discussion of the Census Bureau's decision did appear in an op-ed entitled "Spread the Word," which appeared in the May 1990 issue of the newly inaugurated *Interrace Magazine*.[33] People who did not belong to a local support group or subscribe to *Interrace*—that is, most real or potential members of the community of interracial couples and multiracial individuals—remained in the dark about the new census policy.

"Other" Responses on the 1970, 1980, and 1990 Censuses

Since 1970 responses to the race question (question no. 4) have been based primarily on self-identification when only mail-out and mail-in questionnaires are used. In cases where follow-up interviews were necessary for the 1970 census, however, enumerators were instructed to determine a person's race based on observation. By 1980 this had changed; enumerators were instructed to ask respondents to state their race if there was any question. Following the requirements of Directive No. 15, however, alternative write-in entries in the "other" category had to be "retro-fitted"[34] into the four basic racial categories,[35] but these entries are not publicly available.[36]

Between 1980 and 1990, the number of people who marked "other" race increased by 45 percent (from 6.8 million in 1980 to 9.8 million in 1990). Of the approximately 10 million people (close to 4 percent of the total U.S. population) who wrote in "other," 95.7 percent were Latino. On the 1970 census, Latino entries in the "other" category had been reassigned to the white category unless there was a clear justification for reassigning them otherwise. With the inclusion of the ethnicity question in 1980, Latino write-ins remained in "other."[37] The increased Latino presence in the

United States has presented a significant challenge to the American binary racial project.[38] Indeed, there has been "official ambivalence" about whether Latinos should be considered a separate racial category. For example, the census classified Mexican-descent Americans as "white" from 1940 to 1970 and "of any race" they chose in 1980 and 1990. In 1940, the criterion was that Spanish be the mother tongue. In 1950 and 1960, persons of Spanish surname were recorded as Latino. By 1960, all Mexicans, Puerto Ricans, and other persons of "Latin descent" were counted as "white" unless they were "definitely Negro, Indian, or some other race (as determined by observation)." In 1970, a separate question on "Hispanic" origin was added to the census long form (sent to one-sixth of households). In 1980 and 1990, a separate ethnicity question requesting information on "Hispanic" origins was asked of all households.[39]

The census format typically used includes two separate questions, one on race and another on ethnicity, specifically for collecting information on "Hispanic" origins. Increasingly, however, this format has become meaningless because of increased Latino reporting in the "other race" category, as well as increased reporting inconsistency in the race and ethnicity questions and non-response to both the race and "Hispanic origins" questions.[40] This can be explained in part by the fact that Latinos originate in countries where terms referring to multiracial individuals (e.g., "mestizo," "mulatto") are acceptable means of self-identification. Race in Latin America is often viewed in such a way that not only phenotypical but also social and cultural characteristics are considered. Consequently, racial designations are viewed more as individual markers than determinants of one's reference group.[41] Consequently, one could argue that in some generic sense, Latino identity in the United States is more or less implicitly multiracial.

In the 1990 census, just over half of Latinos counted themselves as racially white and 40 percent as racially "other." However, in matters of public policy and popular culture, "Hispanic" is now treated as a racial category separate from "white." Field tests conducted after the 1990 census to help redesign the race and ethnicity questions on the 2000 census indicate that about one-third of people who identified themselves as Latino on the ethnicity question also listed themselves with recognizable multiracial identifiers, such as "mestizo," "biracial," "multiracial," etc., in the "other" category.[42] Yet a majority of the Latinos reporting in the "other race" category does not appear to be an expression of "multiracial" identity. Rather, they view themselves as neither European *American* nor African *American*, etc., by virtue of their different Latin national-cultural origins, even if they consider themselves racially black, white, mulatto, or mestizo in their respective communities.[43]

The remaining 253,000 write-ins in the "other" category clearly designated a multiracial identity; the largest number (56,000) coming from California.[44] In cases where a multiple response was entered, the data was reassigned to the first race given. For example, the 47,835 respondents who entered "black-white," were counted as black; the 27,926 who wrote in "white-black" were counted as white.[45] Following the 1970 and 1980 census procedures,[46] the 32,505 individuals who wrote in "mixed" on the 1990 census (including those who wrote in "multiracial"), were left in the "other" category, as were the 17,202 respondents who wrote in "interracial" or "biracial."[47] Entries indicating identification with a triracial isolate group—the Issues, Jackson Whites, Melungeons, and so on—have remained in the "other" category since the 1970 census.[48]

It is interesting to note that in 1970 write-in entries such as "Creole" were reassigned to the black category only if the respondent resided in Louisiana. Outside this region the entry remained "other." In 1980 this write-in entry was recoded as black regardless of location.[49] In 1990, however, the 6,244 Creole entries remained in the "other" category regardless of geographical location.[50] This change resulted from pressure from the Creole community to include "Creole American" as a separate official listing on the race question.[51] Words clearly designating African ancestry, e.g., mulatto, quadroon, and octoroon, were reassigned to the black category in 1970 and 1980. In 1990 the 31,708 individuals who used these entries remained in the "other" category.[52]

This change in policy on the 1990 census was an important departure from previous censuses. At no point prior to that census were multiracial individuals enumerated separately from the African American statistical aggregate. On previous censuses the enumeration of African Americans as black and multiracial (mulatto, quadroon, octoroon, etc.), has been essentially a semantic distinction with few if any statistical or social implications. Yet in neither of these cases were individuals actually officially designated as multiracial. These 1990 figures do not, therefore, give an accurate estimate of the actual number of individuals who identify as multiracial, not to mention the vast number of people who checked one box because they were unaware of another alternative. Furthermore, it is impossible to determine from these data how many individuals have an African component in their multiracial identity (except those who identified with terms more clearly associated with African ancestry) or the various other backgrounds with which the larger population of multiracial individuals identify.

The 2000 Census: Reforming the Racial State

In the fall of 1991 Susan Graham and Chris Ashe, two interracially married European American women and the parents of multiracial children, founded Project RACE (Reclassify All Children Equally). They then contacted the AMEA to inquire about strategies for changing official racial categories, both on the decennial census and, more immediately, on public school forms. The AMEA, burdened by more correspondence than its unpaid volunteer staff could handle, was slow to reply, especially because Project RACE was most interested in change at the local level (particularly public schools), while the AMEA's focus was national and concerned primarily with the census, which the AMEA leadership felt had to be reformed before local problems could be tackled.

The founders of Project RACE eventually contacted me in my capacity as a member of the AMEA advisory board and professor of sociology at the University of California, Santa Barbara. I had recently written an article in *Interrace Magazine* entitled "The Census and the Numbers Racket."[53] Graham and Ashe wanted to know how they might implement a stand-alone identifier—the pluralistic format—on public school forms, an idea that was sure to be opposed by African Americans concerned about losing numbers, as I informed them. Since most African Americans were in fact multiracial in background (or "multigenerational"), virtually all of them could check a multiracial box if the term "multiracial" meant anyone having multiple racial ancestries.[54] Furthermore, the AMEA defined as multiracial someone of "multiple backgrounds or heritages," or someone of "more than one" of the current official categories "as indicated by the race or ethnicity of the parents." This gave the impression that the term multiracial was only applicable to first-generation offspring of interracial marriages.[55]

In fact the AMEA leadership deliberately focused on the small but growing population of first-generation offspring, that is, on "biracial" individuals, as those individuals for whom these changes were being requested. They did this in order to sidestep the controversy surrounding multigenerational individuals. Their goal was to gain support for a multiracial identifier by appealing to concerns about children's self-esteem as well as the symbolic importance of multiracial children as manifestations of the American melting pot in action.[56] (Ironically, criticism from the African American community has been directed at the exclusivity of this first-generation definition of multiracial, as well as the more inclusive multigenerational definition. In both cases, however, this criticism was an attempt to point out the weaknesses of or contradictions in the argument for a multiracial identifier, rather than to support one definition over the other.)[57]

I suggested that Project RACE support the combined format that included a separate multiracial identifier in conjunction with multiple boxes or check-offs. I also recommended that the race question include some variation on the phrase, "if you identify as multiracial" or "if you consider yourself multiracial." This definition of the term multiracial relied less on multiple ancestry or backgrounds themselves and more on one's self-identification. I argued that as long as the movement focused on origins, heritages, or backgrounds without simultaneously taking identification into consideration, it would continue to be bogged down with contradictions and remain vulnerable to criticism from African Americans and other communities of color, who would use this contradiction to undermine its goals. Before our conversation, the founders of Project RACE were unaware of the number of multigenerational individuals of African American and European American descent who identified as multiracial. And they had no knowledge of the connection between concerns about multigenerational individuals and the controversy surrounding recommendations for the pluralistic format in the collection of data on multiracial-identified individuals.[58]

Project RACE then began to strategize at the municipal and state levels using the combined format. The organization arrived at a format that focused on the definition of multiracial as someone whose "parents are of more than one race."[59] On the surface this definition gave the impression that the emphasis was on first-generation offspring, in keeping with the AMEA's strategy of appealing to concerns in the African American community. But the phrasing was also intended to address multigenerational concerns by making it possible to interpret the definition of a multiracial individual as either (1) someone whose parents were themselves of more than one race (or racial background), or (2) someone who had parents that were of different racial groups.

As it happened, Project RACE ended up abandoning the combined format because of concerns that it took up too much space. But the organization did define "multiracial" in such a way as to address both first-generation and multigenerational concerns.[60] The AMEA meanwhile continued to define "multiracial" as someone of "multiple backgrounds," "multiple heritages," "multiple origins," or "someone of more than one" of the current official categories "as indicated by the race of the parents." This continued to give the impression that the term was applicable only to first-generation offspring of interracial marriage. The AMEA changed its position on this matter only when Project RACE eventually joined forces with the organization in the effort to make changes at the federal level from 1993 to 1997. Yet the term continued to be framed in a manner that often made it seem applicable to someone with more than one racial background rather than to someone who *identified* with more than one racial background.[61]

Over the next year, the leadership of the AMEA and Project RACE continued to disagree on strategy, and their differences were exacerbated by different leadership styles (Project RACE was more confrontational, while the AMEA tended to be more conciliatory). But Project RACE made significant progress in gaining support at the state and municipal levels using the stand-alone multiracial identifier. By this time I was on the advisory boards of both the AMEA and Project RACE and had become a liaison between the two organizations. I informed Carlos Fernández, the AMEA's president, of Project RACE's successes at the municipal and state levels, and he began to take a more serious look at Project RACE and its strategies.

The process of facilitating a rapprochement between the two organizations was slow and difficult work, however.[62] Tension abated somewhat after I circumvented the AMEA's president and got Susan Graham together with AMEA vice president Ramona Douglass. The easier rapport between these two women did improve the working relationship of the two groups despite Fernández's continued opposition.

The Comprehensive Review Process, 1993–1997

The AMEA and its affiliates failed to get OMB and Census Bureau officials to adopt "multiracial" on the 1990 census. Project RACE therefore sought to politicize racial identities through the traditional means of lobbying state legislators, threatening legal action, and so on.[63] The organization gained support at the state and local levels for a stand-alone multiracial identifier (with the option in several states to break down the numbers in the multiracial category into the minimum single racial categories where necessary for administrative purposes). Project RACE helped lay the foundation for a series of potential conflicts within and between state agencies (i.e., on the question of the stand-alone multiracial identifier at the state and local levels and the demand for single-racial identifiers at the federal level).

State and federal governments responded by closing ranks in order to ensure the relative unity of the racial state, which made opposition more difficult. The forces of change correspondingly made concessions by accepting the "other" category rather than a stand-alone multiracial-identifier; agreeing to a "check one or more" format or a combined format that used a multiracial identifier along with a "check more than one" format. Public schools, for their part, moved toward accommodation of the proposed new changes, while the OMB and the Census Bureau remained entrenched in a protracted struggle to prevent, or at least delay, changes at the federal level.

Nevertheless, beginning in June 1993 federal officials began a comprehensive review process to determine what if any changes could be made to the 2000 census. The AMEA and Project RACE testified at government hearings on the subject between 1993 and 1997. The two organizations had achieved moderate cooperation, especially after Ramona Douglass succeeded Carlos Fernández as president. Still, Project RACE continued to push for a separate identifier at the state level, hoping to use victory there as a lever to force changes at the national level.

From "Other" to "Multiracial"

Thanks to Project RACE, forms for the Operation Desert Shield/Desert Storm Deployment Survey included "multiracial" as a designation for the offspring of returning veterans. In addition, representatives of the organization succeeded in getting elected state officials to sponsor legislation that would add a multiracial category to all state forms used to collect information on race and ethnicity. As a result, in part, of these efforts, Georgia, North Carolina, Ohio, Illinois, Michigan, Indiana, and Texas (pending) included "multiracial" on all official state forms. Similar legislation was passed in Wyoming without the help of Project RACE.[64] The Texas legislation included a multiracial-identifier and requested multiple check-offs. Other states' legislation was worded in such a way as to allow agencies to request and collect data on the multiple components of multiracial-identified individuals whenever necessary for certain tracking purposes.[65]

Georgia, Indiana, and Michigan required a stand-alone multiracial category on all state forms used to collect data on race and ethnicity, including health department forms. The Ohio and Illinois legislation affected only school forms that collect data on race and ethnicity. Florida and North Carolina added a multiracial category (by administrative directive) to school forms that collect information on race and ethnicity.[66] At least eight other states considered legislation adding a multiracial category: California, Massachusetts, New Jersey, New York, Oklahoma, Oregon, Pennsylvania, and Wisconsin. And in May 1998 Maryland added a multiracial identifier in the combined format on official forms. These new state laws specified that if a federal agency did not accept the multiracial data, the reporting state agency should reclassify multiracial-identified individuals according to categories approved by the federal agency, based on the distribution of the general population. However, the term "general population" was not defined in the legislation.[67]

The ACT Testing Service (the alternative to the SAT college entrance exam) included a multiracial identifier. Williams College in Williamstown, Massachusetts, the University of Michigan's Rackham School of Graduate Studies, and several alumni associations (at, for example, UCLA and Tufts) have included a multiracial identifier on official forms. Since 1989 reports prepared by the Center for Assessment and Demographic Studies at Gallaudet University in Washington, D.C., have counted individuals who indicate a multiracial background.[68] For the most part, however, universities have resisted changes in the collection of racial data on admissions forms. A 1994 survey of eight hundred public school districts, conducted by the Education Office for Civil Rights, found considerable variation in the classification of multiracial-identified individuals.[69] Many districts use the mother's racial designation; others use the father's, while approximately 30 percent use a separate category.[70] These practices conflict with Directive No. 15 unless these data can be retrofitted at the federal level into one of the four official racial categories—black; white; Asian/Pacific Islander; American Indian and Alaska Native (and the "Hispanic" identifier, when it is given as an option), or into the figures for each of the single-racial groups with which multiracial individuals identify—including the appropriate historically "underrepresented" racial component(s) in their background—when totaling those individual groups' respective numbers, as is the case on admission forms for Williams College.

In December 1996, A Place For Us/National (APU) filed the 1998 Multiracial/ Multiethnic Children's Initiative with the state of California to begin a petition drive to include a multiracial identifier on the November 1998 ballot. The initiative was approved in February 1997, with a July 11 deadline for obtaining the necessary 800,000 signatures. APU hoped to obtain the required number of signatures by the end of June in celebration of the thirtieth anniversary of *Loving v. Virginia*, but it fell short not only of this goal but of the July 11 deadline as well. Plans to announce the success of the campaign at the Multiracial Solidarity March to be held in Hollywood on August 9 had to be abandoned. Even the march itself was somewhat dismal, as only seventy people turned out, compared to the two hundred who participated in the first Multiracial Solidarity March in July 1996 in Washington, D.C. However, both marches received enthusiastic support from those individuals who attended.[71]

The Third Multiracial Leadership Summit, June 7, 1997

Project RACE and the AMEA mounted massive letter-writing campaigns during the public comment period on each *Federal Register*, recommending that the combined format be used at the federal level, that is, a separate multiracial identifier plus multiple check-offs, though they also advocated that federal agencies be able to break down that information when necessary.[72] Officials in Washington, however, as well as others in traditional communities of color, seemed to believe that the stand-alone identifier was the movement's only goal, perhaps in part because Project RACE gave this impression on several occasions and in some congressional testimony.[73]

By the time of the May 1997 congressional subcommittee hearings, the results of the federal field testing—the Current Population Survey (October 1995), the National Content Survey (December 1996), and particularly the Race and Ethnic Targeted Test (May 1997)—made it clear that if any change was approved at the federal level it would be the integrative format ("check one or more racial groups"), rather than the combined format (a multiracial identifier in combination with the ability to check other boxes). Consequently, the leadership of Project RACE and the AMEA began to consider supporting the inegrative format. Indeed, the success of the movement depended on its ability to generate a wide and flexible variety of strategies and political tactics.

Shortly after the May 1997 Senate subcommittee hearings, the AMEA and Project RACE called a Third Multiracial Leadership Summit to discuss the hearings and a possible compromise. The meeting was held on June 7, 1997, in Oakland, California, and was sponsored by I-Pride. In attendance were AMEA and Project RACE representatives, legal experts, representatives of several educational and support organizations, including Hapa Issues Forum—a national organization that consists of multiracial individuals of partial Asian/Asian American descent—and a representative of the Census Advisory Committee, who was also part of the National Coalition on the Accurate Count of Asian and Pacific Islanders.[74]

A consensus emerged that a separate multiracial box without multiple check-offs was unacceptable. Participants knew that the combined format was unlikely to gain the support of the OMB and that it would also be resisted by traditional civil rights groups. In spite of a general preference for the combined format, the summit leadership withdrew its longstanding support for that format and settled instead on a revised model presented by Project RACE that recommended an integrative format (check more than one box).[75] It was argued, nevertheless, that the movement's goals could be achieved in part by asking some variation on the question "Check One. If you consider yourself to be biracial or multiracial, check as many [boxes] as apply."[76] The word "multiracial" was deliberately included only in the instructions and not as one of the boxes.[77]

This compromised format was drafted as part of a general statement after eight hours of intense and heated discussion. The statement read:

- We the undersigned organizations represent the intersection of traditional racial communities comprised of individuals and families who identify with more than one racial background.
- We advocate a "check one or more" format for the collection of racial data, which will not adversely affect existing civil rights protections. We do not advocate a stand-alone multiracial category on the federal level.
- A "check one or more" format will enable all Americans to respond truthfully on the census and other forms that collect racial data.
- A "check one or more" format will ensure the identification of all Americans who may be at risk for life threatening diseases for which genetic information is critical.[78]

The attendees approved this statement with minor revisions. Both the original statement and the revised version were distributed to various support groups and AMEA affiliates for their endorsement. A representative of Hapa Issues Forum successfully enlisted the support of the Asian American Donor Program and the Japanese American Citizens League (JACL). The JACL is one of the largest traditional civil rights organizations in the United States, with a membership of twenty-five thousand. It is the Japanese American equivalent of the NAACP, and it played a key role for the defense in *Loving v. Virginia*.[79] In addition, a supporter of the AMEA persuaded the American Medical Association to endorse the recommendations.[80]

Many individuals and support groups endorsed the "Oakland Compromise" recommending the "integrative format," but there was strong opposition from those who wanted the "combined format." The strongest resistance came from individuals who wanted a stand-alone multiracial identifier or a multiracial identifier in which checking or writing in all the applicable single-racial groups was optional.[81] In addition, the leadership of Project RACE—perhaps under pressure from its constituents—eventually retracted its support for its own revised model.[82] Consequently, the "Oakland Compromise" created a rift between hard-liners who continued to support the "combined format" and moderates who supported the "integrative format." The former more or less coincided with Project RACE and its supporters and the latter with the AMEA and its affiliates.

The leadership of Project RACE objected to, among other things, the terminology that described multiracial individuals and interracial couples as the "intersection of traditional racial communities." They felt that this language would undermine attempts to gain recognition of specific multiracial identities and the uniqueness of the multiracial experience. The leadership of Project RACE was also critical of the position taken by multiracial adults—who were disproportionately represented at the summit—that the summit statement should emphatically reject a stand-alone identifier. Unlike the executive director of Project RACE, a European American partner in an interracial marriage, these multiracial individuals saw themselves as people of color. Consequently, they rejected any statement that might convey, however unwittingly, a desire to view themselves otherwise as well as any format for the collection of racial and ethnic data that might be interpreted as insensitive to the concerns of the traditional communities of color.[83] In Project RACE's view this emphatic rejection of a stand-alone identifier dismissed the significance of its work at the state and local levels.

More important, their position could jeopardize legislative and administrative decisions at the state and municipal levels where a stand-alone multiracial identifier had been legislated or implemented administratively on state and public school forms.[84] The rejection of a stand-alone multiracial identifier also jeopardized the Petri bill, H.R. 830 (also known as the Tiger Woods bill). This bill, which had been drawn up in 1996 and was pending congressional approval, supported a stand-alone identifier. Introduced in the House by Representative Thomas E. Petri (R-Wisconsin), H.R. 830 was intended as a last resort if the OMB failed to follow through in making changes on its own.[85]

The Interagency Task Force Recommendations, July 9, 1997

When the social changes set in motion by the growth of the multiracial consciousness movement further threatened to disrupt the racial equilibrium, the state was thrown into turmoil. The establishment of a new unstable equilibrium thus became paramount. Reform policies of "absorption" (incorporation) were initiated and deemed potentially effective in achieving this goal. Constituent groups began exploring a range of potential accommodations and possibilities for reconsidering the racial order, and their possible roles in a racial ideology were "rearticulated" and "absorbed" in light of oppositional themes. Accordingly, on July 9, 1997, the OMB announced its recommendations for changes in the collection of racial and ethnic data based on a 150-page report prepared by the Interagency Task Force. This task force—which consisted of some thirty governmental agencies—had been formed by the OMB and the Census Bureau and was charged with making recommendations for possible changes in the collection of racial data. The sources of the information contained in the report included public comments gathered from hearings and responses to OMB notices published in the *Federal Register*, opinions of experts in the area of race and ethnicity, small-scale ethnographic and cognitive laboratory studies, and several national tests sponsored by federal agencies. The recommendations were subject to a sixty-day public review and comment period before the OMB would decide whether to accept them.[86]

The task force unequivocally rejected a stand-alone multiracial identifier, as well as the combined format or indeed any mention of the word "multiracial" in the race question.[87] Instead it recommended unanimously that federal data collection forms be changed so that individuals could check off one or more racial identifications. (Officials in Washington were not yet aware that the "Oakland Compromise" statement had arrived at a similar proposal independently.)

The OMB gave various reasons for its decision. First, there was no general understanding of the definition of the term "multiracial." Second, a stand-alone multiracial identifier would not provide useful information and would in fact adversely affect the historical continuity of data. They also argued that it could heighten racial tensions and further fragment the population. Officials stated that among other things the mark-one-or-more alternative—unlike the combined format—would require fewer changes in formatting on existing forms, take up less space, and allow for the historical continuity of data.[88]

The integrative format they proposed would allow for the continued enforcement and support of existing civil rights legislation and claims aimed at tracking historical and contemporary patterns of discrimination and in arriving at goals for achieving social and economic equity. The data could be retrofitted into the existing official racial categories and figures for each of the single-racial groups with which multiracial individuals identify—including the appropriate historically "underrepresented" racial component(s) in their background—when totaling those individual groups' numbers. (The combined format would also prevent loss of numbers for given racial groups by making it possible to retrofit data into the existing official racial categories and figures for each of the single-racial groups with which multiracial individuals identify while at the same time acknowledging multiracial individuals).

In addition, the task force recommended that the question concerning the Latino population (the "ethnicity question") remain separate from the racial categories but be placed just before the race question. Tests indicated that this format produced more complete data on Latinos, who have been the largest number of respondents in the "other race" category and have failed to respond to the race question if it was asked before questions about ethnic origins. However, this might create some problems for collecting data on individuals who identify with both Hispanic and non-Hispanic origins. They are not permitted to check both Hispanic and non-Hispanic origins on the ethnicity question, nor are they provided with the Hispanic identifier among the various options on the race question.[89]

Officials acknowledged that the multiracial population had grown over the previous thirty years and continued to grow. They recognized that the "check one box only" format had become obsolete and that the task of statistically measuring the multiracial phenomenon eventually would have to be confronted. Adopting a method of reporting more than one race, they argued, would not only increase the accuracy of racial reports reflecting a changing society, but might also eliminate some inconsistencies in racial reporting. Implementing this method would mean that demographic changes could be measured more precisely with a smaller discontinuity in historical data series than if it were adopted at some point in the future.[90] In addition, they maintained, the opportunity to identify with more than one race would promote self-identification, increase self-esteem, and possibly reduce non-response to the race question. Some multiracial individuals also strongly advocated the change, and some states have already begun allowing individuals to identify with more than one race by using a multiracial category.

Allowing respondents in federal data collections to select more than one race, therefore, would be consistent with the trend toward this option at the municipal and state levels, and might encourage the states to conform to a new federal standard. The "select one or more races" format would also require only one question, with fewer write-ins and thus less coding. Although instructions would be needed and the wording would have to be very precise, tabulating a multiple-response option might be more straightforward and consistent across federal agencies than tabulating write-in responses. Another factor favoring the one-or-more format was that the counts for whites and blacks, at least in the short term, would not be affected.[91]

The consensus was that the recommended changes would require data users to understand the impact of those changes in terms of the categories that have been utilized for the past twenty years. New ways of reporting race and ethnicity might require supporting information so that users could assess the magnitude of changes to current time series. To that end, methods of tabulating multiracial responses into the current minimum set of categories would have to be investigated further.[92] Yet the existing standards presented their own problems, including the lack of standardization for classifying data on race and ethnicity across state and federal agencies; less than optimal participation in federal surveys (especially item non-response); misidentification of individuals and groups in surveys; inaccurate counts and rates; inaccurate research; inaccurate program design, targeting, and monitoring; and potential misallocation of funds.

The financial cost of revising forms would be minimal, but the financial expenditure for changing data systems could be substantial. Furthermore, the implementation of new categories might make it necessary for employers to resurvey employees in order to update information on race and ethnicity.[93] Still, most parties agreed that efficiency and accuracy demanded that the changes be made.[94]

As with Directive No. 15, the new OMB recommendations were designed to provide minimum standards for federal data on race and ethnicity. The recommendations continued to permit the collection of more detailed information on population groups in reporting the number of individuals identifying with more than one race to meet the needs of specific data users, provided that additional detail could be aggregated to comply with the minimum standards. However, standardized tabulation rules need to be developed by the federal agencies working in cooperation with one another. When results from data collection activities are reported or tabulated, the number selecting more than one race should be given, assuming that minimum standards for data quality and confidentiality are met.[95]

The new standards were used in the 2000 census, and other data producers should conform as soon as possible. But because data producers were given until January 1, 2003, to conform to the new standards, additional research could be conducted in the context of the different data collection initiatives. This research might estimate the effects in the different settings and evaluate methods for data tabulation to meet users' needs. The 2003 date was chosen because information from the 2000 census will be available then for use in conjunction with other federal data collections.[96]

From "Other" to "Mark One or More Races"

In response to these recommendations, Hapa Issues Forum and the AMEA actively sought the support of traditional civil rights organizations such as the NAACP, JACL, and the Mexican American Legal Defense and Education Fund (MALDEF).[97] Given the longstanding tension between organizations representing multiracial individuals of partial Asian/Asian American descent and those representing black-white individuals, Hapa Issues Forum's involvement was a significant development and aided in mobilization during this phase of the census campaign.

The NAACP and other African American leaders had made it clear that they would oppose a stand-alone multiracial identifier, which they erroneously assumed was the only option acceptable to the multiracial consciousness movement. The Petri bill, along with media coverage of stand-alone identifiers adopted by several states and municipalities, furthered this erroneous impression, although, in fairness, the multiracial movement itself was often confused and unclear in its language and definition of terms.

It did not help matters that Republicans tended to support a multiracial identifier, while Democrats were either neutral or strongly opposed. When President Clinton was asked for his view at an April 1995 press conference in Dallas, he said he supported the addition of a multiracial identifier to the census, only later to equivocate.[98] The Democrats' evasiveness was no doubt the result of fear of alienating their constituents in communities of color and black elected officials. In January 1997 Republican Newt Gingrich—after winning a second term as Speaker of the House—challenged the Democrats on this question when he charged that "many Americans cannot fill out their census because they are an amalgam of races."[99] Gingrich also criticized Clinton's Advisory Committee on Race and its general policy on race,[100] and he wrote the director of the OMB a letter of support for the inclusion of a multiracial identifier on the census and other federal forms.[101] Gingrich and other conservatives argued that a "multiracial category" would help to dilute racial consciousness and thus serve a civic purpose by undermining the obsession with race and ethnicity that fuels identity politics. A multiracial identifier would work against racial divisiveness and what conservatives called the "racial spoils system."[102]

These critics applauded the fact that a "multiracial" category denoted no protected class under the law and thus served no statutory purpose. Data on individuals identifying themselves as "multiracial" would help eliminate the entire racial apparatus for affirmative action purposes. It should be pointed out, however, that some activists in the multiracial consciousness movement have argued that multiracial individuals should be part of a protected group under affirmative action and other civil rights claims. Thus far the majority of activists have not supported these goals.[103] They knew that this would be potentially divisive and would provoke a backlash from communities of color that would see this as a threat to their claims. Activists were thus focused primarily on changing bureaucratic procedures for the collection of data on race and ethnicity.

It is not clear whether Gingrich and other Republican supporters of a multiracial identifier were aware of the implications of the stand-alone identifier as compared to the combined or integrative formats. The former might further the supposed divisiveness and Balkanization they were seeking to move beyond; the latter might move in the more integrative direction they professed to support. In any case, Republican support for a multiracial identifier led many individuals to view the multiracial consciousness movement—particularly the stand-alone identifier—as part of a right-wing "conspiracy." The multiracial movement and its Republican supporters were seen as enemies of civil rights and other claims aimed at achieving social and economic equity and redress. Despite this guilt by association, some activists felt that the Republican majority in the House made their support essential, particularly if it became necessary to pursue this struggle through legislative channels. This was a devil's bargain, but one based more on the political opportunism of some activists in the multiracial movement than on actual support of the Right (although some segments of the multiracial movement have supported the Republican agenda).

By July 1997, when the next round of hearings took place, the "check one or more" format recommended by the Interagency Task Force—in contradistinction to the stand-alone multiracial identifier—had the strong support of traditional African American civil rights organizations such as the NAACP and Urban League, as well as the Congressional Black Caucus.[104] Joseph Lawry of the Southern Christian Leadership Conference, who had previously rejected a stand-alone multiracial identifier, now supported the "mark one or more" option, as did Eric Rodriguez of the National Council of La Raza (NCLR), who had also opposed the stand-alone multiracial-identifier previously.[105] These reversals were the result of intense behind-the-scenes lobbying by the Hapa Issues Forum and the AMEA. Although the traditional civil rights organizations supported the mark-one-or-more format out of concern about the loss of numbers, they voiced concern about how the data would be tabulated (e.g., voter districting, etc.).

In response to the July 9, 1997, *Federal Register* Notice, the OMB received correspondence from approximately eight thousand individuals, some of them members and supporters of the AMEA and Hapa Issues Forum in favor of multiple-race reporting.[106] Project RACE and its supporters, who proposed a stand-alone or combined format, continued to speak out against the Task Force recommendations. In addition, they blasted the AMEA and Hapa Issues Forum for cutting a backroom deal with the NAACP.[107] The OMB's final decision on October 31, 1997, did in fact support the "check one or more" format. The title of the federal standard on racial and ethnic classification was changed from "Directive No. 15" to "Standards Maintaining, Collecting, and Presenting Federal Data on Race and Ethnicity," but the categories themselves remain the same. The recommended instruction forms for the race question read "Mark one or more" and "Select one or more." The format that appeared in the census dress rehearsal form read, "What is this person's race? Mark [X] one or more races to indicate what this person considers herself/himself to be."

This change was achieved in direct response to pressure from the multiracial movement, and it affected the social meaning and political role played by race, as well as the state's part in that drama. The movement managed to achieve this reform only because of decay in the capacity of state policies to organize and enforce the racial status quo. Once the general contours of state reformism were clear, the movement's internal divisions intensified even further. One conflict centered on the format to be used in collecting data on multiracial-identified individuals. The AMEA and its affiliates and supporters advocated a multiple check-off format, along with new state policies. Project RACE and its affiliates hardened in their opposition and became even more adamant about the need for a stand-alone multiracial identifier (and/or the combined format, that is, a separate identifier in combination with the ability to check more than one of the other traditional racial groups). At the very least, Project RACE demanded that the term "multiracial" be retained in the wording of the instructions. Another segment of the movement, represented by the Multiracial Leadership Forum, which was sponsored by a Place for Us/National, wanted to get rid of official racial designations altogether.[108]

Opponents of the multiple check-off format argued that there was no guarantee that federal agencies would actually tabulate data on those who checked more than one box. They were understandably upset that a person who checked both "black" and "white," for example, would be counted as black and tabulated with the data on African Americans in order to comply with the Voting Rights Act and the Civil Rights Act of 1964. They therefore considered the OMB's recommendations no real improvement over previous methods of data collection and tabulation.[109] Opponents also accused the OMB of trying to erase the term "multiracial" from the public's vocabulary because advocates for other communities—most notably the NAACP and the Congressional Black Caucus—were opposed to it. Yet Project RACE believed it had forced federal officials to capitulate to the changes it had helped bring about at the state and municipal levels.

Counting One or More Races and the Task of Tabulations

The greatest challenge ahead is tabulating data on individuals who report more than one race.[110] On February 17, 1999, the OMB issued its recommendations for tabulation of racial and ethnic data in compliance with the new standards. According to a 215-page report entitled "Draft Provisional Guidance on the Implementation of the 1997 Standards for Federal Data on Race and Ethnicity," there are sixty-three potential single- and multiple-race categories, including six for those who marked exactly one race, and fifty-seven categories for those who marked two or more races. The sixty-three mutually exclusive and exhaustive categories of race may be collapsed down to seven mutually exclusive and exhaustive categories by combining the fifty-seven categories of two or more races. These seven categories are: white alone, black or African American alone, American Indian and Alaskan Native alone, Asian alone, Native Hawaiian and Other Pacific Islander alone, some other race alone, and two or more races.[111]

In addition, officials decided that individuals reporting more than one race should not be listed as "multiracial" but as "persons reporting two races," "three races," "four races," "five races," "six races," and so on. The traditional civil rights community and various members of the Census Advisory Committee not only opposed these proposals but also resisted using the term "multiracial" even if a separate tabulation of "multiple racial responses" were allowed. They contended that any attempt to keep a separate tally of individuals who use the term "multiracial" and check more than one box would prove that the whole reform was nothing more than an attempt to undermine affirmative action and other race-based government initiatives.[112]

Under the new regulations, data in the "one race" category and the "two or more races" category can be presented, but data in the latter category can also be broken down into various subcategories.[113] In each case, data on "Hispanic origin" or "not of Hispanic origin" can be reported along with the data on race. However, it does not appear that individuals who identify as both "Hispanic origin" and "not of Hispanic origin" (one Hispanic parent and one non-Hispanic parent), were permitted to check both of these boxes on the ethnicity question, at least not on the 2000 census.

One method of tabulation would be to provide separate totals for those reporting the most common racial combinations, and to collapse the data for less frequently reported combinations. The specifics of the collapsed distributions would have to await the results of particular data collections. In such cases individuals who checked more than one box could be assigned equally to each of the groups with which they identified. In order to avoid compromising the accuracy of data by an overcount of more than 100 percent per person, individuals would not be counted as whole numbers in those groups. Rather, their numbers would be tabulated as part of each group's total percentage of the general population. Another option would be to assign them to the largest or smallest non-white group they marked. These could be ascertained from the racial composition of the population for the relevant geography.[114] Using this method, no change would be needed in the statistical methods currently used by agencies, and, for a few years, those agencies that began collecting data under the new standards would use this allocation method to report new racial data for individuals who select more than one race. This would provide agencies with a measure of the changing racial characteristics in the population and would indicate when the final alternative should be implemented. In other words, this method could be an interim solution used until full implementation of the new standards. Following careful evaluation of 2000 data, decisions could be made that phase in the new standards in an analytically appropriate manner.[115]

Another method would be to report the total, selecting each particular race, whether alone or in combination with other races. Thus, when data were reported it would be possible to determine two counts for each racial group. The lower count, or lower boundary, would include individuals who identify with one race only. The larger count, or upper boundary, adds to the lower boundary individuals who identify with the given racial category and one or more other racial categories. Thus, the upper boundary black count would include everyone who marked black, either alone or in combination with one or more other racial categories. The remainder of the population would consist of those individuals who did not identify as black.

Data from some geographical regions are expected to reflect larger numbers and percentages of respondents reporting themselves as belonging to more than one racial group. In most regions, however, few adults are expected to report themselves as members of more than one racial group. Consequently, the upper and lower boundaries will not be substantially different, at least not initially.[116] The key findings of the comprehensive review favoring the adoption of a method for reporting more than one race were that in self-administered and interviewer-administered surveys—including the 1990 census—only .5 percent of respondents selected more than one race when asked to select only one race. A slightly larger number—between 1 and 1.5 percent—selected a multiracial category when offered an opportunity to do so.[117]

Another approach specifically for Equal Employment Opportunity (EEO) purposes would be to ask respondents to provide a micro-data file containing one record (without specifying their names) for each employee. The micro-record would include the employee's race or races, ethnicity, gender, and occupational category. This approach might be simpler for employers and would provide agencies with the maximum amount of flexibility in using the information. Implementation of this approach appears to be a longer-term solution. The EEO agencies would need to work with respondents in designing and implementing the reporting format and method, and they would need to acquire the relevant software and hardware to process the information.[118] If this type of information became available from all employers, the EEO agencies could use any of the tests, depending on their needs, or they would be able to make the transition to applying the EEO methodology to any groups that become large enough to monitor for EEO purposes, including those that involve more than one race.[119] In some cases, this latter method could be used to compare data collected under the old and new standards. The total number reporting more than one race must be made available, if confidentiality and data quality requirements can be met, in order to ensure that any changes in response patterns resulting from the new standards can be monitored over time. It is also important that users with the same or closely related responsibilities adopt the same tabulation method.[120] In addition, the methods for tabulating data on race and ethnicity must be carefully developed and coordinated among the statistical agencies and other federal data users.[121]

Agencies are still in the process of reviewing the alternative approaches for tabulating data due to the complexities in collecting and using the data reported under the new standards for civil rights enforcement purposes.[122] On March 9, 2000, however, the OMB announced that individuals who check off more than one racial group on the census will be reassigned to one racial category for the purpose of monitoring discrimination and enforcing civil rights laws. Those who designate themselves both as white and as having a "minority" background will be counted as members of the minority background when government officials analyze patterns of discrimination in enforcing the Voting Rights Act, job bias laws, and other civil rights claims. Employers, schools, and others must report the four expected largest multiple-race categories: American Indian and white, Asian and white, black and white, and American Indian and black. Employers also must report any multiracial group that claims more than 1 percent of the population and include a category for any multiracial people not counted in any other group.[123]

The civil rights enforcement agencies agree that they should adopt common definitions for the racial and ethnic categories used to enforce civil rights legislation and other race-based initiatives and regulations. Clearly agencies will need to consider the complex issues related to implementing the new standards, bridging for enforcement purposes data collected under the old standard, and continuing to conduct the important business of ensuring equal employment opportunity during the transition years. Further research will have to be completed before guidelines that meet the requirements of these users can be fully developed. Moreover, just as the OMB's review and decision processes benefited from extensive public input, the OMB needs to discuss tabulation methods with data users both within and outside the federal government.[124]

Additional recommendations will be made after examining the actual 2000 census data. Whatever the outcome for tabulating multiple racial responses, it is clear that the American binary racial project is moving in the direction of a ternary racial project, which will socially and officially recognize three racial groups—white, black, and multiracial.[125]

Part IV

**Black No More
or More Than Black?**

CHAPTER EIGHT

The Illusion of Inclusion:
From White Domination
to White Hegemony

White Makes Right:
The Significance of Color Remains

African American concerns surrounding multiracial identity are not limited to the potential impact it may have on the collection of data needed to support civil rights claims and the tracking of racial discrimination. There are also fears that multiracial identity will undermine the solidarity of African-descent Americans, as "passing," blue-vein societies, Louisiana Creoles of color, and triracial isolate communities have done. Those multiracial identity projects were products of the prevailing Eurocentrism and were responsible for a divisive and pernicious "colorism" among African-descent Americans that has historically driven a wedge between the black masses and the privileged few, who have historically tended to be disproportionately made up of individuals who display more visible European ancestry.

Intraracial stratification among African-descent Americans based on phenotype, particularly skin color, has varied regionally and historically in intensity but is thought to have been significantly reduced by the emergence of the black consciousness movement in the late 1960s and early 1970s. Yet recent research has found a strong correlation between skin color and stratification outcomes for education, occupation, and income among African Americans. This research has found no appreciable difference between data compiled in 1950 and in 1980.[1] Findings revealed that educational attainment, as well as .personal and family income, increased significantly with lighter skin. In addition, the gap between lighter- and darker-skinned African-descent Americans in terms of educational attainment, occupation, and income was as significant as the schism between African Americans and European Americans.

While the 2,107 African Americans in the national survey had approximately the same minimum level of education—twelve years—darker-skinned African Americans earned only seventy cents for every dollar earned by lighter-skinned African Americans. Between all African Americans and all European Americans with approximately the same level of education—twelve years—lighter-skinned African Americans earned about fifty-eight cents for every dollar earned by European Americans. Most revealing, however, were the percentages for both groups of employment in high-status and high-paying professional and managerial occupations. Approximately 29 percent of all European Americans were employed in such jobs, whereas about 15 percent of African Americans were so employed, a nearly two-to-one ratio. This was roughly the same ratio for lighter-skinned African Americans (27 percent), as compared to 15 percent of darker-skinned African Americans. In fact, very light-skinned respondents were substantially more likely to be employed as professional and technical workers than those with a darker complexion, who were more likely to be manual laborers and service workers.[2]

A 1996 Los Angeles study of two thousand male subjects confirms the importance of skin color in determining differences not only in employment but also in unemployment (although a criminal record was a significant variable as well). Being African American and darker-skinned was found to reduce the odds of working by 52 percent. Only 8.6 percent of European Americans were unemployed, as compared to 23.1 percent of African Americans. Lighter-skinned African American men were more likely than their darker-skinned counterparts to be employed, although their rate of unemployment (20 percent) was still higher than that of European American males. Only 10 percent of lighter-skinned African American men with thirteen or more years of schooling were unemployed, as compared to 19.4 percent of their darker-skinned counterparts with similar education. Indeed, the unemployment rate for lighter-skinned African American males was only slightly higher than the 9.5 percent rate for European American males with comparable schooling. Furthermore, the darker-skinned African American males with a criminal record had a jobless rate of 54 percent, as compared to 41.7 percent for lighter-skinned African American males and 25 percent for European American males.[3]

None of this research strongly supports the argument that the correlation between skin color and stratification outcomes among African Americans is merely the result of accumulated benefits passed on to lighter-skinned individuals by virtue of their families' higher educational and socioeconomic status. To the contrary, skin color is a form of "racial capital" that continues to operate as an important stratifier in the larger society—if not among African Americans themselves—independent of family background.

Explanations differ as to how and why this is the case. Hughes and Hertel conclude that skin color continues to operate as a "diffuse status characteristic" in the larger society, although other phenotypical characteristics such as hair texture, eye color, and nose and lip shape are also important. Skin color, however, is the most all-encompassing, and thus most visible, phenotypical feature of the human body.[4] This means that European Americans—particularly males—who are generally responsible for making upper-level management and administrative decisions, are possibly more likely to select for employment individuals who more closely approximate European Americans in physical appearance, even if only unconsciously, believing they are seeing someone who is more competent or more attractive to fill such positions.[5] The normalization of skin color bias makes the phenomenon all the more pernicious because individuals will assume they are making impartial decisions, when in fact this may not be the case.

Keith and Herring, by contrast, hold that this selection process may not be so unconscious and unintentional. Their conclusions are supported by similar research in social psychology and organizational demography that consistently finds an expressed preference for co-workers who are homogeneous by race. These studies employ the similarity-attraction hypothesis, which holds that individuals infer similarity in attitudes based on demographic traits, which in turn serve as an important basis for attraction. Keith and Herring's conclusions are also supported by research on self-categorization theory, which posits that individuals rely on traits to define groups from which they draw positive self-identity.

Nayda Terkildsen, a political scientist then at State University of New York in Stony Brook, reached similar conclusions in research she conducted in 1991 and 1992. Terkildsen used a random sample of 348 European Americans from the jury pool of Jefferson County, Kentucky. She gave each participant a packet of information on one fictitious gubernatorial male candidate—a European American, a light-skinned African American, or a dark-skinned African American. Each candidate was supposedly running for election in a nearby state; all three were created from a photograph of a light-skinned African American that was then altered to make him appear a European American or a darker-skinned African American. Terkildsen deliberately made the candidates' biographies and positions on the issues identical, so that skin color would be the only variable. She asked a series of questions of the participants in order to determine their degree of racial prejudice and their tendency to be self-monitoring—that is, the degree to which they were aware of the negative social consequences of expressing their prejudice.

Overall, the European American candidate received more positive responses than either of the African Americans. This confirmed that race was a significant factor in European Americans' political choices. However, Terkildsen found that the prejudiced voters fell into two subgroups—those who were self-monitoring and those who were not. Those who were not self-monitoring displayed more negative attitudes toward the dark-skinned than toward the light-skinned African American. In other words, they had no qualms about expressing a negative bias toward dark skin. The self-monitoring, prejudiced European Americans were exactly the reverse. They rated the darker-skinned African American more highly than they did the lighter-skinned individual. According to Terkildsen, this suggests that the self-monitoring individuals censored their judgments about the dark-skinned candidate in order to compensate for their prejudice.[6]

Similarly, racial and other demographic differences in a superior-subordinate dyad are linked respectively to comfort and more favorable performance evaluations, or discomfort and less favorable performance evaluations of the other groups. Thus, a "taste for discrimination" appears to be correlated significantly with an individual's self-definition and attraction to others, and has measurable effects in actual work settings. In application to the question of color bias, this means that European Americans may express a preference for lighter-skinned over darker-skinned blacks, because the former are perceived to be closer to whites in terms of racial and assumed behavioral characteristics than the latter.[7]

Whether the preference is based on conscious aesthetic preferences and feelings of comfort that minimize social distance, or simply on unconscious decisions, one is immediately struck by the fact that a significant number of African American "firsts" in the post–civil rights era all have lighter skin. Consider, for example, Thurgood Marshall, the first African American Supreme Court Justice (1966); Edward W. Brooke, the first African American senator to be elected since Reconstruction; Patricia Harris, the first African American woman cabinet member (1976); David Dinkins, the first African American mayor of New York; L. Douglas Wilder, the first African American ever elected governor; General Colin Powell, the first African American chairman of the Joint Chiefs of Staff and Secretary of State (and possibly the only black candidate that could pull in large numbers of votes from the largely white neoconservative Right as a Republican presidential candidate), to mention only a few.[8]

Furthermore, while color selection processes affect the social location of African Americans generally speaking, they have unique implications in terms of gender. The preference for lighter skin is part of a larger trend that provides lighter-skinned African American males with more remunerative employment opportunities and greater access to wealth, power, privilege, and prestige. On the one hand, the negative effect of darker skin color on African American men, aside from a criminal record itself, may be attributed to the fact that dark skin is necessarily viewed as ugly, sinister, and threatening because light skin is the ideal point of reference for attractiveness. On the other hand, it may be the result of the negative stereotyping and fear associated with darker-skinned males, which pervades the larger society and functions independent of socioeconomic class. Darker skin, therefore, may be easily implicated in the subjective assessment of guilt that associates darker-skinned African American males with crime and social disruption (although one could argue that all African American males are potentially subject to this type of vilification).[9] This, in turn, may cause employers to exclude darker-skinned males from certain types of employment, unwittingly believing them to be violent, uncooperative, unstable, and ultimately criminals, as compared to African American males with lighter skin.[10] This places disproportionate limitations on the ability of darker-skinned African Americans males to gain vertical mobility through the "normal" channels available to lighter-skinned African American males. It may also explain in part why residents in the central cities, where unemployment and urban crime are highest, are disproportionately made up of darker-skinned black men.[11]

In politics, the media, the entertainment industry, and the world of high fashion—to name only a few obvious areas—there are advantages for lighter skin due to the Eurocentric aesthetic bias that pervades these cultural spheres.[12] African American anchors for the nationally syndicated news media, both male and female, are disproportionately made up of light-skinned individuals. However, the trend with African American men is more complicated and varies according to the industry, that is, film, modeling, news media. Lighter-skinned males have an advantage over darker-skinned males in terms of overall aesthetic appeal in the mainstream modeling industry and news media, but darker-skinned males may have an edge in the film industry. Yet white advertisers and fashion designers are said to express an almost routine and unabashed preference for white female models, and secondarily for lighter-skinned African-descent American models, if they select African American female models at all.[13] The most prestigious modeling work—magazine cover spreads—is almost the exclusive domain of white or very light-skinned models of African descent. And African American models in general get significantly fewer calls from modeling agencies than white models do.[14]

The Miss America Pageant is perhaps one of the best case studies of this aesthetic bias. African Americans first appeared in the pageant in 1922, when they were cast as "slaves" in His Oceanic Majesty's Court. Until 1950, however, rule 7 of the regulations governing the pageant reportedly stated that contestants had to be in good health and "members of the white race." By the 1970s, African Americans and other groups of color (although in small numbers) were accepted as contestants in the pageant, and by the early 1980s five African American women had been crowned Miss America (Vanessa Williams in 1984; Suzette Charles, who completed Williams's disrupted reign; Debbye Turner in 1990; Marjorie Judith Vincent in 1991; and Kimberly Aiken in 1994).[15]

However, the body types, attire, and hairstyles of these African American women have differed very little, if at all, from those of the European American contestants. Indeed, it is significant that Vanessa Williams, the first Miss America to break the racial barrier, was very light-skinned, with gray-green eyes and sandy hair. Whatever moments of popularity and acceptance "black looks" may have enjoyed in the pageant, the svelte white female represents the dominant somatic norm image in most circles, both public and private. No African American woman has won, or is likely to win, the title of Miss America wearing an Afro, braids, or dreadlocks (or displaying "strong" West African facial features).[16] The fact that a few African American women have been crowned Miss America is an important shift from previous policies of complete exclusion. Yet it far from proves that the commercial beauty culture has acknowledged African Americans as "beautiful" per se. Rather, it suggests that the commercial beauty culture has absorbed, validated, and commodified blackness in a form that is a suitable reproduction of whiteness.[17]

Notwithstanding the negative associations of darker skin, one could argue that socioeconomic mobility for dark-skinned individuals has increased and is on the rise. Larger numbers of African Americans have been able to gain admission to top academic institutions and to get professional, high-paying jobs, regardless of the shade of their skin. But even taking into account the strong positive contribution of socioeconomic status to stratification outcomes and the fact that individual experiences with gender, race, color, and class oppression may vary, there remains a positive correlation between lighter skin color and socioeconomic status. Stratification based on physical appearance—particularly skin color—is one of several different but related and interconnecting systems of stratification that feed on and reinforce each other.[18]

This "matrix of oppression" allots unearned social advantages and rewards to individuals in terms of sex/gender privilege, racial privilege, light-skin privilege, and class privilege. These factors provide advantages to men over women, whites over non-whites, lighter-skinned individuals over those with darker skin, and the bourgeoisie over the proletariat, as these relate to education, occupation, and income.[19] The confluence of these systems of privilege ensures that African Americans, irrespective of gender, race, color, and class, are subject to collective racial oppression. African American women are subject to a "double oppression" in relation to both European Americans and African American men. Darker-skinned African American men also are subject to a "double oppression" originating in the convergence of social inequities based on both race and color; darker-skinned African American women experience a "triple oppression" originating in the convergence of social inequities based on gender, race, and color. This relegates these women to a subordinate position relative to the larger white population and African American men regardless of their skin color.[20]

However, both gendered racism and gendered colorism in social stratification may be mediated by socioeconomic factors. That is, a more privileged socioeconomic status may mitigate the negative impact of a darker skin color, and a lower socioeconomic status may be offset by a lighter skin color for both men and women, particularly women.[21] Darker-skinned African American women from the less privileged socioeconomic classes may actually experience a "quadruple oppression" involving gender, race, color, and class. These women are subordinate not only to less socioeconomically privileged darker-skinned men—and to all African American men—but to the larger European American and African American populations as well.[22]

Therefore, even taking into account a significant reduction in the impact of colorism on the integrity and solidarity of "intragroup" relations among individuals of African descent, changes in the relationship between race and opportunity in "intergroup" dynamics over the last few decades, combined with the persistent Eurocentric bias in the larger society, have actually afforded these individuals a certain racial currency that grants them even greater access to wealth, power, privilege, and prestige. Opponents in the African American community contend that the legitimization of multiracial identity will merely exacerbate this trend. Multiracial individuals, they fear, particularly those who more closely approximate European Americans in terms of physical appearance, will be incorporated into an alliance with whites, while the black masses will be pushed further onto the periphery.[23]

Metaracism and the Color-blind Society: The Increasing Significance of Culture and Class

The official repudiation and discrediting of the ideology of white supremacy, and the dissolution of legalized inegalitarian pluralism, which prevented black equality with whites, have led to the increased integration and affluence of the African American bourgeoisie, particularly in business and politics. These developments also opened some doors to the black proletariat by expanding opportunities for educational achievement. Consequently, the number of individuals who have achieved upper- and middle-class status as large and small capitalists, entrepreneurs, professionals, and white-collar workers, now make up between 16 and 30 percent of African Americans—depending on whether the percentage is measured by ownership or distribution relation to the means of production, occupation, or household income of $35,000 or more.[24]

Many have argued that the growth of the African American bourgeoisie proves that the United States increasingly rewards education and technological expertise largely independent of race, and also that race has declined as a factor in discrimination and social stratification.[25] Racism, through this lens, is viewed less as a cause of poverty among African Americans. Although African Americans may have been subjected to terrible forms of racial discrimination in the past, the situation has been somewhat ameliorated, and now more and more of them have risen into the middle and upper classes.[26] The correlation between race and socioeconomic status is now considered by this camp to be insignificant. Disadvantage is a matter more of class than of race, and of cultural impediments like family instability, unemployment, juvenile delinquency, low aspirations, and so on. It is the historical "culture of poverty" among African Americans, not their skin color, that undermines their chances of upward socioeconomic mobility.[27]

A Decline in the Significance of Race?

This belief—that the United States has transcended racism—commonly referred to as "metaracism,"[28] has become the cornerstone of United States racial etiquette during the last two decades of the twentieth century. But in fact racism has simply gone underground, and racial inequality has become harder to eradicate as a result.[29] Discrimination has become more "refined," and more difficult to discern, to the extent that the actual barriers to achievement are often hidden in a complex web of informal rules and processes. Consequently, attention has been diverted from the fact that only a select few African-descent Americans have moved from the margin to the mainstream and gained increased access to socioeconomic resources, not to mention that many of those structural gains are very circumscribed and easily eroded. Furthermore, the black masses, which make up 70 to 84 percent of the African American population,[30] have been retained disproportionately in service and blue-collar jobs in the secondary labor force, or pushed onto the periphery of society, pariahs who are locked into the ranks of the underemployed and unemployed.[31]

This is not to suggest that the status of African Americans has not improved significantly in many ways. Certainly, their lives are vastly different from what they were at the end of the Great Depression. African Americans made important gains relative to European Americans during the 1940s and the 1960s. But whether they are significantly better off depends on what is being measured, and how. The current average occupational status of African Americans has improved no matter how it is measured. African Americans are included in the economic mainstream in ways that were unheard of half a century ago. Absolute gains in years of formal education are significant. And formal political involvement at both the local and national levels has increased dramatically.[32]

Despite these gains, the condition of African Americans has not improved unambiguously.[33] Although the income gap between African Americans and European Americans has been slowly closing, the gap in socioeconomic status remains enormous. Black adults are still two-and-one-half times as likely as whites to be unemployed. This gap exists at virtually every level of education. If one expands this analysis to include "underemployment"—that is, "falling completely outside the labor force, being unable to find full-time work, or working full-time at below poverty-level wages"—then the black-white ratio in major urban centers over the past two decades has risen from the customary two-to-one disparity, to almost five to one.[34] Conservative estimates are that young, well-educated African Americans with work experience and other characteristics comparable to those of European Americans still earn 11 percent less annually. Even with the national economic boom of the 1990s, there has been sharply rising inequality in wages paid to high- and low-skill workers and a generally sharp rise in the skills that employers demand of workers. Furthermore, adverse market trends, supposedly race-neutral in origin, have a far more deleterious effect on African Americans and worsen their relative position in the labor force.[35]

This contemporary state of black and white America is perhaps best captured by economist and journalist Julianne Malveaux in *Wall Street, Main Street, and the Side Street* (1999). She argues that indeed national economic growth and prosperity on Wall Street in the mid- to late 1990s provided increased opportunities for a few privileged African Americans. But closer examination reveals that, overall, these gains have disproportionately benefited the white male corporate elite, while a disproportionate number of African Americans are still tucked away on the side streets, struggling to survive.[36] In addition, studies have documented continued direct labor-market discrimination against African Americans at both low-skill entry-level and more highly skilled positions. A growing number of studies indicate that even highly skilled and accomplished black managers encounter "glass ceilings" in the corporate sphere. This has prompted some analysts to suggest that African Americans will never be fully admitted into the United States power elite.[37]

The black-white gap in occupation (including employment, unemployment, and underemployment) and earnings almost seems insignificant as compared to differences in wealth, which is in many ways a more reliable indicator than income of one's quality of life.[38] The median net worth (including assets other than earning, such as property, savings, investments, etc.) of the African American household is $4,604 as compared to the median net worth of the European American of $44,408, or ten times greater.[39] In addition, white households with incomes between $7,500 and $15,000 have "higher mean net worth and net financial assets than black households making $45,000 to $60,000."[40] In other words, even European Americans near the lower end of the white income distribution have more wealth than African Americans near the upper end of the black income distribution. Furthermore, the types of assets held by European American households are quite different from the types held by African American households. Almost three-fourths of African American households' assets (as compared to less than half of European American households' assets), are held in durable goods such as housing and vehicles. European American households hold more than three times as much of their wealth in interest-bearing bank accounts or stock shares than do African American households.[41]

African Americans, including the upper and middle classes, also occupy a uniquely disadvantaged position in terms of housing, which demographers Douglas Massey and Nancy Denton describe as "hypersegregation." Hypersegregated groups are "extremely racially isolated from whites on four of five standard measures of residential segregation."[42] Based on 1980 and 1990 census data for large metropolitan areas, African Americans and Latinos rank as hypersegregated from whites, in contrast to the conditions of Asian Americans (although Asian American and Latino groups vary individually in terms of these conditions). There was some modest decline in the level of racial residential segregation of African Americans between 1980 and 1990, but African Americans remain hypersegregated. More important, while both African Americans and Latinos rank high in terms of this dynamic, African Americans are the only group in which this trend does not decrease with increased socioeconomic status. In other words, African Americans remain hypersegregated irrespective of socioeconomic class.[43]

In the past, African Americans of all socioeconomic classes lived largely in the same racially segregated residential enclaves, particularly in cities. Although African Americans of varying class backgrounds on average continue to live in closer proximity to each other than do European Americans, due to persistent racial discrimination in housing, the African American bourgeoisie has gained in residential mobility over the last few decades. Consequently, it is no longer retained in those urban areas to the same extent as previously. Yet this sector of African Americans is still largely shut out of affluent European American residential areas, especially in the suburbs. If and when middle class African Americans succeed in breaking through these residential barriers in numbers that exceed the racial comfort level of European Americans (generally between 10 and 20 percent), whites begin moving out and the neighborhoods eventually become all black. Tired of this "white flight," as well as of the many obstacles to gaining entry to white residential communities, many affluent African Americans who want to live in areas with a "high quality of life" are increasingly settling in predominantly middle-class black communities outside the central cities. This pattern reinforces the growing trend toward "resegregation" that stabilizes identifiably African American enclaves, which are increasingly becoming the communities of choice for many affluent blacks.[44]

In addition, "housing audit studies indicate high levels of direct racial discrimination by realtors and landlords against African Americans" seeking quality housing.[45] There is mounting evidence that mortgage lenders discriminate against African Americans. Some of the more careful studies indicate that racial bias is a significant determinant even after controlling for financial resources and credit history. This in turn has an impact on neighborhood conditions, which may vary greatly in services, school quality, safety, and levels of exposure to a variety of undesirable social conditions. Indeed, this trend certainly exacerbates other disadvantages and cultural impediments in general.[46] A particularly troubling trend is the increasing overlap between suburban and urban locations, races, and distinct political jurisdictions. In extreme cases, a largely black central city (e.g., Detroit) is a separate municipal unit from the surrounding white suburban areas. This urban-suburban divide weakens the possibility of achieving egalitarian integration between blacks and whites in other aspects of social life.[47]

The United States is integrated only to the extent that European Americans and African Americans come into contact with each other more frequently in public places and, significantly less often, in the private sphere. If their lives intersect more than they used to, most European Americans and African Americans still tend to live in separate, mistrustful, unequal, and sometimes downright hostile worlds. Indeed, except perhaps for attendance at church services, housing is the single most inegalitarian pluralist aspect of life in the United States.[48] Moreover, racial patterns in housing and education have made real egalitarianism all but unattainable despite the fact that the United States has perpetuated the grand illusion that racial comity and integration are imminent. The media, television in particular, have produced a "virtual integration,"[49] which many whites accept as if it were real. Images of African Americans on television and in popular films give European Americans the illusion of contact with African Americans without the reality.

Despite the achievements of the civil rights and black consciousness movements of the 1960s, and despite the impressive socioeconomic gains made by a few African Americans since then, these problems of differential employment (and unemployment), wage differentials, disparities in wealth, and racial residential segregation place African Americans in a uniquely disadvantaged position in the United States social order vis-à-vis European Americans. Leonard Steinhorn and Barbara Diggs-Brown, authors of *By the Color of Our Skin: The Illusion of Integration and the Reality of Race,* point out that the achievement of egalitarian integration requires hard work, risk, social engineering, and sacrifice. It also requires a more honest assessment of the factors that continue to keep African Americans in a disadvantaged position, not to mention a more accurate rendering of the historical and cultural forces that put them there in the first place.[50]

Although the relationship between race and opportunity in the United States has changed, the status accorded race in this country remains essentially unchanged. For European Americans—regardless of gender, culture, and class—race locates wealth, power, privilege, and prestige; for African Americans—irrespective of gender, color, culture, or class—race identifies disadvantages and constraints, however informal, subtle, or elusive they may be.[51]

From Racial Apartheid to Racial Amnesia

Beginning with the Reagan-Bush administration in the 1980s, many whites and a few privileged blacks began to assert that civil rights legislation, and the more tolerant attitudes that followed from it, had removed the most egregious racial barriers to African American equality and advancement. Many of these individuals demanded a reduction in the welfare payments, food stamps, and public housing upon which many African Americans rely. They also called for an end to government entitlement programs like affirmative action and racial discrimination regulations in the schools and workplace. In fact, opponents of these compensatory policies have viewed them as actually detrimental to African Americans' quest for self-sufficiency.[52] Some have even gone so far as to argue that policies

like affirmative action are a form of "reverse discrimination" against better qualified European Americans.[53]

Another argument marshaled against these compensatory programs is that they
are contrary to the "color-blind" premises of the American creed, which attribute
success to individual merit and effort alone.[54] And if that is the case, then what purpose is served by collecting data on race? Perhaps racial categories should be abolished altogether, these critics have suggested.[55]

The worthy motives of liberals who support race-neutral policies that would benefit the poor—both African and European American—are not in question.[56] But
class inequality cannot explain away the racial prejudice, discrimination, and
inequality that persist against African Americans regardless of their class status. The
historical context and cycle of poverty in which many Americans of African descent
remain trapped is certainly part of the explanation for the contemporary situation,
but skin color itself also continues to racialize African Americans and to consign
them disproportionately to service and blue-collar jobs, where the minimum wage
is the maximum wage.[57]

Many contemporary analyses ignore these unique features of African American
subordination and operate on the false premise that racial prejudice and discrimination, rather than being built into the American social fabric, are aberrations that
do not represent the nation's core values. These contemporary analyses are merely
the most recent instances of a longstanding tradition of naive egalitarianism that
erroneously assumes that the rights of African Americans were protected by the
founding creed of this nation.[58] Racial beliefs were consciously imprinted into the
very colonial foundations of the social order and codified in the U.S. Constitution.[59]

Although African Americans—as well as liberal and radical European Americans—have used to their advantage the contradiction between the promise that "all
men are created equal" and the reality that this credo applied only to white men
(and only to white men of a certain class, at that), their efforts have been a protracted uphill battle. And the backlash against compensatory racial policies like
affirmative action originates in the fear of losing the advantages of whiteness.[60]

The neoconservative forces that emerged in the 1980s have exploited this fear
and used the principles of individualism and "fairness" embodied in the American
creed to dismantle the very apparatus that was supposedly put into place to bring
about the fulfillment of these principles. This has made it possible for neoconser-
vatives to gain support for their agenda by preying on European American blue-
collar and service workers who fear losing their tenuous economic security to
"unfair" preference given minorities by such policies as affirmative action. These
attitudes have helped roll back many of the gains achieved in the 1960s and 1970s
and have provided a platform for the extremist aims of less benign conservatives
on the far Right. Groups such as the Aryan Nation, the Silent Brotherhood, the
Order, not to mention various sects of the Ku Klux Klan, have appropriated the lan-

guage of egalitarianism for their own political advantage.[61] This rhetorical sleight of hand (or "semantic infiltration") has enabled them to exploit the current racial ecology to advance a pro-white, rather than an anti-black, agenda, by which they mean the preservation of white racial, cultural, social, and political integrity—supposedly free of white racism and supremacy.[62]

Color, Culture, Class, and the New Racial Divide

Although the United States has, for the most part, formally repudiated claims of racial and cultural "purity" and white supremacy, and despite the achievement of relative integration by African-descent Americans and the growth of the African American bourgeoisie in the past few decades, racial inequality persists in United States. Blacks are generally allowed to hold "privileged" positions only to the extent that they do not seriously challenge the racial status quo. They may also be confronted with cooptation and may have to repudiate or in some way compromise their racial identity in order to get ahead.[63]

The ruling European American elite find it tactically expedient to permit a few African Americans to gain entry into the middle class—so long as their social and economic power is not actually threatened. They are quite willing to support a redistribution of what small morsels remain of the loaf after they have taken the lion's share. But they prudently employ the politics of divide-and-rule to encourage excluded groups to fight over the crumbs rather than mobilize against their common oppressor.[64]

By the mid-1980s, the declining economy and increasing inflation helped bring about a shift in attitudes and the abandonment of the rhetoric of black self-determination that had characterized the previous decade. The rising threat of unemployment within the African American community led many to turn their attention to securing a piece of the dwindling economic pie. Idealistic goals of social transformation were relinquished for a more personal and individualistic pursuit of the American dream. Some African Americans were simply overwhelmed by the obstacles to racial progress, psychologically paralyzed by the apparent hopelessness of achieving the fundamental political and social change that would be necessary to bring about racial equality.[65]

The growth, prosperity, and increased integration of the African American elite do not, therefore, necessarily mean that racism has abated. To the contrary, the African American bourgeoisie, disproportionately composed of people who display visible European ancestry and share the sociocultural values of affluent whites because of their class status, has become a vital part of the system of oppression, serving as a double buffer between the dominant European Americans and the darker-skinned black masses. Their partial integration in the white power structure merely furthers the illusion of power sharing without actually requiring European Americans to give up structural control. Even worse, it fosters the belief that the excluded majority of African Americans could surmount their difficulties if only they had the character and drive to do so, as does the included "model minority" of blacks.

Since the late 1980s the concept of the "model minority" has been used largely in discussions of Asian American—particularly Japanese American—achievements in education and the economic sphere. The success of Asian Americans, seen as rooted in their values and family structure, has been singled out not only in the media but also by prominent European American writers as a perfect example of the U.S. meritocracy in action. Yet these stereotypes of Japanese Americans as paragons of hard work and docility carry a negative undercurrent.

Accordingly, the message being sent to other communities of color—specifically African Americans and Latinos—has been that they could achieve the same if they would only buckle down like the Japanese Americans, instead of attempting political change.[66] One could argue, however, that the model minority concept merely proves the point that the Anglo-American power structure will tolerate the advancement by African Americans and others subordinate groups who approximate the dominant ideal in their behavior, cultural norms, values, and physical appearance.

This dynamic downplays racial and ethnic inequality that effectively maintains hierarchy but creates the illusion of equality by means of token gestures of inclusion. Contemporary black-white relations have thus shifted away from the racial apartheid of the past, which was based principally on domination. Although this transition is uneven and truncated, formal exclusion and coercion in the manner of inegalitarian pluralism have been replaced with more informal dynamics. These sit in an uneasy relationship with another, less well-established trend toward inegalitarian integration (or assimilation). Rather than ruling principally through domination (although it is not absent), this trend—which the Italian political theorist and activist Antonio Gramsci describes as "hegemony"—allows dominant groups selectively to include its subjects and incorporate its opposition.[67]

Neither of these trends precludes the formation of cultures of racial resistance that seek to counter racial hierarchy. But neither do they indicate that the hierarchical relationship between blackness and whiteness has been dismantled. They indicate rather that the dichotomization of blackness and whiteness has been attenuated. The significance of the one-drop rule has decreased, that is, as the primary factor determining the social location of African-descent Americans, due to the increased currency of phenotype—particularly skin color—as a form of racial capital, working in combination with the increasing significance of culture and class.[68] W.E.B. Du Bois said that the color line was the problem of the twentieth century, but it may be more accurate to say that the problem was the continuing legacy of racial inequality premised on the *ancestry line* and buttressed by the one-drop rule. This shift from white domination to white hegemony may indicate that the *color line* may actually be the problem of the twenty-first century.

The Doxa and the "Paradoxa"

The balance between colorism in intraracial relations among blacks and the one-drop rule in black-white relations has shifted in the direction of a more generalized "interracial colorism." This reflects the backlash and resurgence of conservative forces that since the 1980s have been redefining political, social, and cultural agendas in the manner of assimilation (or inegalitarian integration), which have been undermining the integrity of the black community.[69] The new multiracial identity as a racial project is not, however, synonymous with this social structural pathology. Rather, this new identity is indicative of an egalitarian dynamic that seeks to resist both the dichotomization and hierarchical valuation of African American and European American cultural and racial differences. Given the insidious toxins in the larger racial ecology, opponents in the African American community contend, nevertheless, that increased interracial marriage, and the growth in the number of multiracial offspring and the legitimization of multiracial identity, will merely exacerbate the trend toward interracial colorism and assimilation.

Individuals who support this position have argued that increased intermarriage between European Americans and Americans of color—including African Americans—allows individuals from subordinate racial groups to achieve vertical mobility by intermarrying into the dominant European American community.[70] Yet this analysis suggests that an interracial union is inherently a one-directional and hierarchical relationship. This view ignores the fact that an interracial marriage is a two-way proposition and provides no convincing psychological motive for European Americans to enter into such unions in the first place (unless for reasons of self-hatred or social rebellion). Moreover, this analysis automatically projects the inequitable intergroup relations between whites and communities of color onto interpersonal relations. Consequently, it overlooks the fact that racial intermarriages may involve individuals who actually view each other as equals.[71]

Critics argue, however, that taken to their logical conclusion increased interracial marriage and greater numbers of multiracial offspring would rearticulate the South African or Brazilian models of multiracial identification, typified by racial apartheid and racial assimilation, respectively. All non-whites have historically been the targets of de facto discriminatory practices in Brazil and officially sanctioned practices in South Africa. Yet multiracial individuals in Brazil and South Africa have been able to avoid the full brunt of racism even though, historically, Brazil has variously extended the privileges of whiteness to "select" multiracial individuals, while South Africa has not. In the United States, these critics allege, this dynamic would integrate as whites those multiracial individuals who physically resemble European Americans. This would not result in a more inclusive transracial/transcultural integration wherein blacks and whites would become similar to each other (Figure 1a). It would lead instead to inegalitarian integration, that is, assimilation (Figure 1b),[72] which would ultimately increase commonalities between blacks and whites by eliminating African American racial and cultural distinctiveness.[73]

Generally speaking, African Americans have not, therefore, sought complete de facto integration in the private sphere, especially as this relates to intermarriage, despite having challenged over the past half-century both the legal and informal inegalitarian pluralism barring integration. Indeed, even within the African American bourgeoisie, which has the highest rate of racial intermarriage among blacks, the majority still marries within the black community. What is envisioned instead is a mosaic of mutually respectful and differentiated, that is, dissimilated (Figure 1c) African American and European American racial/cultural pluralities—egalitarian pluralism . Both whites and blacks would have equal access to all aspects of the public sphere, with the option of integrating in the private sphere—egalitarian integration (Figure 1a). In this case, the selective pattern would be voluntary, rather than mandated by whites, such that if and when blacks choose to integrate they do so as equals.[74]

If it is true, as many have argued, that denial of the right to identify with the fullness of one's racial background is a constant reminder to multiracial individuals that they do not fit in, or even that they do not exist, then any discussion on this topic must necessarily take into consideration its long-term consequences. We should be especially concerned about any half-hearted attack on the Eurocentric paradigm in the manner of interracial colorism that merely weakens rather than eradicates the dichotomization of blackness and whiteness, while leaving intact the racial hierarchy that maintains white privilege.

Yet any analysis that fails to compare the Brazilian and South African with the current situation in the United States will be inconclusive at best and inaccurate at worst. Historical and sociological differences make it difficult to translate the new multiracial identity in the United States into Brazilian or South African terms. And, indeed, the multiracial identity project in the United States does not rearticulate the Brazilian or South African racial projects.[75] Rather, it seeks to dismantle the United States binary racial project and rearticulate a ternary racial project typified by Brazil and South Africa, but without the hierarchical valuation attached to whiteness and blackness. Accordingly, the new multiracial identity may be viewed as a weapon in the war against the colonial past of the United States—and specifically against the one-drop rule.

That said, the United States is now dismantling the one-drop rule and, paradoxically, may be expanding the criteria for racial whiteness through the assimilation of select African-descent Americans who approximate the dominant psychosomatic norm image.[76] This would have the advantage not only of bolstering the numbers of individuals with "insider" status but also of maintaining the United States as an ostensibly "white" nation (Figure 1b). Indeed, this would be of strategic value considering that the currently defined "white" or European American population in the United States will lose its numerical majority status in this century.

It is still not generally accepted in the United States for individuals of African American descent to identify as white. Nevertheless, there are signs that this may be changing, as reflected in the public response to recent DNA evidence confirming the long-disputed contention that Thomas Jefferson—one of the founding fathers and third president of the United States—fathered several children with his mistress, Sally Hemings, who was of partial African descent. The DNA evidence indicates that Jefferson probably fathered at least one of Sally Hemings's sons. In addition, this son or some of his descendants apparently passed as European American. The contemporary descendants of this individual have been socialized as white and had no knowledge of their African American ancestry. At no time during the public discussion of these findings was there any suggestion that these ostensibly European American individuals were now to be seen as black, either legally or informally.[77]

It is possible that these individuals—and the many others who are likely to emerge as more European Americans explore their genealogy—may reconsider the appropriateness of their racial socialization and designation as white.[78] The point is that they did not conceal their African ancestry but allowed it to be reported by the national media, and that there was no interrogation about whether their racial status had changed as a result of the DNA evidence. It is difficult to say whether a white racial identity would be granted a person raised as black but phenotypically European American, or predominantly European American in appearance. There are indications, however, of a shift in this direction in a segment of the *Maury Povich Show* involving two women who identified as African American. Both guests had been socialized in the black community—as had several generations of their antecedents at least since 1840—but were phenotypically indistinguishable from European Americans. Many whites and some blacks in the audience chastised the two women for not embracing both their African American and European American backgrounds, particularly given their white appearance. Some, including some African Americans, even argued that the women were actually white regardless of their socialization and self-identification as African Americans.[79]

If the one-drop rule has historically been an unquestioned and almost sacred social concept or doxa, the shift in the direction of a more generalized interracial colorism indicates that European Americans may have become more willing to bend this rule. African Americans, by contrast, understandably yet paradoxically hold on to the one-drop rule ever more tenaciously—not because they accept its validity as a means of racial oppression but precisely because it has provided a rallying point, for generations, with which to organize in protest. By attempting to exclude and oppress African Americans, the one-drop rule has had the unintended consequence of forging group identity, one that is not easily relinquished.[80]

CHAPTER NINE

The New Millennium: Toward a New Master Racial Project

Keeping the "One-Drop" Rule: Black Essentialism and the Afrocentric Idea

Nowhere is the power of the one-drop rule for cultural and political mobilization more obvious than in currents of Afrocentrist thought that advance the notion of a primordial African "race" and nation. But the effectiveness of any organizing principle as the basis for essentialized collectives (viewed as if they were "natural," static, and eternal units), is inherently fraught with irreconcilable contradictions. Some of the discourses and practices of radical Afrocentrists are not merely pro-black but anti-white, if not actually "racist" in the strict sociological meaning of the concept. Prior to the late 1960s sociological definitions of racism relied heavily on notions of individual psychological biases and discriminatory attitudes. Since the 1960s racism has been viewed as more than simple antipathy and discrimination toward individuals based on individual racial prejudice. It is now defined as an overarching and more systematic implementation of discrimination based on the desire and power of dominant groups to maintain advantages for themselves at the expense of racialized "others." According to this view, racially subordinate groups— which by definition lack structural power—are not capable of "racism."[1]

This is not to suggest that we should dismiss Afrocentric concerns with identity politics, given the pervasiveness of white racism that has prevented the formation of a radical African diasporic subjectivity or plurality. The strengths of Afrocentric discourse are undeniable, notably the fostering of group pride, solidarity, and self-respect, and an interrogation of the ideology of inegalitarian integration (assimi-

lation) and the perpetuation of differences in the manner of inegalitarian pluralism (apartheid).[2] The contradictions and weaknesses of radical Afrocentrism are,
however, also readily apparent. Its exponents often criticize the validity of the concept of "race" on the one hand while reinscribing essentialist notions of black identity on the other.[3] How can they have it both ways?[4]

The "whitening out" of the African participation in the formation of the West is
one of many injustices that have been inflicted on individuals of African descent,
as well as on the whole of human civilization. It is imperative, therefore, to deconstruct the Eurocentric rendering of history.[5] There now seems to be fairly unanimous
agreement on the central African origins of the human species, and few scholars
contest the notion that ancient Egyptian civilization was a specialized variant of Nile
Valley culture—as well as of a broader continental African type—that contained a
largely blended population with strong Africoid geno-phenotypical, ancestral, and
cultural components. There is also general acceptance of the fact that Egyptian civilization significantly antedated and influenced Greek civilization and thus ultimately influenced the early formation of the West. Furthermore, Afrocentrists are
on solid ground in pointing out that even this more modest African presence in
Egyptian civilization, and thus influence on the fountainhead of Western European
civilization, has not traditionally been acknowledged by European historians.

The Demise of Eurocentrism or Eurocentrism in a New Guise?

At the same time, however, radical Afrocentrists' inclusive application of the term
"black" to anyone and anything of African ancestry—no matter how remote in
space or time—ignores the complex ancestral, genetic, and cultural diversity and
blending that has taken place since early humans migrated out of Africa eons ago.
At best it perpetuates a gross oversimplification of prehistory and contemporary history, and at worst a new distortion. Despite the legitimacy of the Afrocentric desire
to give voice to the shared global disillusionment and alienation embedded in the
African diasporic experience, the end result of some strains of Afrocentric revisionism—particularly its more radical variants—is very similar to the oppressive
mechanism of the one-drop rule. If Eurocentrism is to be deconstructed, then the
"either/or" paradigm that has served as its foundation must also be deconstructed.
If anything, the goal should be to move beyond Eurocentrism and radical Afrocentrism in order to embrace a "holocentric" (or postmodern) paradigm based on
"both/neither," which would come closer to the actual "truth."

The reluctance of many African-descent Americans to critique the essentialist
underpinnings of radical Afrocentrism is rooted in the legitimate fear that this
would cause individuals to lose sight of the experience of the African diaspora and
the unique sensibilities and culture that have arisen from that experience.[6] bell
hooks proposes that we can criticize essentialism while emphasizing the significance

of the authority of experience. She argues that there is a significant difference between the repudiation of the idea of an African-derived essence and the recognition that African-derived identity has been forged through the experience of exile and struggle.[7]

The new multiracial identity is part of this process, but it is problematical to many Afrocentrists. Some of their opposition is premised on the belief that a multiracial identity is antithetical and inimical to their goal of forging African Americans into a cohesive political force.[8] Thus they view a multiracial identity as merely one in a series of recent attacks on the integrity of the African American community inspired, however indirectly, by Eurocentric thinking.[9] But this criticism obscures the potential that a multiracial identification may hold for challenging from within and from without the imposition of what Victor Anderson calls a myopic and constricting "ontological blackness."[10]

One of the factors obscuring the compatibility between Afrocentrism and the new multiracial identity is that the term "Afrocentrism" has been used to convey different things, some of which obscure its deeper significance.[11] Although Afrocentrism is significantly related to African history and has emanated from Black Nationalist thought, it is more appropriately described as a paradigm that places African-descent individuals at the center of their analyses. Accordingly, they become subjects rather than simply objects of history. In addition, Afrocentrism is predicated on traditional African philosophical assumptions. Ontologically, Afrocentrism assumes that all elements of the universe are viewed as one and are seen as functionally interconnected. This rejection of clearly delineated boundaries extends to morality, temporality, and the very meaning of reality.[12] Afrocentrism underscores the value of interpersonal relationships. This person-to-person emphasis fosters a human-centered orientation that values interpersonal connections more highly than material objects. Afrocentrists reject Eurocentric dichotomous thinking that divides concepts into mutually exclusive polar opposites.[13] Afrocentricity thus provides a mode through which all individuals can liberate themselves from the restrictive dichotomization and hierarchical concepts of the modern Eurocentric model. It posits a cosmic vision that acknowledges an inheritance that all individuals share as descendants of the first diaspora, when humans migrated out of Africa to populate the globe.

More moderate variants of Afrocentrism *and* of the new multiracial identity both criticize the pathologies of Eurocentrism and also challenge rigid notions of universality and static identity within mass culture and consciousness. They thus provide the occasion for new and more inclusive constructions of self and community absent from more radical Afrocentric discourse. The more inclusive blackness that would emanate from this shift in consciousness would allow African-descent Americans to acknowledge the manner in which the collective African American experience has been altered not only by sex/gender, class, and a host of other categories of experience, but also would take into consideration the empirical conditions of individual lives.[14]

The new multiracial identity, rather than imploding African American identity, can potentially forge more inclusive constructions of blackness (and whiteness). This in turn would provide the basis for new and varied forms of bonding and integration that would accommodate the varieties of African-derived subjectivity without at the same time negating a larger African-derived plurality, or maintaining that plurality as a dichotomous space, which is a photographic negative and complete antithesis of whiteness.[15] Furthermore, this discourse would challenge Eurocentric notions of African-derived identity that represent blackness and whiteness in one-dimensional ways in order to reinforce and sustain white domination and black subordination. Part of the struggle for a radical African American collective subjectivity that furthers black liberation must necessarily be rooted in a process of decolonization that continually challenges and goes beyond the perpetuation of racial essentialism and the reinscription of notions of authentic identity. This process should include the search for ways of constructing self and community that oppose any reification of "the blackness that whiteness created" in the manner of the one-drop rule, by recognizing and embracing the multiple experiences of African-descent identity, which are the lived and empirical conditions that make diverse identities and cultural productions possible.[16] Accordingly, the new multiracial identity, with its nonhierarchical and nondichotomous configuration, is quintessentially Afrocentric in the deepest meaning of the word.[17]

Postcolonial Discourse: Decentering Europe and Deconstructing the West

Any critique of Eurocentrism is inherently predicated on a consciousness that Western European civilization—and its outposts in Asia, the Pacific, Africa, and the Americas—is no longer the "unquestioned and dominant centre of the world."[18] European nation-states reached positions of economic, military, political, and cultural domination through conquest and direct settlement and control of "Others" through both the distant control of resources and direct settlement.[19] The dismantling of these European overseas colonial empires has been one of the most historically significant developments of the twentieth century. It raised the hopes of newly independent countries for the emergence of a truly postcolonial era. Such optimism proved to be short-lived, however. It became apparent that the West had not in fact relinquished control, although it had largely given up colonialism as its primary mechanism of domination and exploitation.

The continuing Western influence is maintained through a flexible yet complex interweaving of economic, political, military, ideological, and cultural hegemonies that has been termed "neocolonialism."[20] "While both 'colonialism' and 'neo-colonialism' imply oppression and the possibility of resistance, 'postcolonialism' neither posits clear domination nor calls for clear opposition."[21] Consequently, it may subtly downplay contemporary forms of hegemony. In fact, by implying that colonialism is over, the term "postcolonial" obscures the traces of colonialism that still exist. It thus lacks a political analysis of contemporary power relations.[22]

Hybridity, Hierarchy, and Hegemony

These ambiguities and contradictions notwithstanding, the term "postcolonial" may be applied to a broader process that involves the dismantling of Eurocentrism.[23] For example, the concept of "hybridity" in postcolonial discourse calls attention to the complex and multilayered identities generated by geographical displacements and interrogates Eurocentric notions of purity, racial and otherwise. Although racial and cultural hybridity have existed from time immemorial, European colonial expansion beginning in the sixteenth century accelerated and actively shaped a new world of practices and ideologies of racial and cultural blending. This is particularly the case in the Americas, which have been the site of unprecedented combinations of indigenous peoples, Africans, and Europeans, and later of immigratory diasporas from all over the world.[24]

On one level, the celebration of hybridity counters the colonialist obsession with racial "purity," which viewed different racial groups as different species created at different times that were therefore forbidden to "interbreed." The hostility to miscegenation—particularly in Anglo-North America—was encapsulated in such pejorative terms as "mongrelization." Yet while rejecting the colonialist obsession with purity, postcolonial hybridity also counterposes itself against the rigid essentialism that underpins Third World discourse, including radical Afrocentrism and much Black Nationalist thought. In addition, the concepts of racial and cultural hybridity in postcolonial theory are admirably honed to deal with the complexities and contradictions "generated by the global circulation of peoples and cultural goods in a mediated and interconnected world."[25] The hybrid globalized human subject is confronted with the challenge of moving among the diverse modalities of sharply contrasting cultural and ideological worlds.

Consequently, hybrid identities are not reducible to a fixed formula; rather, they form a changing repertory of cultural modalities.[26] However, the impetus behind and consequences of the celebration of hybridity is itself "mixed."[27] The deconstruction of dichotomous notions of purity should not obscure the potentially problematic agency of postcolonial racial and cultural hybridity. A celebration of racial and cultural hybridity per se risks downplaying contemporary forms of neocolonialism that effectively maintain racial hierarchy but create the illusion of equality by means of token gestures of inclusion.

From Center to Periphery

Despite these caveats, postcolonial notions of racial and cultural hybridity are part of a broader process instrumental to demystifying or deconstructing Europe and acknowledging the specificity of its development by reading its history through multiple racial and cultural lenses. A closer analysis of the celebrated markers in the historical formation of Europe—Greece, Rome, Christianity, the Renaissance, the Enlightenment—indicates that each is a moment of hybridity and integration: Greece, strongly influenced by, if not an actual colony or outpost of Egyptian, Phoenician, and Asian civilization; Rome, "strongly indebted" to Greece, Egypt, and Carthage; Christianity, originally a religion of Asian origin, whose link with Byzantium, the Nestorians, and Gnostics at times "loomed larger" than it relationship with European, i.e., Latin, Christendom; the Renaissance, "a recovery of Hellenic civilization passed on through Arabic civilization and deeply engaged with non-European cultures"; the Enlightenment, "another period wide open to non-European influences, from China to Egypt."[28]

This linking of the Afro-Asian world with the formation of Western Europe in postcolonial and Afrocentric discourse should come as no surprise given that the scientific and technological achievements of Western Europe have been the benchmark by which "Other" civilizations have been ranked as inferior and superior in terms of how much they approximate or diverge from the modern Western European norm. The participation of Africans and other non-Europeans in the evolution of Western civilization—and the process of civilization generally—has been dismissed, if not excluded, by virtue of their supposed divergence from the European norm. Yet the actual "borders" between the West and the larger non-Western world have been more blurred and porous "frontiers" than Eurocentric rhetoric and imagery have acknowledged.[29] The West was historically both multiracial/multicultural and transracial/transcultural long before it became so demographically in the twentieth century with the arrival of Third World immigrants from previous colonial possessions. Western European domination of others comprises merely one side, albeit an important one, of the historical narrative.

Hybridization originating in the absorption and adaptation of a multiplicity of sources in the form of egalitarian cultural and, not infrequently, racial integration, is the other side of the coin. To a considerable extent what is referred to as European civilization "is actually a universal human heritage that for historical, political, and geographical reasons" has been bequeathed to the modern world "in the guise of a European or Western synthesis."[30] It is significant that the synthesis and stamp are uniquely European. Yet the fact that the sources are plural and intercontinental is equally meaningful.[31] This is particularly so if we consider that the racial and cultural narcissism that buttressed Eurocentrism and European colonialism and imperialism have deliberately obscured these connections. This was done to maintain the purity and thus "superiority" of European identity while furthering the image of "Others" as people without history.[32]

In response to this historical amnesia, and its interrogation of Eurocentrism's totalizing and tyrannizing claims, postcolonial thought is dedicated to redressing outcasts of all sorts, both ideas and individuals. It thus celebrates "Otherness" in almost every guise.[33] Yet this cultural relativism may also mask a romanticization of the "Other" and an appropriation of the experience of "Otherness" to enhance the discourse on difference, or to be "radically chic." Accordingly, this may do non-Europeans an injustice by not contextualizing the historical relationship between the politics of difference in the manner of egalitarian pluralism and the politics of racism in the manner of inegalitarian pluralism.[34]

Interrogating the Concept of Race

As part of the general assault on Eurocentrism, postcolonial discourse not only challenges notions of racial purity but also interrogates the notion that race is an objective reality absolutely fixed in biological datum. Given that modern science has been unable to produce empirical data that would confirm the existence of clearly delineated biophysical racial boundaries, many "deconstructive" postcolonial thinkers recommend that the concept be dispensed with altogether. They tend to present race as a problem, a legacy of the past, and a misconception that should be transcended. Many argue that any kind of racial identification—multiracial or otherwise—is fraught with irreconcilable contradictions. Any notion of transcending race by reifying it through a multiracial identification is thus hopelessly naive if not downright regressive.[35] Note, however, that this opposition to a multiracial identity does not simply originate in a belief in the falseness of the concept of race. It often originates in the misinterpretation of the discourse on multiracial identity as grounded in biological rather than ancestral notions of race. Biological notions of race and those based on ancestry may overlap, but they are not synonymous. The former is based on one's genetic inheritance irrespective of ancestral background. The latter is grounded in the backgrounds in one's lineage or genealogy, irrespective of genetic concerns, and is the basis of the new multiracial identity. Exposure to these backgrounds enhances and unequivocally helps concretize this feeling of kinship. Simple awareness of those backgrounds, however, can catalyze this sentiment, and lack of contact does not preclude its presence.

Critics also dismiss claims that the new multiracial identity is "new" at all, because everyone is in fact "multiracial." While it is true that a multiracial lineage or background is normative among humans, most individuals display single-racial (or monoracial) identities despite the many backgrounds that may make up their genealogy. The new multiracial identity belongs to individuals who feel a sense of kinship with more than one racial community. Those who question the legitimacy of a multiracial identity on the grounds laid out above would probably challenge multiethnic identity on similar grounds. Such a deconstructivist perspective reflects the underlying belief that all categories and identities—racial and otherwise—are sociocultural constructs, mere "fictions" with no basis in "reality."

Other postcolonial thinkers challenge the notion that race is something we can or should somehow move beyond. Many of these "constructive" postcolonial thinkers do agree that the concept of race invokes biologically based human characteristics in the form of "racial traits" but do not view racial categories and boundaries as being absolutely fixed in biological fact. From their perspective the racialization process divides human bodies into presumed exclusive units, and imposes upon them attributes and features that conform to ideological and social values. Racial categories in turn signify and symbolize social conflicts and interests, and represent principles by which society allocates rewards and status. In addition, they argue that the selection of these particular human features for purposes of racial signification has changed over time and is always and necessarily a historical process: Racial categories and identities are understood as unstable and decentered complexes of sociocultural meanings that are constantly being created, inhabited, contested, transformed, and destroyed by political struggle. This constructive postcolonial discourse views racial formation as a major mode of social differentiation grounded in historical consciousness and in the very structure of social institutions. Consequently, a multiracial identity may be thought of not only as an element of social structure but also as a dimension of human cultural representation and signification—rather than an illusion.[36]

In sum, postcolonial thinkers signal the formation of a new master racial project. Deconstructive postcolonial discourse seeks to "transcend race" altogether in pursuit of a universal humanism; constructive postcolonial discourse posits "racial transcendence" by acknowledging a more inclusive identity based on a multiplicity of ancestral backgrounds. The new multiracial identity is part of this broader postcolonial social transformation and consciousness, although it does not dismiss the concept of race. It does, however, interrogate essentialist and reductionist notions of race and decenters racial categories by pointing out the ambiguity and multiplicity of identities that exist within each of us. This makes it possible to acknowledge the way in which those categories are altered by lived experience. The new multiracial identity, along with Afrocentrism, variously interrogates colonial discourse and seeks to bring about the demise of the dominant Eurocentric paradigm.

From "Either/Or" to "Both/Neither": The Postmodern Turn

Any critique of Eurocentrism necessarily challenges the materialist rationalist tradition of the Renaissance and Enlightenment, as well as the notions of

Greco-Roman heritage upon which Europeans have historically predicated their superiority. Eurocentrism, which is based on an almost sacred "Law of the Excluded Middle," has supported an "either/or" paradigm of dichotomous hierarchical ranking of differences, studying things in isolation and acknowledging no shades of gray.[37] Indeed, today's more iconoclastic attitudes toward racial identity—particularly the new multiracial identity—seem themselves to reflect this more fundamental shift in consciousness, frequently referred to as postmodernism, which seeks to incorporate concepts of "partly," "mostly," or "both/neither."[38]

Much like postcolonial thinkers, postmodernists frequently seek to deconstruct dichotomous and hierarchical thinking by exhibiting "marginal" or "hybrid" phenomena that are "undecipherable with reference" to the dichotomy and hierarchy. This demonstrates the difficulties of defining one category of experience without including elements of the other. Rather than reverse the dichotomy, however, this strategy questions the hierarchical "grounds on which the dichotomy is erected."[39] Accordingly, phenomena are seen as relative and complementary rather than as hierarchical and antithetical categories of experiences. In addition, postmodern thinkers interrogate the conception of a linear connection of subjects to an objective world.[40] This has led them to dismiss the notion that the truth can be found in any absolutely impartial sense. They have been instrumental in pointing out that all concepts and categories, racial and otherwise, are largely sociocultural constructs grounded in history, and not fixed and unalterable essences.[41]

Postmodernism emerged in the early 1970s. Its seminal ideas came from the French philosophers Lyotard, Foucault, Baudrillard, Deleuze, Guattari, and Derrida,[42] although the groundwork was laid by their predecessors in Germany, Kant and Hegel, and particularly by Nietszche and Heidegger, who were reacting against the materialist rationalist thought of the Enlightenment.[43] Postmodernist thought, in its early phase, acknowledged and reflected the anxiety surrounding the decline both of religious faith and of confidence in the power of human reason, including embodiments in science and technology and the whole ideology of "progress."[44]

Although postmodernism, as it arose in the late twentieth century, was the culmination of historical trends that began much earlier (as is always and invariably the case with any historical transformation), it signals the collapse of a social order that has more or less prevailed for at least five hundred years. Previous challenges to the modern paradigm operated, for the most part, within its parameters. Now, for many individuals, the sensate culture that had dominated the modern Western world—and the capitalist system associated with it—has been eclipsed and transcended by something new.[45] In an ironic about-face, the postmodern era initiated a "deliberate regression" to recapture all that had been cast aside and marginalized in the progressive ascent into modernity.[46] The postmodern goal has been to avert the most insidious of all confrontations: humanity against humanity, life against itself.[47]

Postmodernism's proponents are engaged in a critique of the pathologies of modernity but not in an attempt to regress to some primordial or premodern integrative state.[48] Many counter-Enlightenment theorists (particularly the Romantics and their late-nineteenth- and twentieth-century Neo-Romantic offshoots), did advocate such a return, condemning modernity as a brutal disruption of a prior harmony, but their vision was often clouded by the very inegalitarian pluralism spawned by modernity.[49] Postmodernism, by contrast, rejects not only modernity's dichotomization but also its hierarchical ranking of differences in the manner of inegalitarian pluralism. In addition, it jettisons modernity's totalizing universalism, which was actually inegalitarian integration (or assimilation in disguise). Postmodernism seeks instead to replace these with a nondichotomous and nonhierarchical dynamic in which egalitarian pluralism becomes a prelude and counterpart to a new, higher egalitarian integration.[50] Deconstructivist, radical, or extreme postmodernists more frequently espouse the pluralistic trend; the integrative trend is more common among more constructivist, moderate, and affirmative postmodernists. Nevertheless, both trends are part of a more generalized assault on the polarization of things into either black or white.

According to philosopher and integral psychologist Ken Wilber, this approach is premised on the notion of holarchy, or nested, normative hierarchy.[51] Differential function, responsibility, and rank are not inherently and necessarily equivalent to differential value and worth. "Lower" and "higher" take on new meanings and become equivalent to different levels of structural organization between an order of increasing and decreasing complexity. In a holarchy of expanding complexity, organization, and depth, atoms are parts of molecules, which are parts of cells, which are parts of individual organisms, which are parts of families, which are parts of cultures, which are part of the total biosphere. "The whole of one level becomes a part of the whole of the next."[52]

Subject and Object

The violent seismic shifts of this "postmodern turn" during the nineteenth and twentieth centuries is comparable in magnitude to the transition from the ideational-dominated worldview of the medieval era to the sensate-dominated worldview of the Renaissance and Reformation.[53] Medieval Europeans "saw themselves embedded in both physical [sensate] and spiritual [ideational] space."[54] Their cosmology included a place not only for the body but also for the soul. Yet with the rise of modern science in the sixteenth and seventeenth centuries, space came to be conceived in purely physical terms, with the universe now seen as a vast machine governed by mathematical laws. Over the next four hundred years physicists developed an ever more sophisticated understanding of physical space, first with the Newtonian conception of space, then relativistic space, and now with contemporary physicists' notion of hyperspace, which proposes that ultimately there is nothing but empty space curled into patterns.

The scientific understanding of space has been extraordinarily successful, but this achievement has come at a price. By removing spiritual space from conceptions of reality, modern humans made any discussion of spiritual phenomena seem unreal, even illegitimate.[55] Paradoxically, the rosy promises of empirical science and technology, and their post-Enlightenment afterglow in the mid- and late nineteenth century (especially in optics and physics), helped destroy the previous materialist rationalism. Matter was reduced to non-sensory dynamic energy patterns that were supposedly organized by an intelligible force through the activity of the mind as intelligence in action. If modern physics disclosed a world at odds with human sensory-intellect, postmodernist physics has uncovered "a radical disjunction between the way things behave and every possible way in which we might try to visualize them."[56]

Previously, the observer and mind were thought to be detached from the objective world of observed material phenomena. The subject doing the reflecting was not really a part of the world that was being mirrored. The subjective and intersubjective domains were reduced to empirical studies and thus humans themselves became "objects of information, never subjects in communication."[57] This led to the belief in one true, preordained reality that was copied onto each individual's subjective consciousness—the representation paradigm—through the process of mimesis, and was objectively represented in scientific models. "If that map is accurate, if it correctly represents or corresponds to the empirical world of objects, then that is 'truth,'" which in turn would provide a means of rationally ordering of the world.[58] All major materialist rationalist theorists, from the Renaissance to the Enlightenment, from Bacon and Descartes to Hobbes, Locke, and Fichte, generally agreed on this point, despite the different philosophical schools. Their legacy was nineteenth-century positivism and twentieth-century scientific rationalism, along with a belief in linear progress, absolute truth, and rational planning of an ideal social order.[59]

If, however, modernity has sought to hold a mirror to the external world, it had not realized that to be human by definition precludes the kind of pure, uninterpreted, value-free data that could give rise to an objective and impartial overview of things—the view of things as they are in themselves, apart from our perspective.[60] By the nineteenth century the limitations of the "mirror view of nature" became clearer. All the prominent counter-Enlightenment theorists, beginning with Kant and running through Hegel, Schopenhouer, Nietzsche, Dilthey, Heidegger, Foucault, and Derrida, have mounted a powerful argument against the notion that there is a single, perceivable empirical or objective world, and that knowledge consists solely of reflecting or mapping this one true world.[61] They argued that the latter was to some extent a passing aspect of the total possibility of perceivable matter as constructed by the mind's focus in space and time. Humans thus stood on the shifting sands of their own socially constructed worldviews and language was deeply involved in this process. The most that could be hoped for was a relative objectivity within the limitations of one's own pluralistic, that is, subjective, vantage point.[62]

Universal and Particular

By virtue of its sensibility, postmodernism—particularly deconstructivist postmodernism—fully recognizes the benefits of pluralism but is relatively less inclined to acknowledge the merits of bonding, that is, integration.[63] Thus, in conjunction with "the essential janiformity" and Faustian nature of centuries' ends, and the extremity of the twentieth century's end as this relates to sensate sociocultural domination, it follows that humans should now most acutely experience themselves, like the times, as multiple. Hegel commented on this phenomenon during the 1790s in his observations on estrangement, and Durkheim made similar comments again during the 1890s in his observations on anomie or normlessness.[64] In the 1990s the appearance of multiple or plural identities, be they racial or otherwise, are not merely symptomatic of the tendency of fin-de-siècle relations between humans to become "deranged" and "disjointed."[65] Rather, the explosion of plural identities at the end of the twentieth century is also indicative of the larger trend that seeks to dismantle modernity's dichotomization and hierarchical valuation of differences, while simultaneously attempting to transcend this loss of continuity by reconnecting and reintegrating humans with the life history of the universal and collective self.

Premodern humans had an inherent experience of universality—at least within their own local communities—but had no concept of it because they lived in communities that were comparatively homogeneous and isolated from each other. In this worldview differences were obliterated by a stronger sentiment: the deep conviction of solidarity with life that bridged over "the multiplicity and variety in its plural forms." Solidarity with life "is an expression of kinship" rather than "a conviction of unity."[66] Although they punished emulation and the transgression of clan, tribal, or communal boundaries, and thus displayed a mistrust of strangers, these communities had to worry less about how to deal with individual pluralism.[67] For modern humans confrontations between different pluralities of cultures have been the norm rather than the exception.[68] This has led to an awareness that people actually see the world differently and thus live in plural realities. If there is no *reality* but only *realities*, then who is to say which is better than another? Late-twentieth pragmatist philosophers, themselves the heirs of a long and complex genealogy, have argued that it is both desirable and possible to evaluate—through open, democratic debate—the relative worth and truth-value of competing versions of reality. Postmodernists, by contrast, profess that these multiple realities are on an equal footing and deserve equal respect in the manner of egalitarian pluralism. In the postmodern era the very concept of universality, or global systems of thought, as well as the search for any foundation upon which to secure a universal and objective reality, has been called into question.[69] On the one hand the upsurge of economic, technological, and ecological forces that "mesmerize the world with fast music, fast computers, and fast food," are binding humanity into a more universalist (or global) network. Yet these same forces also bring with them the real dangers of a bland uniformity and homogeneity. As a result they have spawned reactionary forces that resist the centripetal forces toward global convergence in the name of factitious particularism (racial, ethnic, cultural, religious, etc.), which fly in the face of social and civic cooperation.[70]

The survival of an increasingly global civilization that is at the same time clearly marked by pluralities within pluralities will depend on how successfully humans develop new models of coexistence and cooperation. There is a need to shift from dominator to partnership modes of interaction and simultaneously achieve a renewed and more porous social contract, and a more elastic ethos that nurtures a sense of community without demanding uniformity.[71] It is clear that the continuing quest for domination, be it racial or otherwise, has reached a point where such behavior is not only homicidal but also suicidal.[72] This has been shown with particular urgency by two significant political events in the second half of the twentieth century: the collapse of Western European colonial domination and the fall of communism. It is all the more urgent because other threats to contemporary humanity (e.g., destruction of the natural environment) are growing more serious everyday.[73]

Postmodernity and the "New Age"

Postmodern thinking has also made itself felt in a variety of disparate yet ultimately related phenomena, which in vernacular parlance are frequently grouped under the heading of "New Age." Physicists, philosophers, logicians, linguists, social scientists, administrators, foreign policy analysts, and engineers have all employed similar language and concepts.[74] In the arts the hierarchical distinction between "high" and "popular" art has collapsed and led to an eclectic blending of aesthetic codes.[75] Popular culture itself has become a collage of different styles.[76] In literature and the arts the audience is not simply a passive receptacle of the artist's intention but an active participant in the creative process.[77] In addition, the contrast between illusion and reality breaks down and is replaced by a world of self-referential signs.[78] Technology, particularly the electronic media, gives increased exposure to a multiplicity of perspectives, undermining belief in one objective reality.[79]

As environmentalists in the 1970s increasingly discovered the "web" of nature, "the interconnectedness of species and the wholeness of ecosystems," ecological and systems thinking came to share the same thrust toward the synthesis of information.[80] It is no surprise, therefore, that there is an intimate connection between the environmental movement and the emergence of the women's movement, given the longstanding link that humans have made between women and nature. The revolt against fragmentary thinking fostered by academic apartheid has also received a boost within the university. Calls for interdisciplinary thinking have breached departmental barriers and disciplines that have blocked the cross-fertilization of ideas and knowledge.[81] The emergence of the interdisciplinary approaches of ethnic, feminist, cultural, and postcolonial studies are just a few examples of this trend, although they have not been without territorial battles of their own.[82] In addition, the lines between science, literature and ideology, literature and literary criticism, philosophy and cultural criticism, between "high" cultural criticism and popular criticism, have also blurred considerably.[83]

These changes in secular intellectual culture have been mirrored, and at times served as a catalyst for, changes in religious culture as well. It is no exaggeration to say that the "religion" of modernity has been science. But religious cultures, traditional or otherwise, although overshadowed by science since the seventeenth century, did not atrophy—far from it. The attraction to Eastern religions, for example, has been a strong attraction to those seeking postmodern religious expression. These traditions recognize the individuality of things but at the same time acknowledge that all differences and contrasts are relative within an all-embracing unity. In the West, this trend has historically been limited to a tiny fringe among the European and European American bourgeoisie. But beginning in the 1960s and 1970s, thousands of individuals in the West began in earnest their conversion to the spiritual traditions of the East, as the contradictions in the schizo-cultural logic of late capitalism and the postindustrial economy became increasingly apparent.[84]

This trend has led to a "privatization" of religious expression and experience in which individuals feel free to cross, erase, and redraw all kinds of religious boundaries that were previously viewed as sacrosanct. The resulting plethora of hybrid religious perspectives borrow from multiple religious meta-narratives—as well as from alternative metaphysical sources (e.g., astrology, the I Ching, etc.), and have created new alternatives to the mainstream Western religions of Judaism, Christianity, and Islam. The Baha'i' faith, for example, originated in Iran and is anchored in a transcultural validation and incorporation of various metaphysical systems. The faith posses its own unique tenets, yet its adherents see no incompatibility between simultaneously espousing Judeo-Christian, Hindu, Moslem, Buddhist, or any other beliefs. The universal tenets underlying all systems of religious thought and ritual are viewed by the Baha'i' as compatible. There is one spiritual journey, but many paths.[85]

In medicine, the need to integrate the spiritual, intellectual, emotional, and physical dimensions of the individual has served as the underlying premise of the "holistic" health movement. Although the movement has often blended quackery with serious medical innovation, it gained enormous strength in the late 1970s. Since then interest in alternative healing methods has increased dramatically. In the field of mental health, the notion of a static unified self has fallen into disrepute among psychologists who view the individual as a member of many communities and networks, a participant in many discourses. Mental health professionals have thus arrived at new techniques, such as radicalized Jungian analysis with an eco-spiritual bent, the anti-psychiatry of R. D. Laing, gestalt and Reichian therapy, depth psychology, and so on.[86] Feminist therapy has been especially helpful in providing men and women with more androgynous images of masculinity and femininity, as well as an understanding of the relationship between these socially constructed models. New models of sexuality have challenged notions of clearly delineated heterosexual and homosexual orientations and have replaced them with more continuous and ambisensuous configurations of sex.[87]

These techniques, along with their more popular variants (Life Spring, EST, The Forum, Landmark, etc.), seek to treat the "whole person" and to increase human potential. This process involves helping individuals negotiate a dynamic and kaleidoscopic personal identity. Individuals learn to accommodate ambiguity and navigate the paradoxical and constantly changing unity amid their diverse conscious and unconscious personas in both their personal and collective dimensions. The goal is to help individuals learn to celebrate their multiple selves in lived experience through a process of integrating their sensory awareness, perceptions, and relationship with the outside world.[88] These approaches embrace the notion of an underlying "thematic self" that provides a sense of connection to developmental variations that emerge historically. The subject is conceptually grounded in something akin to Bordieu's "habitus," which is "the cumulative, durable totality of cultural and personal experiences" that humans carry with themselves.[89] This subject or self has its own characteristics, its own structures, its own development and currents of its own development, its own history, and its own evolution. Although the subject is empirical, habitus cannot be structured or aggregated. It is the strategic interplay and balancing of multiple inputs that is unique to each individual and defies scientific generalization.[90]

With the rise of global capitalism, after the collapse of socialist and communist models of economic planning (which were more failures of implementation than flaws in these paradigms themselves), the tentacles of unbridled corporate greed have reached multinational proportions. Yet the excesses of individualism have led to anarchy, while the excesses of collectivism have resulted in totalitarianism. A merging of the assets of both the capitalist and socialist-communist modes of economic production and distribution would seem to meet the demands for a viable society. This might lead to a more ethical or compassionate capitalist dynamic, one that would still allow a certain amount of free enterprise, but not at the expense of the health, welfare, and security of the masses.[91]

Japan may have gone further in this direction than either the United States or any of the socialist or socialist-democratic countries of the West.[92] Nevertheless, in the West, the business world, which is the sensate mode's economic domain par excellence, has not gone untouched by the new paradigm. Intuitive business leadership is challenging the logocentric management styles of modernity. Among other things, new directives take into account the executive's appreciation of the inner resources that are available but frequently not used, and the changes in institutions and society that are accompanying the "awakening" of employees and the public at large. The new corporate models emphasize innovation and a work environment that foster the development of creativity. Corporations and other organizations are increasingly viewed not as hierarchical structures fitting a traditional organization charter, but rather as adaptable organisms that exist in interaction with a larger whole. Organizational purpose is not chosen arbitrarily by select members of the organization but is in large part "given" by the system.[93]

This emphasis on holocentric thinking has also included a shadow-side of activities ranging from the psychedelic phenomenon of the 1960s to the cult phenomenon since the 1970s and 1980s. It should not be confused, however, with these more aberrant flights from reason. Furthermore, "holocentrism" does not mean that humans must take leave of their senses and completely repudiate the materialist rationalism bequeathed by modernity. Along with sensate culture's negative psychological and sociocultural consequences have come many physical comforts and technological benefits. The postmodern challenge is to acknowledge and embrace— that is, to integrate—modernity's successes and the rational-industrialization inherent in the sensate mode, yet to transcend its excesses. In the new holocentric vision, rationality, objectivity, and technology would be viewed as components of a more inclusive "transmodern" conversation with ideational culture that would incorporate—and limit—rationality, objectivity, and industry.[94] This process must necessarily be part of a new global value sphere premised on integrative pluralism (or pluralistic integration) that encourages respect for differences in the manner of egalitarian pluralism but need not imply that all differences are viewed as equally valuable or useful.[95] The search for community would be based on general agreement or consensus.[96] This transformation will defuse some problems but will also create its own challenges, challenges that we would do well not to underestimate but to approach with due sobriety and openness.[97]

EPILOGUE

Beyond Black or White: A New United States Racial Project

A New United States Racial "Commonsense": Beyond the One-Drop Rule

The new multiracial identity reflects a fundamental postmodern shift in consciousness premised on the "Law of the Included Middle," which seeks to incorporate concepts of "partly," "mostly," or "both/neither," and acknowledges shades of gray. Although embodied in individuals, the new multiracial identity is perhaps best characterized as a cluster of new possibilities in the nation's collective racial consciousness that seeks to transform traditional racial categories and boundaries by expanding definitions of blackness and whiteness.[1] While the new multiracial identity is a flagship for this alternative consciousness, it should not be viewed as the solution, in and of itself, to racism and racial inequality. It remains to be seen how many individuals will actually live out the promise of the new multiracial identity and help create a more egalitarian racial order in the United States. There is no single multiracial voice but many different voices, including those of reactionaries and radical visionaries. Some individuals will reinscribe racial hierarchies associated with previous multiracial identity projects. Those who display the new multiracial identity, however, resist pressures to conform to the existing racial order, with its inequitable power relations. Many will devote their energies to developing institutions that address the needs and interests of multiracial individuals in the manner of egalitarian pluralism, as other groups have done in their ethnogenesis in the United States. At the same time they will seek to build bridges across the racial divide in the manner of egalitarian integration. In the process, these individuals will become part of the larger antiracist struggle for human liberation.

Ethnoempathy and the Law of the Included Middle

As long as public policy deems it necessary to collect data on race and ethnicity—particularly as a means of tracking the nation's progress in achieving social equity—the inclusion of a multiracial identifier, no matter what the format, will not only provide a more accurate picture of contemporary demographics but also help alleviate the psychological oppression imbedded in current methods of data collection, which support and are supported by the one-drop rule. A multiracial identifier is a logical step in the progression of civil rights, with the potential to change social attitudes. The multiracial phenomenon helps deconstruct the notion of racial "purity" by challenging the notion of mutually exclusive racial categories, which are the very means by which racist ideology and racial privilege are perpetuated in the United States.[2] The option to identify oneself as multiracial should encourage more people to question the artificially fixed and static nature of racial and ethnic categories as they now exist. Ultimately, multiracial identity can initiate a long overdue national conversation about the shared ancestral connections that have been obscured by centuries of racism.

Discussion should not center, however, on multiracial identity, which is not inherently problematic in itself. Being multiracial in a hierarchical system, whether pluralist or integrationist or both, can mean being a little less black, and thus a little less subordinate, but it does not assure equality with whites. The critical challenge is completely to dismantle the Eurocentric underpinnings of the racial order in the United States by deconstructing both the dichotomous and hierarchical relationship between blackness and whiteness and making a genuine socal commitment to affirming the equality of differences in the manner of egalitarian pluralism (Figure 1d), while at the same time nurturing the equality of commonalities in the manner of egalitarian integration (Figure 1a). This transformative consciousness seeks to achieve equality of similarity without advocating assimilation, to encourage unity without perpetuating uniformity, and to build new kinds of community without promoting conformity.[3]

The acceptance of multiracial identity should in time work in the minds and hearts of European Americans greater sensitivity to the experience of African Americans, or what sociologist John Cruz has called "ethnosympathy."[4] Ultimately both African Americans and European Americans would develop a greater level of identification with and appreciation of each other's experiences in the manner of "ethnoempathy." Such a development would hold promise for moving race relations beyond the assimilation model toward a new multiracial synthesis, a horizontal process of transracial/transcultural amalgamation. In such a model, African American and European American heritage would become relative and complementary rather than absolute and antithetical. Black and white would be extremes on a continuum of blended grays, with no one color or heritage being superior or inferior to another.

A New American Revolution: Toward a "Declaration of Interdependence"

The removal of legal barriers to black equality and the growth of the black middle class have neither eradicated white racism nor achieved the egalitarianism promised by the American creed. Yet the African American struggle for racial equality has been the most powerful assertion in recent times of the American revolutionary tradition embodied in the Declaration of Independence. The success of collective African American resistance provides the nation with a lesson in what political scientist Richard Merelman calls "supportive interdependence."[5]

Unlike European American ethnic groups, African Americans have never been permitted to lose what W.E.B. Du Bois calls the "twoness" of their identity as hyphenated Americans. Despite its painful consequences this twoness has provided African Americans with a shared experience of racial subjugation and a common racial fate—however varied this may be in terms of sex/gender, color, culture, or class—that has historically required blacks to support and depend on each other in the face of white domination.[6] African Americans thus bring to the national conversation on race a sense of bonding that has been forged in isolation, exclusion, and out of the experience of "Otherness" and difference, but one that can serve as a springboard for a renewed national sense of community.[7] As the United States enters the twenty-first century, European Americans must embrace the supportive interdependence of the African American value sphere.

Racial domination has historically made whites dependent on each other. Unlike blacks, however, many whites are unconscious of their interdependence in a racial collective subjectivity. Unlike African Americans, European American ethnic groups have been largely permitted or encouraged—if not actually forced—to lose the doubleness of their identity as hyphenated Americans in exchange for the benefits of white racial privilege. The apparent "racelessness" (and "culturelessness") that seems to have emerged in this process has imbued whiteness with a pervasive and universal status as the hegemonic "Other" against which all other "Otherness" is posited. Consequently, whiteness often appears to operate as an unmarked racial category.

But just as African American resistance to racial domination has developed a value sphere premised on supportive interdependence, the practice of racial domination on the part of European Americans has paradoxically imbued them with the values of individualism (or universal particularism). Unfortunately, white racism is

deeply embedded in American society and intertwined with the ideas of individualism, merit, and standards of excellence associated with the "American Dream."
The myth that European Americans achieved their power solely through individual merit and excellence is a powerful one, but it leaves their racial advantage as
whites out of the equation. This is not to suggest that individual European Americans have not had to struggle for success, or that all European Americans benefit
equally from the advantages of white racial privilege. Nor can individual European
Americans be blamed for slavery, Jim Crow segregation, or other racially discriminatory practices and inequities. Yet European Americans as a racial plurality have
a structural edge in the pursuit of the American Dream, quite apart from questions
of individual merit and excellence. Indeed, one of the privileges of being white is
not even having to think about the fact of one's race.[8]

That said, the individualism that whites espouse originates in the idea of universal pluralism and can bring to the national conversation on race a new individualism based on "supportive independence." Such a contribution would also provide
African Americans with a lesson in the importance of dissent within the African
American community. Generally speaking, the experience of oppression diminishes
tolerance of internal dissent because subordinate groups must be as unified as possible in order to survive; and nonconformists and dissidents have often been silenced
or expelled. Yet receptivity to dissent is a crucial part of fighting domination.[9]

In the European American case, individualism has been allowed to hypertrophy
and has consequently degenerated into a pathological sense of disconnection and
dissociation that isolates individuals from each other. By contrast, individualism
that permits open debate among African Americans would strengthen arguments
against outside domination and unite its members in a collective effort to overcome
subjugation. By forcing proponents of resistance to make their strongest case, dis-
sident members of subordinate groups play an indispensable role in the struggle
for liberation.[10] An openness to internal dissent can disabuse groups of what may
be only an illusion of unity—which frequently degenerates into coercion—by
replacing it with the more dynamic notion of communion.[11] The European American value sphere's emphasis on individualism in the manner of supportive independence could be an antidote to this dis-ease.[12]

A "Trans-American" Value Sphere

The United States must, therefore, meld the African American and European American value spheres into a new trans-American value sphere based on supportive independence and interdependence. This new value sphere could serve as the foundation for a new racial contract based on integrative pluralism that would unite
European Americans, African Americans, and other Americans of color in a new consciousness.[13] In a system of integrative pluralism, differences become the basis upon

which to forge a web of interdependent yet flexibly integrated racial and cultural pluralities.

These dynamics acknowledge the reality of black-white differentiation but maintain porous boundaries that are easily crossed. Group pluralism functions in tandem with individual pluralism that is integrated under a larger national consciousness and identity.[14] A value sphere based on integrative pluralism is greater than the sum of its parts—it exists at a deeper level of organization than either the American creed of individualism or the African American ideal of community alone.[15]

The people of the United States must come together in support of a new consciousness based on the founding principles of individualism while simultaneously making a commitment to a "Declaration of Interdependence" based on the principles of communion and mutual support. Otherwise, race relations will continue to deteriorate. Cities will become more unlivable, and whites will continue to retreat—psychologically into themselves and physically into the suburbs. The racial divide will widen and the nation will lose both economic power and cultural capital, as both African Americans and European Americans abandon the promise of the American Dream.[16]

From Racial Dictatorship to Racial Democracy

The achievement of integrative pluralism will necessarily depend on "social engineering, constant vigilance, government authority, official attention to racial behavior," and a willingness by U.S. citizens to relinquish at least some individual rights for the greater national good.[17] Ironically, this presents the United States with a new "American Dilemma" perhaps even more daunting than the one described by Gunnar Myrdal half a century ago. The very values that are essential to achieving a new racial order run directly counter to some of the nation's deepest and most cherished beliefs about authority, self-determination, and individual rights. African Americans may be more willing than European Americans to compromise these ideals, because they stand to gain. Most whites, on the other hand, are reluctant to give up any authority, self-determination, or rights, and have little to gain from that kind of sacrifice.[18]

Its is doubtful that a majority of European Americans genuinely desire contact with African Americans as equals in more than token numbers. Even if they do, achieving more than token contact would exact a price that most whites are probably not willing to pay.[19] Genuine integrative pluralism is unlikely to be achieved on a large scale until the nation is willing to make a commitment to the social engineering and the sacrifice necessary to achieve it.[20] As long as European Americans refuse to confront notions of white privilege (and lingering beliefs of white supremacy, however subtle), even the best-intentioned efforts to eradicate racial equality will be continually thwarted.[21]

By now, the lessons of history should have taught the nation that neither political reform nor appeals to conscience alone can solve issues of racial inequality in the United States. Yet a new trans-American value sphere based on supportive independence and interdependence would help coordinate political action and public policy. This in turn would serve as a means of building other issue-based coalitions, regardless of racial and ethnic group differences, to work toward an inclusive politics that recognizes the complexity of various types of oppression and how each feeds on the others in order to thrive.[22] This kind of politics would create a constructive and beneficial relationship between the different groups, one marked by mutual respect, interdependence, a balance of power, and a shared commitment to commuity.[23]

Forging this consciousness will require both blacks and whites to disabuse themselves of the illusions and falsehoods spawned by history.[24] There must be a genuine commitment to undermining hierarchical and dichotomous thinking, particularly in the media and the classroom. The current multicultural curriculum, however—which tends to emphasize differences in the manner of group pluralism—is not likely to meld the African American and European American value spheres into an integrative pluralism. Multiculturalism without a simultaneous commitment to transculturalism could easily harden into a pernicious isolationism, despite its egalitarian premises and goals. What is needed instead is a comprehensive and nationally coordinated curriculum at the pre-school, K–12, and university levels that explores and validates not only racial and cultural diversity (egalitarian pluralism), but also shared racial and cultural commonalities (egalitarian integration). A comprehensive anti-bias curriculum and a program that teaches skills in conflict mediation must buttress this agenda.[25] Both European Americans and Americans of color would be taught to embrace their own "colorfulness" without internalizing "white guilt" or "minority victimization," respectively.[26]

The new multiracial identity, which seeks to transform traditional racial categories and boundaries, is emblematic of this transformative consciousness. As multiracial-identified individuals climb over the walls, cross the borders, erase and redraw the boundaries that separate them, everyone will be reminded that they actually live most of their lives in the liminal gray space between the extremes of black and white, whether or not they are conscious of that fact.[27] Taken to its logical conclusion, a new national consciousness grounded in integrative pluralism would lead whites and blacks and everyone in between to transcend their separate and hostile worlds.[28] It would ensure that wealth, power, privilege, and prestige were more equitably distributed than has ever been the case before in this country. Such a transformation in thought and behavior would move the United States closer to the ideal of a land of equal opportunity for all.

Notes

Preface

1. The term *mulatto* is popularly thought to have evolved from the Portuguese word for mule (*mulo*) and was considered an epithet (i.e., a mule is the sterile offspring of a donkey and a horse). The mulatto, as the offspring of a black and a white, was imagined to be degenerate and at least low in fertility, if not actually sterile, like its zoological counterpart. There is linguistic evidence to suggest, however, that the word is a legacy of the Islamic occupation of the Iberian Peninsula and derives from the Arabic word for blended individuals of African/Arab descent—*muwallad*—which may have evolved into the Portuguese word *mulato* to refer to Afro-Europeans (or Eurafricans). The word *mulatto* can be used with derogatory connotations but it is more often used simply to describe individuals of blended African and European backgrounds. See Jack D. Forbes, *Black Africans and Native Americans: Color, Race and Caste in the Evolution of Red-Black Peoples* (London: Blackwell, 1988), 131–50.

2. Philip V. Tobias, "The Meaning of Race," in *Race and Social Difference*, ed. Paul Baxter and Basil Sansom (London: Penguin Modern Sociology Series, 1972), 19–43.

3. Jack D. Forbes, "The Manipulation of Race, Caste, and Identity: Classifying Afro-Americans, Native Americans, and Red-Black People," *Journal of Ethnic Studies* 17 (1990), 37–38.

4. F. James Davis, *Who Is Black?: One Nation's Definition* (University Park, Pa.: Pennsylvania State University Press, 1991), 19–23.

5. Ibid.

6. Michael Omi and Howard Winant, *Racial Formation in the United States from the 1960s to the 1990s* (New York: Routledge, 1994), 54–55; Audrey Smedley, *Race in North America: Origin and Evolution of a Worldview* (Boulder: Westview Press, 1993), 18–21.

7. Smedley, *Race in North America*, 20–21; Elaine K. Ginsberg, "Introduction: The Politics of Passing," in *Passing and the Fictions of Identity*, ed. Elaine K. Ginsberg (Durham: Duke University Press, 1996), 8. The individual significance of race, sex/gender, class, etc., will vary depending on the context. But the disruptive power of race is perhaps most apparent in the formation of labor, women's, and gay/lesbian movements, to mention only a few examples. These social movements have historically been rife with racial divisions that have presented

challenges to mobilizing on questions of class, gender, and sexual orientation, among others.

8. Omi and Winant, *Racial Formation*, 55–60.

9. Ibid.

10. Ibid.

11. Ibid., 83–85.

12. Ibid.

13. Ibid.

14. J. Milton Yinger, *Ethnicity: Source of Conflict? Source of Strength?* (Albany: State University of New York Press, 1994), 3–4, 16, 25.

Introduction

1. George Schuyler, *Black No More: Being An Account of the Strange and Wonderful Workings of Science in the Land of the Free, A.D. 1933–1940* (Boston: Northeastern University Press, 1989; 1931), 25.

2. Ibid., 219–21.

3. bell hooks, "Postmodern Blackness," in *Yearning: Race, Gender, and Cultural Politics* (Boston: South End Press, 1995), 23–31; Patricia Hill Collins, "Setting Our Own Agenda" *Black Scholar* 23 (fall–winter 1993): 52–55; Victor Anderson, *Beyond Ontological Blackness: An Essay on African American Religious and Cultural Criticism* (New York: Continuum Publishing, 1995), 1–19.

4. hooks, "Postmodern Blackness," 23–31; Manning Marable, *Beyond Black and White: Transforming African American Politics* (New York: Verso, 1995), 121–22; Jerome H. Schiele, "Afrocentricity for All," *Black Issues in Higher Education* (September 26, 1991), 27; Kwame Nantambu, "Pan-Africanism Versus Pan-African Nationalism: An Afrocentric Analysis," *Journal of Black Studies* 28 (May 1998): 561–74.

5. Marable, *Beyond Black and White*, 122; Ali Rattansi, "'Western' Racisms, Ethnicities and Identities in a 'Postmodern' Frame," in *Racism, Modernity, and Identity*, ed. Ali Rattansi and Sallie Westwood (Cambridge: Polity Press, 1994), 57; Molefi Asante, *Afrocentricity: The Theory of Social Change* (Buffalo: Amulefi, 1980), 105–8; Molefi Asante, *Kemet, Afrocentricity, and Knowledge* (Trenton, N.J.: Africa World Press, 1990), 17–22.

6. Schiele, "Afrocentricity for All," 27; Asante, *Kemet, Afrocentricity, and Knowledge*, (Trenton, N.J.: Africa World Press, 1990), 5, 26, 28, 39.

7. hooks, "Postmodern Blackness," 23–31.

8. Ella Shohat and Robert Stam, *Unthinking Eurocentrism: Multiculturalism and the Media* (New York: Routledge, 1994), 1–54; Jan Nederveen Pieterse, "Unpacking the West: How European Is Europe?" in *Racism, Modernity and Identity: On the Western Front*, ed. Ali Ratanssi and Sallie Westwood (Cambridge: Polity Press, 1994), 130–46.

9. Pieterse, "Unpacking the West," 130–46.

10. Candice West and Sarah Fenstermaker, "Doing Difference," *Gender and Society* 9 (February 1995), 19.

11. Davis, *Who Is Black?*, 12, 14; Candy Mills, "Blue-Eyed Indians: Celebrity Native Roots," *Interrace* 3 (May/June 1992): 4.

12. See Tomás Almaguer, *Racial Fault Lines: The Historical Origins of White Supremacy in California* (Berkeley: University of California Press, 1994), 1–74; Mario Barrera, *Race and Class in the Southwest: A Theory of Racial Inequality* (Notre Dame: University of Notre Dame Press, 1979), 1, 8, 49–50; Rodolfo Acuña, *Occupied America: A History of Chicanos*, 3rd ed. (New York: Harper Collins, 1988), 1, 117; Jack D. Forbes, "Black Pioneers: The Spanish-Speaking Afro-Americans of the Southwest," in *Minorities in California History*, ed. George E. Frakes and Curtis B. Solberg (New York: Random House, 1971), 30–33.

13. Joseph Logsdon and Caryn Cosé Bell, "The Americanization of Black New Orleans, 1850–1900," in *Creole New Orleans: Race and Americanization*, ed. Arnold R. Hirsch and Joseph Logsdon (Baton Rouge: Louisiana State University Press, 1992), 205–7.

14. Virginia Meachum Gould, "The Free Creoles of Color of the Antebellum Gulf Ports of Mobile and Pensacola: A Struggle for the Common Ground," in *Creoles of Color of the Gulf South*, ed. James H. Dorman (Nashville: University of Tennessee Press, 1996), 40–44.

15. U.S. Government, Office of Management and Budget (hereafter OMB), *Federal Register* 62: 36876–909, July 9, 1997; Virginia R. Domínguez, *White by Definition: Social Classification in Creole Louisiana* (New Brunswick, N.J.: Rutgers University Press, 1986), 272–77.

16. Ellen Goodman, "Challenging Racial Categories," *Boston Globe* (April 13, 1995).

17. James W. Loewen, *The Mississippi Chinese: Between Black and White*, 2d ed. (Prospect Heights, Ill.: Waveland Press, 1988), vii–xii, 1–7, 58–71, 73–93.

18. Karen Sacks, "How Did Jews Become White Folks," in *Race*, ed. Steven Gregory and Roger Sanjek (New Brunswick, N.J.: Rutgers University Press, 1994), 78–102; Michael Rogin, *Blackface, White Noise: Jewish Immigrants in the Hollywood Melting Pot* (Berkeley: University of California Press, 1996), 3–18; David R. Roediger, *The Wages of Whiteness: Race and the Making of the American Working Class* (London and New York: Verso, 1991), 6–40; Noel Ignatiev, *How The Irish Became White* (New York: Routledge, 1995), 1–6, 178–88; Richard Williams, *Hierarchical Structures and Social Value: The Creation of Black and Irish Identities* (New York: Cambridge University Press, 1990), 15–48, 77–87, 131-47; Alexander Saxon, *The Rise and Fall of the White Republic: Class Politics and Mass Culture in Nineteenth-Century America* (London: Verso, 1990), 1–20; Lou Decaro, "Mixed Relations: The Italian African-American Dis-Connection," *Interrace* 3 (May/June 1992), 17–19; George E. Cunningham, "The Italian, A Hindrance to White Solidarity in Louisiana, 1890–1898," *Journal of Negro History* 1 (July 1965), 22–36; Ian F. Haney López, *White by Law: The Legal Construction of Race* (New York: New York University Press, 1996), 111–53; Thomas Sowell, *Ethnic America: A History* (New York: Basic Books, 1981), 43–68.

19. Joe R. Feagin and Clairece Booher Feagin, *Racial and Ethnic Relations*, 5th ed. (Upper Saddle River, N.J.: Prentice-Hall, 1996), 35–38, 280–82.

20. Ibid., 44–55, 280–82.

21. Paul R. Spickard, "The Illogic of American Racial Categories," in *Racially Mixed People in America*, ed. Maria P. P. Root (Thousand Oaks, Calif.: Sage Publications, 1992), 12–13.

22. Shirley Taylor-Haizlip, "Black Relatives Meet White Relatives," *Oprah Winfrey Show*, July 17, 1995.

23. Davis, *Who Is Black?*, 9–11.

24. Ibid.

25. Domínguez, *White by Definition*, 2.

26. Davis, *Who Is Black?*, 10–11.

27. Domínguez, *White by Definition*, 3.

28. Davis, *Who Is Black?*, 9–11.

29. Domínguez, *White by Definition*, 3.

30. Davis, *Who Is Black?*, 10–11.

31. Domínguez, *White by Definition*, 4–5, 53.

Chapter One

1. Carter A. Wilson, *Racism: From Slavery to Advanced Capitalism* (Thousand Oaks, Calif.: Sage Publications, 1996), 37–47; Smedley, *Race in North America*, 14–16.

2. Pitrim Sorokin, *Social and Cultural Dynamics: The Study of Change in Major Systems of Art, Truth, Ethics, Law and Social Relationships,* rev. and abr. (Boston: Porter Sargent Books, 1957), 15, 226–30.

3. Jeremy Rifkin, *Biosphere Politics: A Cultural Odyssey from the Middle Ages to the New Age* (San Francisco: Harper, 1991), 15; Sorokin, *Social and Cultural Dynamics,* 226–30, 272–75.

4. Thomas Goldstein, *The Dawn of Modern Science: From the Arabs to Leonardo da Vinci* (Boston: Houghton Mifflin, 1980), 191–98; Ankie M. M. Hoogvelt, *The Sociology of Developing Societies,* 2d ed. (London: Macmillan Press, 1978), 41.

5. Bruce Mazlish, *A New Science: The Breakdown of Connections and the Birth of Sociology* (New York: Oxford University Press, 1989), 24–26, 32; Rifkin, *Biosphere Politics,* 15; Ken Wilber, *The Eye of the Spirit: An Integral Vision for a World Gone Slightly Mad* (Boston: Shambhala Press, 1996), 38–51.

6. Samir Amin, *Eurocentrism,* trans. Russell Moore (New York: Monthly Review Press, 1989), 79–81; Hoogvelt, *Sociology of Developing Societies,* 41.

7. Hoogvelt, *Sociology of Developing Societies,* 41–42; Roland N. Stromberg, *An Intellectual History of Modern Europe,* 2d ed. (Englewood Cliffs, N.J.: Prentice-Hall, 1975), 44; Morris Berman, *Coming to Our Senses: Body and Spirit in the Hidden History of the West* (New York: Bantam Books, 1989), 111–12.

8. Bryce Little, "Rationalism and the Rise of the Sensate," unpublished paper, 1989; Mazlish, *A New Science,* 3–9, 12–14; Brain Easlea, *Witch-hunting, Magic, and the New Philosophy* (Sussex, England: Harvester Press, 1980), 201, 216–18, 241–42; Amaury de Riencourt, *Sex and Power in History* (New York: David McKay Co., 1974), 262–63.

9. The term "man" is not used here generically to refer to both men and women. Rather, it is deliberately used to emphasize the patriarchal domination that accompanied the detachment of humanity from nature.

10. Daniel Chirot, *How Societies Change* (Thousand Oaks, Calif.: Pine Forge Press, 1994), 66–67.

11. Amin, *Eurocentrism,* 71–76, 85.

12. George Ritzer, *Sociological Theory,* 5th ed. (New York: McGraw Hill, 2000), 6–7; Ken Morrison, *Marx, Durkheim, Weber: Formations of Modern Social Thought* (Thousand Oaks, Calif.: Sage Publications, 1995), 6–16.

13. Wilson, *Racism,* 41–47.

14. Ibid.

15. Ibid.

16. Omi and Winant, *Racial Formation*, 61–62.

17. Ibid.

18. Ibid.

19. Colonialism was a specific phase in the history of Western imperialism beginning in the fifteenth century. Between 1870 and 1914 there occurred an accelerated phase of European imperialist expansion into Africa and parts of Asia and the Pacific called by historians the "New Imperialism." Although the causes and nature of the "New Imperialism" remain a source of heated controversy among historians, it is sufficient for this account to say that it was marked by a systematic search for both markets and mechanisms to absorb export capital. In a broader sense, over time, this phase of imperialism included the export of the capitalist mode of production and mass culture, as well as the concomitant destruction of precapitalist forms of social organization. See Ella Shohat and Robert Stam, *Unthinking Eurocentrism: Multiculturalism and the Media* (New York: Routledge, 1994), 1–54; Patrick Williams and Laura Chrisman, "Colonial Discourse and Post-Colonial Theory: An Introduction," in *Colonial Discourse and Post-Colonial Theory: A Reader*, ed. Patrick Williams and Laura Chrisman (New York: Columbia University Press, 1994), 1–19; Helen Tiffin, "Introduction," in *Past the Last Post: Theorizing Post-Colonialism and Post-modernism*, ed. Ian Adam and Helen Tiffin (Calgary, Alberta, Canada: University of Calgary Press, 1990), vii–xvi.

20. Robert Young, "Egypt in America," in *Racism, Modernity, and Identity*, ed. Ali Rantansi and Sallie Westwood (Cambridge: Polity Press, 1994), 160–65; Shohat and Stam, *Unthinking Eurocentrism*, 1–54; Williams and Chrisman, "Colonial Discourse and Post-Colonial Theory," 1–19; Tiffin, "Introduction," vii–xvi.

21. Smedley, *Race in North America*, 14, 18; Omi and Winant, *Racial Formation*, 61–62.

22. Ivan Van Sertima, *They Came before Columbus: The African Presence in Ancient America* (New York: Random House, 1976), 108–10; Edith Sanders, "The Hamitic Hypothesis: Its Origin and Function in Time Perspective," *Journal of African History* 10 (1969): 521–32; Anton L. Allahar, "When Black First Became Worth Less," *International Journal of Comparative Sociology* 34 (1993), 39–55; Kathryn A. Manzo, *Creating Boundaries: The Politics of Race and Nation* (Boulder: Lynn Rienner Publishers, 1996), 46–53.

23. David Brion Davis, *The Problem of Slavery in Western Culture* (New York: Cornell University Press, 1967), 186.

24. St. Claire Drake, *Black Folk Here and There*, vol. 1 (Los Angeles: UCLA Center for African American Studies, 1987), 31, 62–75; Franz Fanon, *Black Skin, White Mask* (New York: Grove Press, 1967), 167, 177, 188–92; Winthrop D. Jordan, *Black over White: American Attitudes toward the Negro, 1550–1812* (Chapel Hill: University of North Carolina Press, 1968), 248, 253; Joel Kovel, *White Racism: A Psychohistory* (New York: Columbia University Press, 1970), 14–20, 62–64.

25. Sanders, "The Hamitic Hypothesis," 524.

26. Kovel, *White Racism*, 16–19.

27. Ibid.

28. Smedley, *Race in North America*, 14–18.

29. Ibid.

30. Ibid.

31. Ibid.

32. Ibid., 25–29.

33. Ibid., 27.

34. Ibid., 18; Amin, *Eurocentrism*, 94–97; Martin Bernal, *Black Athena: The Afroasiatic Roots of Classical Civilization*, vol. 1 of *The Fabrication of Ancient Greece, 1785–1885* (New Brunswick, New Jersey: Rutgers University Press, 1987), 31–33.

35. Amin, *Eurocentrism*, 94–97.

36. Smedley, *Race in North America*, 18, 26–29.

37. Ibid.

38. Ibid.

39. Ibid.

Chapter Two

1. Hoetink uses the terminology "somatic norm image" to describe the clusters of phenotypical traits, particularly skin color, that every racial/ethnic group accepts as the norm for that group and that can become a primary determinant in developing inter/intragroup prejudice and discrimination against individuals and groups that diverge from that norm. Serious inequities arise in the distribution of wealth, power, privilege, and prestige when one group has the power to establish its somatic norm image as the dominant one in a given society. Hartimus Hoetink, *Slavery and Race Relations in the Americas: Comparative Notes on Their Nature and Nexus* (New York: Harper & Row, 1973), 197–98, 200, 201; Hoetink, *Caribbean Race Relations: A Study of Two Variants* (London: Oxford University Press, 1967), 88–89, 122.

2. Carl N. Degler, *Neither Black nor White: Slavery and Race Relations in Brazil and the United States* (Madison: University of Wisconsin Press, 1986), 198–99.

3. G. Reginald Daniel, "Multiracial Identity in the United States and Brazil," in *We Are a People: Narrative and Multiplicity in the Construction of Ethnic Identity* (Philadelphia: Temple University Press, 2000), 153–78.

4. Ibid., 154.

5. Gary B. Nash, *Red, White, and Black: The Peoples of Early America*, 4th ed. (Englewood Cliffs, N.J.: Prentice-Hall, 2000), 162, 279; Marvin Harris, *Patterns of Race in the Americas* (New York: Norton, 1963), 79–94.

6. Mechal Sobel, *The World They Made Together: Black and White Values in Eighteenth-century Virginia* (Princeton: Princeton University Press, 1987), 3–20; Nash, *Red, Black, and White*, 141, 170–78, 185–97; William D. Piersen, *Black Legacy: America's Hidden Heritage* (Amherst: University of Massachusetts Press, 1993), 99–100.

7. K. F. Dyer, "Patterns of Gene Flow between Negroes and Whites in the U.S.," *Journal of Biosocial Science* 8 (October 1976): 309–33; Ira Berlin, *Slaves without Masters: The Free Negro in the Antebellum South* (New York: Pantheon, 1974), 10–11; Paul R. Spickard, *Mixed Blood: Intermarriage and Ethnic Identity in Twentieth-Century America* (Madison: University of Wisconsin Press, 1989), 237; Laurence R. Tenzer, *A Completely New Look at Interracial Sexuality: Public Opin-*

ions and Select Commentaries (Manahawkin, N.J.: Scholar's Publishing House, 1990), 56–68; Martha Hodes, *White Women, Black Men: Illicit Sex in the Nineteenth-Century South* (New Haven: Yale University Press, 1997), 1–15; Ira Berlin, *Many Thousands Gone: The First Two Centuries of Slavery in North America* (Cambridge: Harvard University Press, 1998), 44–46.

8. David H. Fowler, "Northern Attitudes towards Interracial Marriage: A Study of Legislation and Public Opinion in the Middle Atlantic States and the States of the Old Northwest" (Ph.D. diss., Yale University, 1963), 23–81.

9. Winthrope D. Jordan, "American Chiaroscuro: The Status and Definition of Mulattoes in the British Colonies," *William and Mary Quarterly* 19 (April 1962), 183–200; Davis, *Who Is Black?*, 49, 54, 62–63; Tenzer, *A Completely New Look*, 56–68; Naomi Zack, *Race and Mixed Race* (Philadelphia: Temple University Press, 1994), 33; Spickard, *Mixed Blood*, 238–39, 244–45; Berlin, *Slaves without Masters*, 5; Dyer, "Patterns of Gene Flow," 309–33; Fowler, "Northern Attitudes towards Interracial Marriage," 23–81; A. Leon Higginbotham, Jr., *In The Matter of Color: Race and the American Legal Process, The Colonial Period* (New York: Oxford University Press, 1978), 40–46.

10. Dyer, "Patterns of Gene Flow," 309–33; Tenzer, *A Completely New Look*, 56–68.

11. Fowler, "Northern Attitudes towards Interracial Marriage," 62–81. Six of the southern colonies passed laws penalizing interracial sexual relations between blacks and whites, and four of these (South Carolina and Delaware excepted) enacted legal prohibitions against marriage between blacks and whites. Among the seven northern colonies only Massachusetts and Pennsylvania implemented restrictions. Yet both colonies prohibited interracial sexual relations as well as interracial intermarriage.

12. Spickard, *Mixed Blood*, 244–45.

13. Higginbotham, *In The Matter of Color*, 40–46; Ginsberg, "Introduction," 5.

14. Nash, *Red, Black, White*, 282, 285; Ginsberg, "Introduction," 5.

15. Roediger, *The Wages of Whiteness*, 6–17, 133–56; John C. Mencke, *Mulattoes and Race Mixture: American Attitudes and Images, 1865–1918* (Ph.D. diss., University of North Carolina, 1976), 5; Eric Lott, *Love and Theft: Blackface Minstrelsy and the American Working Class* (New York: Oxford University Press, 1995), 70–71, 94–96, 191–92; Theodore W. Allen, *The Invention of the White Race: Racial Oppression and Social Control*, vol. 2 (New York: Verso, 1994), 14; Joel Williamson, *New People: Mulattoes and Miscegenation in the United States* (New York: New York University Press, 1984), 8–11.

16. *Negro Population in the United States, 1790–1915* (Washington, D.C.: Government Printing Office, 1918), 210.

17. Berlin, *Slaves without Masters*, 137; David W. Cohen and Jack P. Greene, "Introduction," in *Neither Slave nor Free: The Freedmen of African Descent in the Slave Societies of the New World*, ed. David W. Cohen and Jack P. Greene (Baltimore: Johns Hopkins University Press, 1972), 10, 14.

18. Berlin, *Slaves without Masters*, 216; Mencke, *Mulattoes and Race Mixture*, 15.

19. Mencke, *Mulattoes and Race Mixture*, 19; Berlin, *Slaves without Masters*, 216.

20. Berlin, *Slaves without Masters*, 110; Berlin, *Many Thousands Gone*, 332–38, 354–57.

21. Ibid., 7–9, 49, 90–97; Williamson, *New People*, 10, 11, 25; Davis, *Who Is Black?*, 34; Spickard, *Mixed Blood*, 49, 98; Higgenbothem, *In The Matter of Color*, 42, 48, 62, 175.

22. Berlin, *Slaves without Masters*, 97–98.

23. Mencke, *Mulattoes and Race Mixture*, 8–9; Berlin, *Slaves without Masters*, 97–99, 163.

24. Ibid., 8–9; Berlin, *Slaves without Masters*, 98–99, 163.

25. Davis, *Who Is Black?*, 55–58.

26. A more lengthy discussion of this topic can be found in Myrdal's *An American Dilemma: The Negro Problem and Modern Democracy* (New York: Harper and Bros., 1944).

27. Young, "Egypt in America," 160–65.

28. Robert Young, *Colonial Desire: Hybridity in Theory, Culture, and Race* (New York: Routledge, 1995), 118–41; Edith Sanders, "The Hamitic Hypothesis," 521–32.

29. Bernal, *Black Athena*, vol. 1, 1–2, 29.

30. Bernal's Revised Ancient Model accepts the invasions from the north by Indo-European speakers but also supports the stories of Egyptian and Phoenician colonization of Greece set out in the Ancient Model, though he sees them as beginning somewhat earlier, in the first half of the second millennium BCE. See Bernal, *Black Athena*, 2.

31. Amin, *Eurocentrism*, 77, 90–100.

32. Bernal, *Black Athena*, 7.

33. Recent scholarship acknowledges Egyptian influence on Greece and vice versa but continues to challenge, as did nineteenth-century historians, the accuracy of the Ancient Model's claims of Egyptian colonization. By virtue of the lack of direct empirical evidence, this scholarship also rejects the anecdotal accounts passed on orally to Greek thinkers by Egyptian priests claiming that Greek philosophers such as Plato and Aristotle studied in Egypt. See Mary Lefkowitz, *Not Out of Africa: How Afrocentrism Became an Excuse to Teach Myth As History* (New York: Basic Books, 1996), 53–90, 134–54. Other scholars argue that from the pre-Christian seventh century onward, Egyptian law, science, art, architecture, religion, and philosophy had a dramatic impact on Greek civilization and that Greek civilization also influenced Egyptian culture dramatically. The extent to which Egypt influenced Greek civilization needs to be further explored. This is particularly the case given the paucity of definitive sources and the questionable reliability of some evidence.

34. Sanders, "The Hamitic Hypothesis," 521–32.

35. St. Claire Drake, *Black Folk Here and There*, vol. 1, 132–37.

36. John S. Haller, Jr., *Outcasts from Evolution: Scientific Attitudes of Racial Inferiority, 1859-1900* (Urbana: University of Illinois Press, 1971), 72.

37. Sertima, *They Came before Columbus*, 108–10.

38. Young, "Egypt in America," 163–68.

39. William Lee Miller, *Arguing about Slavery: The Great Battle in the United States Congress* (New York: Knopf, 1996), 12; Kenneth James Lay, "Sexual Racism: A Legacy of Slavery," *National Black Law Journal* 13 (spring 1993): 165.

40. Thomas F. Gossett, *Race: The History of an Idea in America* (New York: Oxford University Press, 1963), 54–83.

Chapter Three

1. Everett V. Stonequist, *The Marginal Man: A Study in Personality and Culture Conflict* (New York: Russell and Russell, 1937), 184.

2. G. Reginald Daniel, "Passers and Pluralists," in *Racially Mixed People in America*, ed. Maria P. P. Root (Thousand Oaks, Calif.: Sage Publications, 1992), 107.

3. Caroline Bond Day, *A Study of Some Negro-White Families in the United States* (Cambridge: Harvard University Press, 1932), 7–12; Joel Williamson, *New People: Mulattoes and Miscegenation in the United States* (New York: New York University Press, 1984), 101, 125–26.

4. Daniel, "Passers and Pluralists," 2; Lynell George, "Guessing Game," *Los Angeles Times Magazine* (February 21, 1999), 18–21, 34, 36.

5. G. Reginald Daniel, *Going Underground: The Phenomenon of Racial Passing*, unpublished manuscript, 1991, 2; Spickard, *Mixed Blood*, 335; Davis, *Who Is Black?*, 56.

6. Daniel, *Going Underground*, 2; Adrienne Piper, "Passing for White, Passing for Black," *Transition* 58 (1992): 13–15.

7. St. Clair Drake and Horace Cayton, *Black Metropolis: A Study of Negro Life in a Northern City*, rev. ed., vol. 1 (New York: Harper Torchbooks, 1962), 162–63.

8. Daniel, *Going Underground*, 2–3.

9. Ibid., 4.

10. Daniel, "Passers and Pluralists," 93.

11. Davis, *Who Is Black?*, 21–22.

12. Berlin, *Slaves without Masters*, 160.

13. Gary B. Nash, *Forbidden Love: The Secret History of Mixed-Race America* (New York: Henry Holt, 1999), 106; Lucia Stanton and Dianne Swann-Right, "Bonds of Memory: Identity and the Hemings Family," and Joshua D. Rothman, "James Callender and Social Knowledge of Interracial Sex in Antebellum Virginia," both in *Sally Hemings and Thomas Jefferson: History, Memory, and Civic Culture*, ed. Jan Ellen Lewis and Peter S. Onuf (Charlottesville: University Press of Virginia, 1999), 107, 165–70.

14. Davis, *Who Is Black?*, 21–22; Williamson, *New People*, 102.

15. Spickard, *Mixed Blood*, 336.

16. Williamson, *New People*, 100–103.

17. Thomas G. Mathews, "The Question of Color in Puerto Rico," in *Slavery and Race Relations in Latin America*, ed. Robert Brent Toplin (Westport, Conn.: Greenwood Press, 1974), 299–323.

18. John H. Burma, "The Measurement of Negro 'Passing,'" *American Journal of Sociology* 52 (1946): 18–20.

19. Stonequist, *Marginal Man*, 186–88; Adrienne Piper, "Passing for White, Passing for Black," 4–32.

20. Daniel, "Passers and Pluralists," 94; Drake and Cayton, *Black Metropolis*, 166–67.

21. Spickard, *Mixed Blood*, 335–36.

22. Davis, *Who Is Black?*, 56; Daniel, "Passers and Pluralists," 94.

23. Teresa Wiltz, "Can We Tell Who Is White or Black? Generations after Slavery, Issues of Identity Are Confusing, Complex," *Chicago Tribune* (Sunday, February 26, 1995), 1, 4.

24. Daniel, *Going Underground*, 6.

25. Gregory Howard Williams, *Life Along the Color Line: The True Story of a White Boy Who Discovered He Was Black* (New York: Dutton, 1995), 33.

26. Shirlee Taylor Haizlip, *The Sweeter the Juice: A Family Memoir in Black and White* (New York: Simon and Schuster, 1994).

27. Ibid., 89.

28. Ibid., 34.

29. Willard B. Gatewood, *Aristocrats of Color: The Black Elite, 1880–1920* (Bloomington: Indiana University Press, 1990), 37, 46, 53.

30. Judith Berzon, *Neither White nor Black: The Mulatto Character in American Fiction* (New York: New York University Press, 1978), 162–87.

31. Philip S. Foner, *History of Black Americans: From Africa to the Emergence of the Cotton Kingdom,* vol. 1 (Westport, Conn.: Greenwood Press, 1975), 498.

32. Berlin, *Slaves without Masters,* 3.

33. Mencke, *Mulattoes and Race Mixture,* 9, 22.

34. Berlin, *Slaves without Masters,* 178–79, 218, 245; Foner, *History of Black Americans,* 501.

35. Gatewood, *Aristocrats of Color,* 45–46.

36. Kathy Y. Russell, Midge Wilson, and Ronald Hall, *The Color Complex: The Politics of Skin Color among African Americans* (New York: Harcourt Brace Jovanovich 1992), 25.

37. Gatewood, *Aristocrats of Color,* 45–46, 68.

38. Ibid., 46.

39. Ibid., 50.

40. Mencke, *Mulattoes and Race Mixture,* 24.

41. Russell, Wilson, and Hall, *The Color Complex,* 25.

42. Berzon, *Neither White nor Black,* 164–87; Mencke, *Mulattoes and Race Mixture,* 25; George C. Wright, *Life Behind a Veil: Blacks in Louisville, Kentucky, 1865–1930* (Baton Rouge: Louisiana State University Press, 1985), 134–37.

43. Ibid., 39, 44.

44. Gatewood, *Aristocrats of Color,* 52, 60–61.

45. Ibid., 42–43.

46. Ibid., 44, 52.

47. Ibid., 27, 63.

48. Ibid., 44.

49. Berzon, *Neither White nor Black,* 168; Mencke, *Mulattoes and Race Mixture,* 24–26.

50. Daniel, "Passers and Pluralists," 95–96; Wright, *Blacks in Louisville,* 134–37; Gatewood, *Aristocrats of Color,* 272–73, 298–99.

51. Russell, Wilson, and Hall, *The Color Complex,* 28, 30; Gatewood, *Aristocrats of Color,* 44, 61.

52. Berzon, *Neither White nor Black,* 168; Gatewood, *Aristorcrats of Color,* 62.

53. Lawrence Otis Graham, *Our Kind of People: Inside America's Black Upper Class* (Harper Collins, 1999), 42–43; Russell, Wilson, and Hall, *The Color Complex,* 25.

54. Daniel, "Passers and Pluralists," 97; Davis, *Who Is Black?,* 11–12, 57; Sharon Lee, "Racial Classification in the U.S. Census: 1890–1990," *Ethnic and Racial Studies* 16 (1993): 77; Williamson, *New People,* 114.

55. Mencke, *Mulattoes and Race Mixture,* 2.

56. Davis, *Who Is Black?,* 35; Smedley, *Race in North America,* 270, 276, 285–87.

57. Lee, "Racial Classification," 77.

58. Gatewood, *Aristocrats of Color,* 64.

59. Zack, *Race and Mixed Race,* 98–99.

60. Cary D. Wintz, *Black Culture and the Harlem Renaissance* (Houston: Rice University Press, 1988), 13.

61. Ibid.

62. Zack, *Race and Mixed Race*, 98–99; Wintz, *Black Culture*, 7–8.

63. Graham, *Our Kind of People*, 42–43; Russell, Wilson, and Hall, *The Color Complex*, 25.

64. Mencke, *Mulattoes and Race Mixture*, 3, 23–24; Williamson, *New People*, 81, 87–88; Gatewood, *Aristocrats of Color*, 300–322.

65. Mencke, *Mulattoes and Race Mixture*, 24; Williamson, *New People*, 121, 129.

66. Gatewood, *Aristocrats of Color*, 147–48.

67. Ibid.

68. Zack, *Race and Mixed Race*, 96; Williamson, *New People*, 113, 118–23.

69. Davis, *Who Is Black?*, 55.

70. Mencke, *Mulattoes and Race Mixture*, 28; Williamson, *New People*, 112–14, 125.

71. William M. Banks, *Black Intellectuals* (New York: Norton, 1996), 47; W.E.B. Du Bois, "The Talented Tenth," (1903) in *Writings by W. E. B. Du Bois in Periodicals Edited by Others*, ed. Herbert Aptheker (Millwood, N.Y.: Kraus-Thomson, 1982), 75.

72. Zack, *Race and Mixed Race*, 98; Wintz, *Black Culture*, 13–14.

73. Wintz, *Black Culture*, 20.

74. Zack, *Race and Mixed Race*, 98; Wintz, *Black Culture*, 14, 27–29.

75. Zack, *Race and Mixed Race*, 99.

76. George Hutchinson, *The Harlem Renaissance in Black and White* (Cambridge: Harvard University Press, 1995), 1–28; Susan Gubar, *Racechanges: White Skin, Black Face in American Culture* (New York: Oxford University Press, 1997), 95–133, 153–56; Sieglinde Lemke, *Primitivist Modernism: Black Culture and the Origins of Transatlantic Modernism* (New York: Oxford University Press, 1998), 17–20; Jon Woodson, *To Make a New Race: Gurdjieff, Toomer, and the Harlem Renaissance* (Jackson: University of Mississippi Press 1999), 7–9.

77. Hutchinson, *The Harlem Renaissance in Black and White*, 61–77, 42–61.

78. Marlon Riggs, *Ethnic Notions*, video recording (San Francisco: California Newsreel, 1986).

79. Ann duCille, *The Skin Trade* (Cambridge: Harvard University Press, 1996), 27. On the surface it may appear that many blacks also "appropriate" European American attitudes and looks. However, the political dimensions of their actions are very different. Appropriation suggests the power to do so, whereas the African American response is much more akin to assimilation, however superficial this internalization of whiteness may be. Whites may appropriate practices that make them appear more African American, but for many African Americans embracing whiteness is often a matter of economic, social, or political survival. This phenomenon parallels the experience of other subordinated groups that may chose the route of assimilation as a means of gaining access to those few opportunities available for vertical mobility, which to some extent require that one display at least public conformity to the dominant psychosomatic norm image. See Russell, Wilson, and Hall, *The Color Complex*, 54–55.

80. Zack, *Race and Mixed Race*, 99; Nash, *Forbidden Love*, 141–45.

81. Zack, *Race and Mixed Race*, 100–101.

82. Ibid., 100–101; Kevin K. Gaines, *Uplifting the Race: Black Leadership, Politics, and Culture in the Twentieth Century* (Chapel Hill: University of North Carolina Press, 1996), 9–10.

83. Zack, *Race and Mixed Race,* 100–101.

Chapter Four

1. Brewton Berry, *Almost White: A Study of Certain Racial Hybrids in the Eastern United States* (New York: Macmillan, 1963), 31–33.

2. A reader wrote in to Walter Scott's "Personality Parade" in *Parade Magazine,* "I belong to a Native American tribe called the Lumbee, and Locklear is a common last name. That makes me wonder: Is Heather Locklear part Native American?" Locklear, who was contacted by the magazine about the question, responded, "Yes, I *am* part Lumbee—way, way back on my father's side." Her maternal ancestors were predominantly Scottish. Walter Scott, "Walter Scott's Personality Parade," in *Parade Magazine,* August 23, 1998: 2. Ms. Locklear received the 1999 First Americans in the Arts Award for her continuing role on Fox TV's "Melrose Place." First Americans in the Arts is a nonprofit organization dedicated to improving the image and visibility of Native Americans in the entertainment industry. Proceeds from the annual First Americans awards ceremony go to a scholarship fund for Native American students pursuing careers in entertainment. Other honorees include entertainer Wayne Newton (Cherokee-Powhatan) and actor Wes Studi (Cherokee). Miramax Pictures' "Smoke Signals" won three awards, including Evan Adams's win for Outstanding Performance by an Actor in a Film, Outstanding Achievement in Directing, and Outstanding Achievement in Writing. The newspaper *Indian Country Today* received the Will Sampson Memorial Award ("First Americans in the Arts Awards To Be Presented," *OCB Tracker,* February 1999).

3. N. Brent Kennedy and Robyn Vaughan Kennedy, *The Melungeons: The Resurrection of a Proud People, An Untold Story of Ethnic Cleansing in America,* 2d rev. ed. (Macon, Ga.: Mercer University Press, 1997), 91, 92, 99–102, 164.

4. Ibid., 13–14.

5. Mariah Wilkins, "The Triracial Isolates," unpublished manuscript, 1989, 1–2.

6. Karen I. Blu, *The Lumbee People: The Making of an American Indian People* (New York: Cambridge University Press, 1980), 3, 39–51.

7. Berry, *Almost White,* 1–41.

8. Ibid.

9. Blu, *The Lumbee People,* 1–8.

10. Wilkins, "The Triracial Isolates," 1–2.

11. Berry, *Almost White,* 179.

12. Ibid., 180.

13. Ibid.

14. Ibid.

15. Ibid., 181.

16. Ibid., 182.

17. Ibid., 183.

18. Ibid.

19. Ibid., 11–12, 33, 166–71; Wilkins, "The Triracial Isolates," 11–12.

20. Charles Crowe, "Indians and Blacks in White America," in *Four Centuries of Southern Indians,* ed. Charles M. Hudson (Athens: University of Georgia Press, 1975), 158–61.

21. Fergus M. Borowich, *Killing the White Man's Indian: Reinventing Native Americans at the End of the Twentieth Century* (New York: Doubleday, 1996), 17–18; Crowe, "Indians and Blacks," 158–61; C. Matthew Snipp, "Who Are American Indians? Some Observations about the Perils and Pitfalls of Data for Race and Ethnicity," *Population Research and Policy Review* 5 (1986): 247–51.

22. Feagin and Feagin, *Racial and Ethnic Relations,* 224–28, 280–83.

23. Berry, *Almost White,* 1–9.

24. Ibid., 7–9.

25. Jack D. Forbes, *Black Africans and Native Americans,* 203; Wilkins, *Triracial Isolates,* 1.

26. "Cultural and Historical Information of the Lumbee Tribe," Official Home Page of the Lumbee Tribe, "The Lumbee Tribe of North Carolina," Dalton B. Brooks, Tribal Chairman, Society of Native American Cultures (SNAC): <http://www.lumbee.org>.

27. Ibid.

28. Ibid.

29. Ibid.

30. Mark Stinnford, "Lumbee Tribe to Address Federal Recognition," Fayetteville (N.C.) *Observer-Times,* January 25, 1997; Paul Woolverton, "Measure Could Benefit Lumbees," Ibid., May 21, 1998.

31. Ibid.

32. Ibid.

33. Berry, *Almost White,* 137–38; Blu, *The Lumbee Problem,* 77–90; Borowich, *Killing the White Man's Indian,* 60–65, 74–83; Russell Thornton, *American Indian Holocaust and Survival: A Population History since 1492* (Norman: University of Oklahoma Press, 1987), 210–12; U.S. Bureau of the Census, 1980.

34. Berry, *Almost White,* 106–7, 115–18, 188; Brewton Berry, "America's Mestizos," in *The Blending of Races: Marginality and Identity in World Perspective,* ed. Noel P. Gist and Anthony Gary Dworkin (New York: Wiley-Interscience, 1972), 200–201.

35. Berry, *Almost White,* 157, 163; U.S. Bureau of the Census, 1980.

36. Berry, *Almost White,* 185–86, 190; Blu, *The Lumbee Problem,* 43, 182. Recently there seems to have been a change in these attitudes. After becoming almost extinct, Melungeon identity is experiencing resurgence, as indicated by the Melungeons' web site at <http://www.melungeons.org>. There has also been a surge of research culminating in the "First Union: Melungeon, Appalachian Research Conference" held July 25–27, 1997, at Clinch Valley College of the University of Virginia in Wise, Virginia. A second conference was held in 1998 and a third in 2000. Melungeon-identified individuals and others seeking to recapture Melungeon history and examine contemporary issues and concerns of the Melungeon community organized the conferences. This "new" Melungeon identity differs from the "old" Melungeon identity in that it seeks to deconstruct the elitist and hierarchical premises upon which the previous identity was based by acknowledging and embracing the African ancestry.

37. Berry, *Almost White,* 173, 188.

38. Berlin, *Slaves without Masters;* Mencke, *Mulattoes and Race Mixture,* 10–11; Berlin, *Many Thousand Gone,* 77–92; Williamson, *New People,* 14–15: Gwendolyn Midlo-Hall, "The Formation of Afro-Creole Culture," in *Creole New Orleans: Race and Americanization,* ed. Arnold R. Horsch and Joseph Logsdon (Baton Rouge: Louisiana State University Press, 1992), 58–90.

39. Laura Foner, "The Free People of Color in Louisiana and St. Domingue: A Comparative Portrait of Two Three-Caste Slave Societies," *Journal of Social History* 3 (1970): 406–30.

40. Berlin, *Many Thousands Gone,* 195–216; David C. Rankin, "The Impact of the Civil War on the Free Colored Community of New Orleans," *Perspectives in American History* 11 (1977–78): 379–416.

41. Berlin, *Slaves without Masters,* 130–132; Leonard Richard Lempel, "The Mulatto in United States Race Relations: Changing Status and Attitudes." Ph.D. diss., Syracuse University, 1979, 54–56; Russell Garvin, "The Free Negro in Florida before the Civil War," *Florida Historical Quarterly* 46 (July 1967), 1–17; David Y. Thomas, "The Free Negro in Florida before 1865," *South Atlantic Quarterly* 10 (October 1911), 335–37; Jane Landers, *Black Society in Spanish Florida* (Urbana: University of Illinois Press, 1999), 1–28, 229–53.

42. Berlin, *Slaves without Masters,* 5, 110–12.

43. Williamson, *New People,* 22–23; Mencke, *Mulattoes and Race Mixture,* 11–14.

44. Gary B. Mills, *The Forgotten People: Cane River's Creoles of Color* (Baton Rouge: Louisiana State University Press, 1977), 78.

45. Kimberly S. Hanger, *Bounded Lives, Bounded Places: Free Black Society in Colonial New Orleans, 1769–1803* (Durham, N.C.: Duke University Press, 1997), 25; Hall, *Africans in Colonial Louisiana,* 276.

46. Hanger, *Bounded Lives, Bounded Places,* 7.

47. Katrina Hazzard-Gordon, "The Interaction of Sexism and Racism in the Old South: The New Orleans Bals Du Cordon Bleu," *Minority Voices,* 2d series 6 (fall 1989), 14–25.

48. Domínguez, *White by Definition,* 24; Rankin, "The Impact of the Civil War on the Free Colored Community," 381.

49. Hanger, *Bounded Lives, Bounded Places,* 7–8; Gwendolyn Midlo Hall, *Africans in Colonial Louisiana: The Development of Afro-Creole Culture in the Eighteenth Century* (Baton Rouge: Louisiana State University Press, 1992), 276; Caryn Cossé Bell, *Revolution, Romanticism, and the Afro-Creole Protest Tradition, 1718–1868* (Baton Rouge: Louisiana State University Press, 1997), 29.

50. Jerah Johnson, "Colonial New Orleans: A Fragment of the Eighteenth-Century French Ethos," in *Creole New Orleans: Race and Americanization,* ed. Arnold R. Horsch and Joseph Logsdon (Baton Rouge: Louisiana State University Press, 1992), 52–53; Domínguez, *White by Definition,* 23–24; Hazzard-Gordon, "The Interaction of Sexism and Racism in the Old South," 15; Rankin, "The Impact of the Civil War on the Free Colored Community," 380; Berlin, *Slaves without Masters,* 108–14.

51. H. E. Sterkx, *The Free Negro in Antebellum Louisiana* (Rutherford: Farleigh Dickinson University Press, 1972), 94.

52. Berlin, *Slaves without Masters,* 114–17; Haskins, *Creoles of Color,* 32–33; Johnson, "Colonial New Orleans," 53; Mencke, *Mulattoes and Race Mixture,* 14–19; Rankin, "The Impact of the Civil War on the Free Colored Community," 380–82.

53. Berlin, *Many Thousands Gone,* 290–357; Berlin, *Slaves without Masters,* 114–17.

54. Domínguez, *White by Definition,* 113–15.

55. The linguistic divide was more apparent in Mobile than in Pensacola. In that region, the representatives of the three nations spoke English, Spanish, and French, respectively. Even though a large portion of the population was culturally French, Spanish was the predominant language and the lingua franca in the port. See Gould, "The Free Creoles of Color of the Antebellum Gulf Ports," 40–41.

56. Logsdon and Bell, "The Americanization of Black New Orleans," 201–61; Gould, "The Free Creoles of Color of the Antebellum Gulf Ports," 28–50; Domínguez, *White by Definition,* 28–50, 134–40.

57. Logsdon and Bell, "The Americanization of Black New Orleans," 189–261.

58. Domínguez, *White by Definition,* 141–48, 150–53.

59. Haskins, *The Creoles of Color,* 50; Rankin, "The Impact of the Civil War on the Free Colored Community of New Orleans," 387.

60. Gatewood, *Aristocrats of Color,* 84.

61. Domínguez, *White by Definition,* 134–37; Haskins, *The Creoles of Color,* 50–57.

62. Logsdon and Bell, "The Americanization of Black New Orleans, 1850–1900," 204.

63. Bell, *Revolution, Romanticism,* 280–81.

64. Haskins, *The Creoles of Color,* 61.

65. Bell, *Revolution, Romanticism,* 280.

66. *The Thin Disguise: The Turning Point in Negro History—Plessy v. Ferguson, A Documentary Presentation (1864–1896),* ed. Otto H. Olsen (New York: Humanities Press, 1967), 74.

67. Ibid.

68. Ibid.

69. Ibid., 280–81.

70. Ibid.

71. Ibid.

72. Ibid.

73. Ibid., 81–85.

74. Ibid., 112; Davis, *Who Is Black?* 8–9, 52–53.

75. Davis, *Who Is Black?,* 8–9, 52–53.

76. Haskins, *The Creoles of Color,* 118–20.

77. Ibid.

78. Ibid.

79. Domínguez, *White by Definition,* 223–24; Haskins, *The Creoles of Color,* 64.

80. Mills, *The Forgotten People,* xvii–xxx, 247–50; Williamson, *New People,* 21–22.

81. Omi and Winant, *Racial Formation,* 80–81; Howard Winant, "Dualism at Century's End," in *The House That Race Built: Black Americans, U.S. Terrain,* ed. Wahneema Lubiano (New York: Pantheon Books, 1997), 91–93.

82. Daniel, "Passers and Pluralists," 91–92.

83. Cheryl Harris, "Whiteness as Property," in *Critical Race Theory: The Key Writings That Formed the Movement,* ed. Kimberlé Crenshaw, Neil Gotanda, Gary Peller, Kendall Thomas (New York: New Press, 1995), 276–91; Ginsberg, "The Politics of Passing," 3.

84. Ginsberg, "Introduction," 3–5.

85. Ibid.

86. Ibid.

87. Ibid., 16. Passing has been applied discursively to disguises of other elements of an individual's presumed "natural" or "essential" identity including ethnicity, as well as class and gender. These categories of experience were usually effected by deliberate alterations of physical appearance and behavior, including cross-dressing.

88. Berzon, *Neither White nor Black*, 162–87.

89. Ibid., 107.

90. Daniel, "Passers and Pluralists," 95.

91. Ibid.

92. Gatewood, *Aristocrats of Color*, 67–68, 347–48.

93. Ibid.

94. G. Reginald Daniel, "Beyond Black and White," in *Racially Mixed People in America*. ed. Maria P. P. Root (Thousand Oaks, Calif.: Sage Publications, 1992), 333–41; Daniel, "Passers and Pluralists," 91–107; Daniel, "Black and White Identity in the New Millennium," in *The Multiracial Experience: Racial Borders as the New Frontier*, ed. Maria P. P. Root (Thousand Oaks, Calif.: Sage Publications, 1996), 121–39.

95. Gatewood, *Aristocrats of Color*, 84.

96. Berzon, *Neither White nor Black*, 162–87.

97. For example, on the 1970 census "Creole" write-in entries were reassigned to the black category only if the respondent resided in Louisiana. Outside this region the entry remained in the "other" category. In 1980, this write-in entry was recoded as black, regardless of location (U.S. Bureau of the Census, 1970, 1980).

98. Berzon, *Neither White nor Black*, 162–87.

99. Mencke, *Mulattoes and Race Mixture*, 3, 23–24; Williamson, *New People*, 81, 87–88.

100. G. Reginald Daniel, *Louisiana Creoles of Color; The French Resistance*, unpublished manuscript, 1991, 9.

101. Ibid., 10; Domínguez, *White by Definition*, 172–76; James H. Dorman, "Louisiana's 'Creoles of Color': Ethnicity, Marginality, and Identity," *Social Science Quarterly* 73 (September 1992): 620–21; James H. Dorman, "Ethnicity and Identity: Creoles of Color in Twentieth-Century South Louisiana," in *Creoles of Color of the Gulf Coast*, ed. James H. Dorman (Knoxville: University of Tennessee Press, 1996), 166–79; Haskins, *The Creoles of Color*, 127–28; Arnold Hirsch, "Simply a Matter of Black and White: The Transformation of Race and Politics in Twentieth-Century New Orleans," in *Creole New Orleans: Race and Americanization*, ed. Arnold R. Hirsch and Joseph Logsdon (Baton Rouge: Louisiana State University Press, 1992), 262–319.

102. Lynell George, *No Crystal Stair: African Americans in the City of Angels* (New York: Verso, 1992), 222.

103. Arthé A. Anthony, "Collective Memory and Ethnicity: The Black Creole Community in Los Angeles, 1940s–1990s," 1–3, paper presented at the Conference on Ethnicity and Multiethnicity: The Construction and Deconstruction of Identity, hosted by the Division of Social Sciences and the Institute of Polynesian Studies, Brigham Young University, Laie, Hawaii, 1995.

104. Dorman, "Louisiana's 'Creoles of Color,'" 622–23; Dorman, "Ethnicity and Identity," 166–79.

105. Arthé Anthony, "Collective Memory and Ethnicity," 9, 33, 38–40.

106. Daniel, "Louisiana Creoles of Color," 11–12; Lillian Comas-Dias, "Latinegra: Mental Health Issues," in *The Multiracial Experience: Racial Borders as the New Frontier*, ed. Maria P. P. Root (Thousand Oaks, Calif.: Sage Publications, 1996), 167–90.

107. Daniel, "Louisiana Creoles of Color," 11–12; George, *No Crystal Stair*, 240–43.

108. Omi and Winant, *Racial Formation*, 163 n.8, 195 n.11.

109. Mike McGlothlen, *Melungeons and Other Mestee Groups* (Gainesville, Fla.: McGlothlen Publishers, 1994); N. Kennedy and Kennedy, *The Melungeons*.

110. Kennedy and Kennedy, *The Melungeons*, xiii.

111. Ibid.

112. Ibid.

Chapter Five

1. Daniel, "Beyond Black and White," 335; Daniel, "Black and White Identity in the New Millennium," 128.

2. Nancy Brown and Ramona Douglass, "Making the Invisible Visible: The Growth of Community Network Organizations," in *The Multiracial Experience: Racial Borders as the New Frontier*, ed. Maria P. P. Root (Thousand Oaks, Calif.: Sage Publications, 1996), 323–40.

3. Daniel, "Beyond Black and White," 335; Daniel, "Black and White Identity," 121–39.

4. Roger Whitlaw, *Black American Literature: A Critical History* (Totowa, N.J.: Littlefield, Amas, and Co.: 1974), 81–83; Robert A. Bone, *The Negro Novel in America*, rev. ed. (New Haven: Yale University Press, 1965), 80–89; Addison Gayle, *The Way of the New World: The Black Novel in America* (New York: Anchor Press, 1976), 117–23; Woodson, *To Make a New Race*, 28–46; Arna Bontemps, "Introduction," in *Cane* by Jean Toomer (New York: Harper and Row, 1969), vii–viii.

5. Bontemps, "Introduction," viii.

6. Woodson, *To Make a New Race*, 29, 31–33, 45.

7. Bontemps, "Introduction," viii.

8. Cynthia Earl Kerman, *The Lives of Jean Toomer: A Hunger for Wholeness* (Baton Rouge: Louisiana State University Press, 1987), 341–46; George Hutchinson, "Jean Toomer and American Racial Discourse," *Texas Studies in Literature and Language* 35 (summer 1993), 226–50.

9. Zack, *Race and Mixed Race*, 110–11; Woodson, *To Make a New Race*, 31–45.

10. Kathryn Talalay, *Composition in Black and White: The Tragic Saga of Harlem's Biracial Prodigy* (New York: Oxford University Press, 1995), 60, 93, 191.

11. Ibid., 179–80, 200, 265.

12. Daniel, "Beyond Black and White," 335; Spickard, *Mixed Blood*, 302, 333.

13. Drake and Cayton, *Black Metropolis*, 145–46.

14. Forrest Cozart, *The Manasseh: A Story of Mixed Marriages* (Atlantic City, N.J.: State Register Publishing Co., 1909), 27–33.

15. Drake and Cayton, *Black Metropolis*, 145–46.

16. Gatewood, *Aristocrats of Color*, 177–78.

17. Drake and Cayton, *Black Metropolis,* 145–46; Gatewood, *Aristocrats of Color,* 177–78.

18. Robert E. T. Roberts, "Black-White Intermarriage in the United States," in *Inside the Mixed Marriage: Accounts of Changing Attitudes, Patterns, and Perceptions of Cross-Cultural and Interracial Marriages* (Lanham, Md.: University Press of America, 1994), 57–74; Davis, *Who Is Black?,* 68–73; Spickard, *Mixed Blood,* 278–79; Belinda M. Tucker and Claudia Mitchell-Kernan, "New Trends in Black American Interracial Marriage: The Social Structural Context," *Journal of Marriage and the Family* 52 (February 1990): 209–19.

19. Maryland's repeal of its prohibitions against interracial marriage, Md. Laws 1967, c. 6, left Virginia and fifteen other states with statutes outlawing interracial marriage: Alabama, Ala. Const., Art. 4, 102, Ala. Code, Tit. 14, 360 (1958); Arkansas, Ark. Stat. Ann. 55-104 (1947); Delaware, Del. Code Ann., Tit. 13, 101 (1953); Florida, Fla. Const., Art. 16, 24, Fla. Stat. 741.11 (1965); Georgia, Ga. Code Ann. 53-106 (1961); Kentucky, Ky. Rev. Stat. Ann. 402.020 (Supp. 1966); Louisiana, La. Rev. Stat. 14:79 (1950); Mississippi, Miss. Const., Art. 14, 263, Miss. Code Ann. 459 (1956); Missouri, Mo. Rev. Stat. 451.020 (Supp. 1966); North Carolina, N.C. Const., Art. XIV, 8, N.C. Gen. Stat. 14-181 (1953); Oklahoma, Okla. Stat., Tit. 43, 12 (Supp. 1965); South Carolina, S. C. Const., Art. 3, 33, S. C. Code Ann. 20-7 (1962); Tennessee, Tenn. Const., Art. 11, 14, Tenn. Code Ann. 36-402 (1955); Texas, Tex. Pen. Code, Art. 492 (1952); West Virginia, W. Va. Code Ann. 4697 (1961). "United States Supreme Court Case: Loving v. Virginia," *Multiracial Activist;* Roberts, "Black-White Intermarriage," 57–74.

20. Roberts, "Black-White Intermarriage," 57–74.

21. Ibid.

22. Ibid.

23. Ibid.

24. Lise Funderburg, *Black, White, Other: Biracial Americans Speak about Race and Identity* (New York: William Morrow, 1994), 26; Jewelle Taylor-Gibbs, "Biracial Adolescents," in *Children of Color: Psychological Interventions with Minority Youth* (San Francisco: Jossey-Bass, 1989), 323; Mitchell-Kernan and Tucker, "New Trends in Black American Interracial Marriage," 209–19; Sylvestre Monroe, "Love in Black and White: The Last Racial Taboo," *Los Angeles Times Magazine* (December 9, 1990), 14.

25. Roberts, "Black-White Intermarriage," 57–74.

26. Ibid.

27. Ibid., 59–74.

28. Ibid., 57–74.

29. Maria P. P. Root, *Love's Revolution* (Philadelphia: Temple University Press, 2000), 6–8.

30. Roberts, "Black-White Intermarriage," 57–74.

31. Spickard, *Mixed Blood,* 307–11.

32. Antonio McDaniel, "The Dynamic Racial Composition of the United States," in *An American Dilemma Revisited: Race Relations in a Changing World,* ed. Obie Clayton, Jr. (New York: Russell Sage Foundation, 1996), 282; Roger Sanjek, "Intermarriage and the Future of Races" in *Race,* ed. Steven Gregory and Roger Sanjek (New Brunswick: Rutgers University Press, 1994), 105, 113–14; Douglas Besharov and Timothy Sullivan, "One Flesh: America Is Experiencing an Unprecedented Increase in Black-White Intermarriage," *The New Democrat* 8 (1996): 19–21; Mitchell-Kernan and Tucker, "New Trends in Black American Interracial Marriage," 209–19; Stanley Lieberson and Mary Waters, *From These Strands: Ethnic and Racial*

Groups in Contemporary America: The Population of the United States in the 1980s, A Census Mono-graph Series (New York: Russell Sage Foundation, 1988), 171.

33. Robert Staples, "An Overview of Race and Marital Status," in *Black Families*, ed. Harriette Pipes McAdoo (Thousand Oaks, Calif.: Sage Publications, 1988), 187–90; Laura B. Randolph, "Black Women/White Men: What's Goin' On?" *Ebony* (March 1989), 154, 156–62.

34. U.S. Government Office of Management and Budget (hereafter OMB), *Federal Register* (July 9, 1997):36901; Sanjek, "Intermarriage and the Future," 110–14.

35. OMB, *Federal Register* (July 9, 1997): 36901; Bettina Boxall and Ray F. Herndon, "Far from Urban Gateways, Racial Lines Blur in Suburbs, *Los Angeles Times* (August 15, 2000), A1, A25.

36. OMB, *Federal Register* (July 9, 1997): 36901; Margaret L. Usdansky, "For Interracial Kids, Growth Spurt," *USA Today* (December 11, 1992), 7A.

37. OMB, *Federal Register* (July 9, 1997): 36901.

38. Ibid., 36901; Funderburg, *Black, White, Other*, 11–12; Taylor-Gibbs and Hines, "Negotiating Ethnic Identity," 223; Roberts, "Black-White Intermarriage," 57–74. It should be pointed out that analysis of the change in the numbers of births in which one parent is African American and the other is some other race is complicated by the increasing number of births for which the race of the second parent, usually the father, is not given on the birth certificate—40 percent in 1994 as compared to 24 percent in 1968. However, it can be inferred from births for which both parents' races are known that births involving one African American parent and a second parent of another race (other than European American) also are increasing.

39. OMB, *Federal Register* (July 9, 1997): 36901; Funderburg, *Black, White, Other*, 11–12; Taylor-Gibbs and Hines, "Negotiating Ethnic Identity," 223.

40. Christine C. Iijima Hall, "Please Choose One: Ethnic Identity Choices for Biracial Individuals," in *Racially Mixed People in America*, ed. Maria P. P. Root (Thousand Oaks, Calif.: Sage Publications, 1992), 250–64.

41. Francis Wardle, "Are You Sensitive to Interracial Children's Special Identity Needs?" *Young Children* (January 1987), 55.

42. Daniel, "Beyond Black and White," 335; Daniel, "Black and White Identity," 121–39.

43. G. Reginald Daniel, "Two Parent Ethnicities and Parents of Two Ethnicities: Generational Differences in the Discourse on Multiethnic Identity: A Preliminary Study," unpublished manuscript (1994, 1998), 7–8. Data was obtained between 1988 and 1998 through observations of the public behavior of students attending the University of California at Los Angeles, Santa Barbara, and Santa Cruz, and from individuals participating in several California support groups and attending regional and national conferences on multiracial identity.

44. Daniel, "Beyond Black and White," 335; Daniel, "Black and White Identity," 128; Daniel, "Two Parent Ethnicities and Parents of Two Ethnicities," 8.

45. Daniel, "Two Parent Ethnicities and Parents of Two Ethnicities," 8.

46. Ibid., 8–9.

47. Ibid.; Daniel "Black and White Identity," 128–29.

48. Maria P. P. Root, "Resolving 'Other' Status: Identity Development of Biracial Individuals," in *Complexity and Diversity in Feminist Theory and Therapy*, ed. Laura Brown and Maria P. P. Root (New York: Hayworth, 1990), 185–205.

49. Brenda-Jean Winchester, "More Than Just A Pretty Face," *Interrace* (April/May 1995), 36.

50. Daniel, "Two Parent Ethnicities," 8–9.

51. Ibid., 10–11.

52. Ibid.

53. Davis, *Who Is Black?*, 128–29.

54. Daniel, "Two Parent Ethnicities," 11–12; Daniel, "Black and White Identity," 129.

55. Daniel, "Two Parent Ethnicities," 11–12.

56. Ibid., 130.

57. Forbes, *Black Africans and Native Americans*, 271.

58. "Biracial Children of Interracial Divorce," *Oprah Winfrey Show*, October 7, 1994.

59. Manuel Ramirez, III, *Psychology of the Americas: Mestizo Perspectives on Personality and Mental Health* (New York: Pergamon Press, 1983), 100–117.

60. Daniel, "Black and White Identity," 134.

61. Peter S. Adler, "Beyond Cultural Identity: Reflections on Cultural and Multicultural Man," in *Topics in Cultural Learning*, ed. R. Brislin, vol. 2 (Honolulu: East-West Center, 1974), 23–40; Philip M. Brown, "Biracial Identity and Social Marginality," *Child Adolescent Social Work* 7 (August 1990): 319–37.

62. Adler, "Beyond Cultural Identity," 29.

63. Gloria Anzaldúa, *Borderlands: La Frontera—The New Mestiza* (San Francisco: Spinsters/Aunt Lute, 1987), 77–91; Daniel, "Black and White Identities," 134; Adler, "Beyond Cultural Identity," 25. Liminality (from the Latin *limen*, "boundary or threshold") also can be seen in the rites associated with the initiation of adolescent youth from boyhood into manhood among traditional peoples. A similar dynamic can be observed in individuals who are simultaneously members of two or more culturally distinct groups (second-generation immigrants or recent migrants from country to city, and women in nontraditional female roles). These categories follow a similar path from "either/or" to "both/neither." See Bob Trubshaw, "The Metaphors and Rituals of Place and Time: An Introduction to Liminality, or Why Christopher Robin Wouldn't Walk on the Cracks," originally published in *Mercian Mysteries* (February 1995); see the web site of "At the Edge" at <http://www.gmtnet.co.uk/indigo/edge> copyright 1995, 1996, "At the Edge," Bob Trubshaw <bobtrubs@gmtnet.co.uk>, created April 1996 and updated May 1998; Victor Witter Turner, *The Ritual Process: Structure and Anti-Structure* (New York: Cornell University Press, 1969), 94–130.

64. Daniel, "Black and White Identity," 121–39; George Kitahara Kich, "In The Margins of Sex and Race: Difference, Marginality, and Flexibility," in *The Multiracial Experience: Racial Borders as the New* Frontier, ed. Maria P. P. Root (Thousand Oaks, Calif.: Sage Publications, 1996), 263–76; Root, "Resolving 'Other' Status," 185–205.

65. Robert E. Park, "Human Migration and the Marginal Man," *American Journal of Sociology* 33 (1928): 881–93; Stonequist, *The Marginal Man*, 10–11, 24–27.

66. Leonard Richard Lempel, *The Mulatto in United States Race Relations: Changing Status and Attitudes*, Ph.D. diss., Syracuse University, 1979, 247–99.

67. Aaron Antonovsky, "Toward a Refinement of the 'Marginal Man' Concept," *Social Forces* 35 (1956): 57–67; Milton M. Goldberg, "A Qualification of the Marginal Man Theory," *American Sociological Review* 6 (1941): 52–58; Arnold W. Green, "A Re-examination of

the Marginal Man Concept," *Social Forces* 26 (1947): 167–71; Alan C. Kerchkhoff and Thomas C. McCormick, "Marginal Status and Marginal Personality," *Social Forces* 34 (1955): 48–55.

68. Noel P. Gist, "Cultural Versus Social Marginality: The Anglo-Indian Case," *Phylon* 28 (1967): 361–65; Robin Miller, "The Human Ecology of Multiracial Identity," in *Racially Mixed People in America*, ed. Maria P. P. Root (Thousand Oaks, Calif.: Sage Publications, 1992), 24–36; Carlos W. S. Poston, "The Biracial Identity Model: A Needed Addition," *Journal of Counseling and Development* 69 (November/December 1990): 152–55; R. D. Wright and S.D. Wright, "A Plea For A Further Refinement of the Marginal Man Theory," *Phylon* 33 (1972): 361–68.

69. Maria P. P. Root, "Within, Between, and Beyond Race," in *Racially Mixed People in America*, ed. Maria P. P. Root (Thousand Oaks, Calif.: Sage Publications, 1992), 3–11.

70. Chiaroscuro is a baroque technique of defining space by the interpenetration of light and animating space by the flowing movement of shadows, rather than through clear delineation, in order to bring new psychological profundity to portraiture.

71. Carla Bradshaw, "Beauty and the Beast," in *Racially Mixed People in America*, ed. Maria P. P. Root (Thousand Oaks, Calif.: Sage Publications, 1992), 77–90; Lynda Field, "Piecing Together the Puzzle: Self-Concept and Group Identity in Biracial Black/White Youth," in *The Multiracial Experience: Racial Borders as the New Frontier*, ed. Maria P. P. Root (Thousand Oaks, Calif.: Sage Publications, 1996), 211–26; Hall, "Check One Please," 250–64; Deborah Johnson, "Developmental Pathways: Toward an Ecological Theoretical Formulation of Race Identity in Black-White Biracial Children," in *Racially Mixed People in America*, ed. Maria P. P. Root (Thousand Oaks, Calif.: 1992), 37–49; Agnetta Mitchell, "Cultural Identification, Racial Knowledge and General Psychological Well-Being Among Biracial Young Adults," Ph.D. diss., California School of Professional Psychology, Los Angeles, 1990, x–xii, 47–66; Root, "Resolving 'Other' Status," 185–205; Root, "Within, Between, and Beyond Race," 3–11; Kerry Rockquemore, "Between Black and White: Exploring the Biracial Experience," *Race and Society* 1: 197–212; Daniel, "Two Parent Ethnicities," 15–16; Rockquemore, "Socially Embedded Identities: Theories, Typologies, and Processes of Racial Identity among Biracials," unpublished manuscript, 2000; Barbara Tizard and Ann Phoenix, *Black, White, or Mixed Race: Race and Racism in the Lives of Young People of Mixed Parentage* (London: Routledge, 1993), 44–66.

72. Daniel, "Two Parent Ethnicities," 15–16; Daniel, "Black and White Identity," 135–36.

73. Ramirez, *Psychology of the Americas*, 100–117.

74. Daniel, "Two Parent Ethnicities," 16; Ramirez, *Psychology of the Americas*, 100–117.

75. David Morley and Kuan-Hsing Chen, "Introduction," in *Stuart Hall: Critical Dialogues in Cultural Studies*, ed. David Morley and Kuan-Hsing Chen (New York: Routledge, 1996), 9; Isaac Julien and Kobena Mercer, "De Margin and De Centre," in *Stuart Hall: Critical Dialogues in Cultural Studies*, ed. David Morley and Kuan-Hsing Chen (New York: Routledge, 1996), 456; Ian F. Haney López, *White by Law: The Legal Construction of Race* (New York: New York University Press, 1996), 155–95.

76. Adler, "Beyond Cultural Identity," 23–40.

77. Daniel, "Two Parent Ethnicities," 17–18.

78. Ibid.

79. Adler, "Beyond Cultural Identity," 23–40; Daniel, "Beyond Black and White," 333–41.

80. Daniel, "Two Parent Ethnicities," 18; Daniel, "Black and White Identity," 136; Ramirez, *Psychology of the Americas*, 100–117.

81. Daniel, "Two Parent Ethnicities," 19.

82. Ibid., 19–20.

83. Daniel, "Beyond Black and White," 333–41.

Chapter Six

1. Anthony W. Marx, "Contested Citizenship: The Dynamics of Racial Identity and Social Movements," *International Review of Social History* 40, supplement 3 (1995): 159–60; Stephen Cornell and Douglas Hartmann, *Ethnicity and Race: Making Identities in A Changing World* (Thousand Oaks, Calif.: Pine Forge Press, 1998), 86.

2. Cornell and Hartmann, *Ethnicity and Race*, 73–80, 85, 101.

3. West and Fenstermaker, "Doing Difference," 19.

4. Ibid., 19, 21–24.

5. Cornell and Hartman, *Ethnicity and Race*, 73–80, 85, 101.

6. Adler, "Beyond Cultural Identity," 23–40.

7. Ibid., 87.

8. Observation of students at the University of California at Los Angeles, Santa Barbara, and Santa Cruz, and public behavior at local support group meetings, as well as regional and national conferences on the topic of multiracial identity and interracial marriage; *Multiracial Couples: Black and White Voices*, ed. Paul C. Rosenblatt, Terri A. Karis, and Richard D. Powell (Thousand Oaks, Calif.: Sage Publications, 1995), 32–33; Rita J. Simon and Howard Alstein, *Transracial Adoptees and Their Families: A Study of Identity and Commitment* (New York: Praeger, 1987), 33–91; Matt Kelley, "Transracial Adoptees: Creating an 'Other' Identity," *Mavin: The Mixed Race Experience* 3 (Fall, 1999): 12, 15–19: Ruth G. McKay and Christine C. Iijima Hall, "Transracial Adoptions: In Whose Best Interest?" in *The Multiracial Experience: Racial Borders as the New Frontier*, ed. Maria P. P. Root (Thousand Oaks, Calif.: Sage Publications, 1996), 63–78.

9. Observation of students at the University of California at Los Angeles, Santa Barbara, and Santa Cruz, and public behavior at local support group meetings, as well as regional and national conferences on the topic of multiracial identity and interracial marriage; Michael Thornton, "Is Multiracial Status Unique? The Personal and Social Experience," in *Racially Mixed People in America*, ed. Maria P. P. Root (Thousand Oaks, Calif.: Sage Publications, 1992), 321–25.

10. Cornell and Hartmann, *Ethnicity and Race*, 98.

11. Ibid., 87–89; Richard Jenkins, *Rethinking Ethnicity: Arguments and Explorations* (Thousand Oaks, Calif.: Sage Publications, 1997), 122.

12. Christine C. Iijima Hall, "The Ethnic Identity of Racially Mixed People: A Study of Black-Japanese," Ph.D. diss., University of California, Los Angeles, 1980, 2–3.

13. Observation of students at the University of California at Los Angeles, Santa Barbara, and Santa Cruz, and public behavior at local support group meetings, as well as regional and national conferences on the topic of multiracial identity and interracial marriage; Rodney Morales, "Literature," in *Multicultural Hawai'i: The Fabric of a Multiethnic Society*, ed. Michael Haas (New York: Garland Publishing, 1998), 121.

14. Itabari Njeri, former staff writer of the *Los Angeles Times,* provided some of the most important articles on the topic of multiracial identity and intermarriage in the popular media during the late 1980s and early 1990s, although individuals in the movement often questioned her motives and her objectivity.

15. Personal communication with Paul R. Spickard, November 23, 1999; William E. Cross, Jr., *Shades of Black: Diversity in African American Identity* (Philadelphia: Temple University Press, 1991), 118–19.

16. Ibid.

17. Ibid.

18. Ibid.

19. Ibid.

20. Ibid.

21. Adler, "Beyond Cultural Identity," 23–40; Brown, "Biracial Identity and Social Marginality," 319–37.

22. Ibid.

23. Cornell and Hartmann, *Ethnicity and Race,* 82–89.

24. Spickard, *Mixed Blood,* 276–77.

25. Observation of public behavior at local support group meetings, as well as regional and national conferences on the topic of multiracial identity and interracial marriage.

26. Participant observation of attendees at founding meeting of the AMEA, November 1989.

27. Paul R. Spickard, *Mixed Blood,* 276–77.

28. Omi and Winant, *Racial Formation,* 95–98.

29. Ibid., 80–81; Winant, "Dualism at Century's End," 91–93.

30. Ibid.

31. Omi and Winant, *Racial Formation,* 96–97.

32. Ibid., 69.

33. Ibid., 101–12; Ringer and Lawless, 151–69.

34. Ringer and Lawless, 151–69.

35. Ibid.

36. Ibid.

37. "Backlash," produced by Queen of Hearts Production in association with Louisiana Broadcasting, 1991.

38. Ibid.

39. Omi and Winant, *Racial Formation,* 96.

40. Ibid.

41. "Introduction," in *Cultural Politics and Social Movements,* ed. Marcy Darnovsky, Barbara Epstein, and Richard Flacks (Philadelphia: Temple University Press, 1995), xii–xv; Hank Johnston, Enrique Laraña, and Joseph R. Gusfield, "Identities, Grievances, and Social Movements," in *New Social Movements: From Ideology to Identity,* ed. Hank Johnston, Enrique Laraña, and Joseph R. Gusfield (Philadelphia: Temple University Press, 1994), 7; Robert Alberto, "The New Social Movements: A Theoretical Approach," in *Social Science Information* 19: 199–226; Robert Alberto, "The Symbolic Challenge of Contemporary Social Movements," *Social Research* 52 (1985): 789–816; Omi and Winant, *Racial Formation,* 90.

42. Omi and Winant, *Racial Formation*, 97.

43. Observation of public behavior between 1989 and 1998 at local support group meetings, as well as regional and national conferences on the topic of multiracial identity and interracial marriage.

44. Pierre Bordieu, *Outline of a Theory Practice*, trans. Richard Nice (New York: Cambridge University Press, 1977), 159.

45. Spickard, *Mixed Blood*, 333.

46. Lieberson and Waters, *From Many Strands*, 16.

47. Mary Waters, "Multiple Ethnicities and Identity Choices: Some Implications for Race and Ethnic Relations in the United States," in *We Are a People: Narrative and Multiplicity in Ethnic Identity*, ed. Paul R. Spickard and Jeffrey Burroughs (Philadelphia: Temple University Press, 2000), 30–31.

48. Carlos Fernández, "Testimony of the Association of Multiethnic Americans before the Subcommittee on Census, Statistics and Postal Personnel of the U.S. House of Representatives, Washington, D.C." (June 30, 1993), 4; Fernández, "Government Classification of Multiracial and Multiethnic People," in *The Multiracial Experience: Racial Borders as the New Frontier*, ed. Maria P. P. Root (Thousand Oaks, Calif.: Sage Publications, 1996), 36n.12.

49. Ibid.

50. Brown and Douglass, "Making the Invisible Visible," 323–40.

51. Daniel, "Beyond Black and White," 335; Gabe Grosz, "From Sea to Shining . . . : A Current Listing of Interracial Organizations and Support Groups Across the Nation," *Interrace* 1 (1989): 24–29; Brown and Douglas, "Making the Invisible Visible," 323–40.

52. Kim Williams, personal correspondence, April 2000. Williams is a graduate in political science from Cornell University who has done extensive interviews with members of support groups across the nation for her dissertation research. This has been confirmed by my own observations of attendees at various local, regional, and national conferences between 1988 and 1998 sponsored by local and national support groups for interracial couples and multiracial-identified individuals.

53. Other organizations include My Shoes, a support group for multiracial individuals who appear phenotypically European American. Carlos A. Fernández, "Census Nonsense," *I-PRIDE (Interracial/Intercultural Pride) Newsletter* 10 (May 1988), 1–4; Carlos A. Fernández, "Testimony of the Association of Multiethnic Americans Before the Subcommittee on Census, Statistics, and Postal Personnel of the U.S. House of Representatives," in *American Mixed Race: The Culture of Microdiveristy*, ed. Naomi Zack (New York: Rowan & Littlefield, 1995), 191–210; Fernández, "Government Classification of Multiracial/Multiethnic People," in *The Multiracial Experience*, ed. Maria P. P. Root, 15–36; Brown and Douglass, "Making the Invisible Visible," 323–40; Root, "The Multiracial Experience: A Significant Frontier," xiii–xxviii; Tucker and Mitchell-Kernan, "New Trends," 209–19; participant observation of public behavior between 1989 and 1998 at local support group meetings, as well as regional and national conferences on the topic of multiracial identity and interracial marriage; Kim Williams, personal correspondence, April 2000.

Chapter Seven

1. Omi and Winant, *Racial Formation*, 55–56, 71–75.

2. William Petersen, *Ethnicity Counts* (New Brunswick, N.J.: Transaction Publishers, 1997), 51–72; Marx, "Contested Citizenship," 159–83.

3. Omi and Winant, *Racial Formation*, 77–90.

4. Ibid.

5. Ibid.

6. The Bureau of the Census, the Bureau of Labor Statistics, the National Center for Education Statistics, the Centers for Disease Control and Prevention, and the National Center for Health Statistics are among the various federal agencies that collect data on race and ethnicity. However, one of the principal driving forces in the 1970s for the development of the current standards in Directive No. 15 was the need to monitor enforcement of civil rights legislation by agencies such as the Equal Employment Opportunity Commission (EEOC), the U.S. Commission on Civil Rights, the Civil Rights Division of the Department of Justice, the Office of Federal Contract Compliance Programs in the Department of Labor, the Office for Civil Rights in the Department of Education, and the Office for Civil Rights in the Department of Health and Human Services. Agencies also use racial and ethnic data for administrating federal programs, and analyses of social, economic, and health trends for population groups. State and local governments, educational institutions, and private sector employers also use the categories when providing data on race and ethnicity to meet federal reporting requirements. Lawrence Fuchs, *American Kaleidoscope: Race, Ethnicity, and the Civic Culture* (Hanover, N.H.: University Press of New England, 1990), 405–24; Deborah A. Ramirez, "Multiracial Identity in a Color Conscious World," in *The Multiracial Experience: Racial Borders as the New Frontier*, ed. Maria P. P. Root (Thousand Oaks, Calif.: Sage Publications, 1996), 49–62.

7. Frank Parker, "Eradicating the Continuing Barriers to Effective Minority Voter Participation," in *From Exclusion to Inclusion: The Long Struggle for African American Political Power*, ed. Ralph C. Gomes and Linda Faye Williams (Westport, Conn.: Praeger, 1995), 73–83; Walter Hill, "Redistricting in the 1990s: Opportunities and Risks for African Americans," in *From Exclusion to Inclusion: The Long Struggle for African American Political Power*, ed. Ralph C. Gomes and Linda Faye Williams (Westport, Conn.: Praeger, 1995), 164–171; Omi and Winant, *Racial Formation*, 74; Fuchs, *American Kaleidoscope*, 425–43; OMB, *Federal Register* (July 9, 1997), 36884, 36909.

8. OMB, *Federal Register* (July 9, 1997), 36884.

9. Ibid., 36876–77.

10. Ira Lowry, "The Science and Politics of Ethnic Relations," paper presented at the annual meeting of the American Association for the Advancement of Science in San Francisco (January 3–8, 1980), 1–25; OMB, *Federal Register* (July 9, 1997), 36879.

11. Lee, "Racial Classification in the U.S. Census: 1890–1990," 75–94.

12. Fernández, "Testimony of the Association of Multiethnic Americans," 191–210; Fernández, "Government Classification," 15–36.

13. Lowry, "The Science and Politics of Ethnic Relations," 15; Ramona Douglass, "Socio-Political Consequences of Racial Classification in the U.S.," *Interracial/Intercultural Connection:*

The Newsletter of the Biracial Family Network (November/December 1985), 1–3; Elizabeth Radcliffe, "Round One Lost," *The Communiqué: Newspaper of the Interracial Family Alliance* (Fall 1988): 1–2; Evelyn Thompson, "From the Editor," *Spectrum: The Newsletter of Multiracial Americans of Southern California* (May 1988): 1, 4; Fernández, "Testimony of the Association of Multiethnic Americans," 191–210; Fernández, "Government Classification," 15–36; Lee, "Racial Classification in the U.S. Census," 75–94.

14. John G. Brown, president of Interracial Family Circle, Atlanta, Georgia; correspondence with Multiracial Americans of Southern California (MASC), Los Angeles, March 26, 1988; Thompson, "From the Editor," 1, 4; Njeri, "A Sense of Identity," *Los Angeles Times* (June 5, 1988), F1, F8–F9; Douglass, "Socio-Political Consequences," 1–3; Radcliffe, "Round One Lost," 1–2; Yemi Tourér, "Census Bureau Stopped," *Challenger* (August 31, 1988): 31.

15. Lieberson and Waters, *From Many Strands*, 16, 46, 48.

16. F. Finley McRae, "Watson Fears Use of 'Mixed Race' on Census Forms," *Los Angeles Sentinel* (September 22, 1988), A12; Trudy S. Moore, "Black Lawmakers Oppose Michigan Bill That Makes New Multiracial Class," *Jet* 88 (June 1995): 46; Tom Morganthau, Susan Miller, Gregory Beals and Regina Elam, "What Color Is Black?" *Newsweek* (February 13, 1993), 63–65.

17. Douglass, "Socio-Political Consequences," 1–3; Radcliffe, "Round One Lost," 1–2; Lowry, "The Science and Politics of Ethnic Relations," 15; Thompson, "From the Editor," 1, 4.

18. "Backlash," Louisiana Broadcasting, 1991.

19. McRae, "Watson Fears Use of 'Mixed Race.'"

20. OMB, *Federal Register* (July 9, 1997), 36880.

21. Observation of public behavior at founding meeting of the AMEA, November 12, 1988.

22. Fernández, "Testimony of the Association of Multiethnic Americans," 191–210; House Subcommittee, Testimony by Carlos Fernández (June 30, 1993), 130.

23. Observation of public behavior at founding meeting of the AMEA, November 12, 1988, at Multiracial Americans of Southern California (MASC) general meetings in Los Angeles, and Kaleidoscope, the annual conference sponsored by MASC in fall 1988, 1989, 1990.

24. Susan Graham, "The Real World," in *The Multiracial Experience: Racial Borders as the New Frontier,* ed. Maria P. P. Root (Thousand Oaks, Calif.: Sage Publications, 1996), 37–48; Kathleen Rand Reed, president of Necronomics, personal correspondence with J. Eugene Grigsby, III, Director of UCLA Center for Afro-American Studies, October 9, 1993; Personal communication with Kathleen Rand Reed, November 12, 1993; personal communication with Susan Graham, executive director of Project RACE, December 16, 1993.

25. Ibid.

26. Ibid.

27. Of course, this would not preclude adding a "Hispanic" or "Latino" category to the race question to allow individuals to identify themselves as both "Hispanic" and "non-Hispanic" (e.g., for persons identifying themselves as part Latino and part African American or European American).

28. Observation of public behavior at founding meeting of the AMEA, November 12, 1988, and Kaleidoscope, the annual conference sponsored by MASC in fall 1988, 1989, 1990.

29. Ibid.

30. Steven Cheney-Rice, "Kaleidoscope: Annual Conference of MASC (Multiracial Americans of Southern California)," *Spectrum: Newsletter of Multiracial Americans of Southern California* 1 (November–December 1988), 1-7; Douglass, "Socio-Political Consequences of Racial Classification," 1–3; Itabari Njeri, "A Sense of Identity," F1, F8–F9; Njeri, "Call for Census Category Creates Interracial Debate," *Los Angeles Times*, January 13, 1991, E1, E9–E11.

31. Nancy Brown, President of MASC, personal correspondence, September 20, 1989; Carlos Fernández, president of AMEA, personal correspondence, November 10, 1989.

32. Pat Edwards, Interracial Family Circle (IFC), Washington, D.C., personal correspondence with Ms. Edna Paisano, Acting Chief, Racial Statistics Branch, Population Division, Bureau of the Census, November 27, 1989; Pat Edwards, IFC, personal correspondence with MASC, November 28, 1989, and December 18, 1989; Nampeo R. McKenney, Assistant Division Chief, Special Population Statistics, Population Division, U.S. Census Bureau; correspondence with Ms. Darlene Y. Willoth, Interracial Family Circle, Atlanta, Georgia, December 18, 1989.

33. Pat Edwards, "Open Forum," *Interrace Magazine* (March/April 1989): 20.

34. Maria P. P. Root, "The Multiracial Experience: The Borders as the New Frontier," keynote address at the third annual Students of Mixed Heritage statewide conference, University of California, Santa Cruz, April 29–30, 1995.

35. Lee, "Racial Classification in the U.S. Census," 75–94.

36. Fernández, "Testimony of the Association of Multiethnic Americans," 191–210.

37. Lee, "Racial Classification in the U.S. Census," 75–94. Evaluations of the results from the 1980 Census, the 1980 Current Population Survey, the 1990 Census, the 1990 Panel Study of Income Dynamics, and the 1991 Current Population Survey have shown that approximately 40 percent of Latinos select the "other" category, although the use of this category varies by group and geographical region, OMB, *Federal Register* (July 9, 1997), 36911.

38. Morganthau et al., "What Color Is Black?" 63–65; Thomas Skidmore, "Bi-Racial U.S.A. vs. Multi-racial Brazil: Is the Contrast Still Valid?" *Journal of Latin American Studies* 25 (1993): 383–86.

39. Review of Federal Measurements of Race and Ethnicity, Hearings Before the Subcommittee on Census, Statistics and Postal Personnel of the Committee on Post Office and Civil Service House of Representatives, 103rd Congress, First Session, April 14, June 30, July 29, November 3, 1993. (Washington, D.C.: U.S. Government Printing Office, 1994), 10, 25, 32, 40; U.S. Bureau of the Census: Census of 1990; U.S. Bureau of the Census: Census of 1970, 1980; U.S. Bureau of the Census: Census of 1990; U.S. Bureau of the Census: Census of 1970, 1980, 1990; U.S. Bureau of the Census: Census of 1970, 1980; U.S. Bureau of the Census: Census of 1990; OMB, *Federal Register* (July 9, 1997), 36909–13.

40. Morganthau et al., "What Color Is Black?" 63–65; Skidmore, "Bi-Racial U.S.A.," 383–86.

41. OMB, *Federal Register* (July 9, 1997), 36909–13.

42. Jonathan Tilove, Newhouse News Service, July 3, 1991; MSNBC News, "Talking about Race, National Identity"; Roberto Rodriguez and Patricia Gonzales, "Census Bureau Paints the U.S. White," *Chronicle Features*, January 14, 1996.

43. Clara E. Rodriguez, *Puerto Ricans Born in the U.S.A* (Boston: Unwin Hyman, 1989), 49–84; Clara E. Rodriguez, *Changing Race: Latinos, the Census, and the History of Ethnicity in the United States* (New York: New York University Press, 2000), 3–26, 129–52.

44. Review of Federal Measurements of Race and Ethnicity, 1994; Karen E. Downing, "1990 Census Statistics 'Other' Category," Multiracial/Multicultural Group of the University of Michigan, October 1992; Barbara Vobeja, "Categorizing the Nation's Millions of 'Other Race,'" *Washington Post* (April 29, 1991), A9.

45. U.S. Bureau of the Census: Census of 1990.

46. U.S. Bureau of the Census: Census of 1970, 1980.

47. U.S. Bureau of the Census: Census of 1990.

48. U.S. Bureau of the Census: Census of 1970, 1980, 1990.

49. Ibid.

50. Louis H. Metoyer, "Creoles Stand Up," *Bayou Talk: A Cajun Creole Community Newspaper* 4 (March 1990): 2.

51. Ibid.

52. U.S. Bureau of the Census: Census of 1970, 1980, 1990.

53. G. Reginald Daniel, "The Census and the Numbers Racket," *Interrace Magazine* 2 (1991): 20; personal communication with Chris Ashe and Susan Graham, co-founders of Project RACE, September 10, 1991.

54. Ibid.

55. Carlos A. Fernández, "AMEA Proposed Revised Minimum Reporting Standards with Multiracial Multiethnic Categories," in *American Mixed Race: The Culture of Microdiversity,* ed. Naomi Zack (New York: Rowan and Littlefield, 1995), 210.

56. House Subcommittee on Census, Statistics, and Postal Personnel, Committee on Post Office and Civil Service, *Hearings on the Review of Federal Measurements of Race and Ethnicity,* testimony by Carlos Fernández (June 30, 1993), 130.

57. African Americans were the first and remained the most vocal community to express concerns about this multigenerational definition of the term "multiracial." However, it would have a similar impact on Latinos, Native Americans, and various other communities in the United States that have a long history of miscegenation, particularly with European Americans.

58. Personal communication with Susan Graham, January 28, 1992.

59. House Subcommittee on Census, Statistics, and Postal Personnel, Committee on Post Office and Civil Service, *Hearings on the Review of Federal Measurements of Race and Ethnicity,* testimony by Susan Graham (June 30, 1993), 115.

60. Personal communication with Susan Graham, May 19, 1992.

61. Ramona Douglass (AMEA) and Susan Graham (Project RACE) to Katherine Wallman (Office of Regulatory Affairs, OMB), September 29, 1995; House Subcommittee on Census, Statistics, and Postal Personnel, Committee on Post Office and Civil Service, *Hearings on the Review of Federal Measurements of Race and Ethnicity,* testimony by Susan Graham (June 30, 1993), 115.

62. G. Reginald Daniel, personal communication with Susan Graham and Carlos Fernández, October 22, 1992, November 11, 1992, November 18, 1992.

63. One such lawsuit was filed against the OMB by Loretta Edwards—the mother of two biracial children—with the support of Project RACE. Personal correspondence with Susan Graham, December 1, 1995.

64. Susan Graham, Project RACE, personal communications, March 5, 1992; March 15, 1995; April 3, 1995; May 10, 1995; Graham, "Grassroots Advocacy," 185–90; Graham, "The Real World," 185–90.

65. Ibid.

66. OMB, *Federal Register* (July 9, 1997), 36903.

67. These states have enacted the following legislation: Ohio Am. Sub. H.B. No. 154, effective 1992, Governor Voinovich; Illinois Senate Bill No. 421, effective January 1, 1996, Governor Edgar; Georgia Senate Bill 149, effective July 1, 1994, Governor Miller (this legislation covers all school forms, state agency forms, employment forms, and applications); Indiana House Enrolled Act No. 1592, effective July 1, 1995, Governor Bayh; Michigan House Bills 5399 and 5400, 1995, Governor Engler. The following states have adopted the multiracial identifier by administrative mandate: North Carolina (accepted by the State Department of Education on October 1, 1994); Florida (accepted by the State Department of Education in August 1995). The following states introduced legislation in 1997: Minnesota Senate File #449 (introduced by Senator Don Betzold on February 10); Texas SB851 (sponsored by Senator Rodney Ellis). Project RACE members worked with the Maryland Task Force on Multiracial Designations to make this change. This legislation allows respondents to choose more than one racial category and includes instructions that multiracial respondents may select all applicable categories.

68. UCLA School of Education Survey, 1991; Anim Steel, Williams College, Williamstown, Massachusetts, personal communication, May 1995; Center for the Assessment of Demographic Studies, Gallaudet University, Washington, D.C., Annual Survey, 1989.

69. Review of Federal Measurements of Race and Ethnicity, 1994.

70. Ibid., 28. A similar policy for classifying the offspring of interracial unions has been used for census purposes. In 1970 they were assigned the father's racial identity; since 1980, they have been assigned the mothers identity. See Lee, "Governmental Classification," 75–94.

71. Susan Graham, personal communication, June 5, 1996; Ramona Douglass, personal correspondence, February 21, 1997.

72. Although the leadership of the AMEA and Project RACE would support the combined format at the federal level, recent data collected by Kim Williams, a graduate in political science from Cornell, indicate that 36.7 percent of the leadership of various support groups preferred the integrative format and 40 percent the stand-alone multiracial identifier. See Kim Williams, personal correspondence, April 2000.

73. Graham, "The Real World," 44–45.

74. Observation of public behavior at Third Multiracial Leadership Summit, June 7, 1997, Oakland, California.

75. Ibid.

76. Previously Susan Graham had experimented on several talk shows, where she used the wording "if you identify as multiracial," as well as "if you consider yourself multiracial." Listeners and viewers were less supportive of the former formulation, which explains in part the wording in the summit proposal. Susan Graham, personal communication, May 5, 1997.

77. One of the reasons for doing this was to gain the support of representatives of the Hapa Issues Forum who preferred the term "mixed-race" to "multiracial."

78. Third Multiracial Leadership Summit, June 7, 1997, Statement and Attachment C Model for OMB Statistical Directive 15.

79. Ramona Douglass, personal correspondence with Greg Mayeda, president of Hapa Issues Forum, June 16, 1997.

80. Ramona Douglass, personal communication, July 11, June 25, 1997.

81. Ramona Douglass, "Endorsements of the Multiracial Leadership Summit, *Interracial Voice* (June 21, 1997); Nathan Douglas, "I Solemnly Swear," *Interracial Voice* (May 1997); Nathan Douglas, "Leaving The Scene Of A Crime" and "What We're Up Against," *Interracial Voice* (March–April 1998); Charles Byrd, "The Political Color Continuum," *Interracial Voice* (July–August 1997); Charles Byrd, "Leftist Socialism or Multiracial Libertarianism," *Interracial Voice* (November–December 1997); Charles Byrd, "Our Community's Two Choices?," *Interracial Voice* (November–December 1997); <www.webcom.com/intvoice>; Charles Byrd, "*Interracial Voice* will not oppose or support," letter from Charles Michael Byrd, editor of *Interracial Voice*, to multiracial community (June 18, 1997).

82. Susan Graham, communication to multiracial community, June 14, 1997.

83. Observation of public behavior at Third Multiracial Leadership Summit, June 7, 1997, Oakland, California.

84. Ibid.

85. Susan Graham, personal communication, May 25, 1997.

86. OMB, *Federal Register* (July 9, 1997), 36937–43.

87. Ibid., 36906–7.

88. Ibid.

89. Ibid.

90. Ibid.

91. Ibid.

92. Ibid.

93. Ibid.

94. Ibid., 36885.

95. Ibid., 36906–7.

96. Ibid.

97. Personal correspondence with Ramona Douglass, June 19, 1997.

98. Kristina Falkerstein-Jordan, "Clinton Needs to Hear from You," *Spectrum: The Newsletter of Multiracial Americans of Southern California* (June 1995): 4.

99. Susan Graham, "Newt Said It," (January 7, 1997); "From the Speaker," (July 1, 1997); "The Speaker Says," (July 19, 1997); "Newt Confirms," (July 15, 1997), all found on the "Hot News" feature on Project RACE's web site at <www.projectrace.com>.

100. Eun-Kyung Kim, "Gingrich against Affirmative Action," *Associated Press* (June 6, 1997).

101. Charles Byrd, "The Speaker's Apparent Endorsement of a Multiracial Classification," *Interracial Voice* (June 20, 1997); letter from Speaker of the U.S. House of Representatives to Franklin D. Raines, director of the OMB, July 1, 1997.

102. Dinesh D'Sousa, "The One-Drop-of-Blood-Rule," *Forbes Today* (December 2, 1996); George Will, "Census: Should the 'Other' Category Be Expanded?" *Washington Post*, October 5, 1997.

103. Observation of public behavior at Third Multiracial Leadership Summit, June 7, 1997. Indeed, one segment of the movement, represented in the Multiracial Leadership Forum in Washington, D.C., publicly came out in support of this agenda.

104. Personal communication with Ramona Douglass, July 21 1997; House Subcommittee on Government Management, Information, and Technology, Committee on Gov-

ernment Reform and Oversight, Hearings on Federal Measures of Race and Ethnicity and the Implications for the 2000 Census, testimony by Harold S. McDougall, May 22, July 25, 1997. McDougall was eventually appointed as the NAACP representative on the Census 2000 Advisory Committee delegated with the task of making recommendations concerning tabulations. His resignation from that position left a serious void in the discussions.

105. "The Color Code," *MSNBC Evening News*, July 10, 1997.

106. OMB, *Federal Register* (October 30, 1997), 58784.

107. Charles Michael Byrd, "OMB's Preliminary Recommendations and an IV Commentary," July 12, 1997; "Leftist Socialism or Multiracial Libertarianism," *Interracial Voice* (November–December 1997); "Compensation's Secret," *Interracial Voice* (December 26, 1998); "Census 2000 Protest: Check American Indian," *Interracial Voice* (January 7, 1998); "Government Officially Nixes Multiracial Category," *Interracial Voice* (December 30, 1997).

108. Among those individuals present at this meeting were Charles Byrd of *Interracial Voice*, James Landrith of the *Multiracial Activist*, Ward Connerly, UC Regent and founder of the American Civil Rights Institute, and Steve and Ruth White of *A Place for Us*. Charles Michael Byrd, "From the Editor—The Political Realignment: A *Jihad* against 'Race'-consciousness," *Interracial Voice* (September–October 2000); Ward Connerly, "*Loving* America," *Interracial Voice* (September–October 2000); Herbert A. Sample, "Connerly Joins Foes of 'Silly' Queries on Census Forms: He Weighs Ballot Drive to Limit Race Data," *Bee Washington Bureau* (April 1, 2000).

109. Susan Graham, "From the Executive Director," (October 29, 1997); "Advocates to Continue to Fight For Multiracial Classification," (July 25, 1997); "The Illegitimate Birth of 'Multiple Race People,'" (January 5, 1998); "You Call This a Race Commission," (January 5, 1998); Susan Graham and James Landrith, "Blood Pressure," *Project RACE Website* (April 21, 1999); Nathan Douglas, "I Solemnly Swear," *Interracial Voice* (May 22, 1997); "Leaving the Scene of a Crime," *Interracial Voice* (July 12, 1997); "What We're Up Against," *Interracial* Voice (May–June 1998); "The Kinky Hair Machine," *Project RACE Website* (January 5, 1998).

110. Ramona Douglass, personal communication, June 19, 1997.

111. Ibid.

112. Ramona Douglass, personal communication, September 26, September 27, September 30, and October 1, 1997.

113. If an individual of African American and European American backgrounds checked "black" and "white" on her employment application, she would be counted as black for tabulation purposes, since it is the largest non-white group marked. If her supervisor discriminated against the employee based on her race, and if she tried to file a claim with the EEOC as a multiracial individual, she would have no grounds because she was classified as black rather than multiracial.

114. OMB, Tabulation Working Group Interagency Committee for the Review of Standards for Data on Race and Ethnicity, "Draft Provisional Guidance on the Implementation of the 1997 Standards for Federal Data on Race and Ethnicity," 41–51.

115. Ibid.

116. Ibid.

117. OMB, *Federal Register* (July 9, 1997), 36906. Preliminary data from the 2000 Census released in March 2001 indicate that nearly 7 million people, or about 2 percent of the

U.S. population, identified with more than one race. This figure is somewhat higher than expected, but the number of people who identified with more than one racial group is still minuscule in comparison to the number who identified with only one racial group.

118. Ibid.

119. Ibid.

120. OMB, *Federal Register* (October 30, 1997), 58782–88.

121. "Draft Provisional Guidance on the Implementation of the 1997 Standards for Federal Data on Race and Ethnicity," 41–51.

122. OMB, *Federal Register* (October 30, 1997), 58782–88.

123. OMB, *Guidance on Aggregation and Allocation of Data on Race for Use in Civil Rights Monitoring and Enforcement*, OMB Bulletin no. 00-02, March 9, 2000.

124. There are at least four areas in which further exploration is needed. Equal employment opportunity and other antidiscrimination programs have traditionally provided the number of people in the population by selected characteristics, including racial categories, for business, academic, and government organizations to use in evaluating conformance with program objectives. Because of the potentially large number of categories that may result from application of the new standards, many with very small numbers, it is not clear how this need for data will be satisfied in the future. The number of people in distinct groups based on decennial census results are used in developing sample designs and survey controls for major demographic surveys. For example, the National Health Interview Survey uses census data to increase samples for certain population groups, adjust for survey non-response, and provide weights for estimating health outcomes at the national level. The impact of having data for many small population groups with a multiple racial identity must be explored. Vital statistics data include birth and death rates for various population groups. Typically the numerator (number of births or deaths) is derived from administrative records, while the denominator comes from intercensal population estimates. Birth certificate data on race are likely to have been self-reported by the mother. Over time, these data may become comparable to data collected under the new standards. An observer, such as a mortician, physician, or funeral director, however, frequently fills out death certificate data. These data, particularly for the multiracial-identified population, are likely to be quite different from the information obtained when respondents report about themselves. Research to define comparable categories to be used in both numerators and denominators is needed to assure that vital statistics are as accurate and useful as possible. More generally, statistical indicators are often used to measure change over time. Procedures that will permit meaningful comparisons of data collected under the previous standards with those that will be collected under the new standards need to be developed.

125. OMB, *Federal Register* (October 30, 1997), 58782–88.

Chapter Eight

1. Michael Hughes and Bradley R. Hertel, "The Significance of Color Remains: A Study of Life Chances, Mate Selection, and Ethnic Consciousness Among Black Americans," *Social Forces* 68 (1990): 1105–20; Verna M. Keith and Cedric Herring, "Skin Tone and Stratification in the Black Community," *American Journal of Sociology* 97 (1991), 760–78. The sample for

the National Survey of Black Americans (NSBA) was drawn according to a multistage-area probability procedure designed to ensure that every African American household in the United States had an equal probability of being selected for the study. Within each household in the sample, one person aged eighteen or older was randomly selected to be interviewed from among those eligible for the study. Only self-identified African Americans who were also United States citizens were eligible. Trained African American interviewers, yielding a sample of 2,107 respondents, carried out face-to-face interviews. The response rate was approximately 69 percent. For the most part, the NSBA is representative of the national African American population enumerated in the 1980 census, with the exception of a slight overrepresentation of females and older blacks and a small underrepresentation of southerners. James S. Jackson and Gerald Gurin, *National Survey of Black Americans 1979–1980* (Ann Arbor: Institute of Social Research, 1987).

2. Hughes and Hertel, "The Significance of Color," 1105–20.

3. James H. Johnson, Jr. and Walter C. Farrell, Jr., "Race Still Matters," *Chronicle of Higher Education* (July 7, 1995): A48.

4. Hughes and Hertel, "The Significance of Color," 1116.

5. Ibid., 1116–18; Keith and Herring, "Skin Tone and Stratification," 765; Anne S. Tsui, Terri D. Egan, and Charles A. O'Reilly III, "Being Different: Relational Demography and Organizational Attachment," *Administrative Science Quarterly* 37 (1992): 549–79. Sue Shellenbarger, "Work-force Study Finds Loyalty Is Weak, Divisions of Race and Gender Are Deep," *Wall Street Journal*, September 3, 1993, B1.

6. David K. Shipler, *A Country of Strangers: Black and White in America* (New York, Knopf, 1997), 240–41.

7. Tsui, Egan, and O'Reilly III, "Being Different: Relational Demography and Organizational Attachemnt," 549–79; Shellenbarger, "Work-force Study Finds Loyalty Is Weak, Divisions of Race and Gender Are Deep," B1. Russell, Wilson, and Hall, *The Color Complex*, 127–28. A policy of selecting lighter-skinned African-descent Americans can be seen in other sectors of the public sphere, as was the case with the integration of the faculties of previously all-white public schools in places such as Louisville, Kentucky, in the 1960s.

8. Russell, Wilson, and Hall, *The Color Complex*, 36–37; ABC *Nightline*, "Light and Dark," February 28, 1997.

9. Ibid., 37–38; Ronald E. Hall, "The Color Complex: The Bleaching Syndrome," *Race, Class, and Gender* 2 (winter 1995): 103.

10. Russell, Wilson, and Hall, *The Color Complex*, 37–38; Joleen Kirschenman and Kathryn M. Neckerman, "We'd Love to Hire Them, But . . . : The Meaning of Race for Employers," in *The Urban Underclass*, ed. C. Jencks and P. E. Peterson. (Washington, D.C.: Brookings Institute Press, 1991), 203–34. This was most vividly displayed in the darkening of O. J. Simpson's skin on the cover of *Time* magazine during his trial for the murder of his former wife Nicole Brown Simpson and her friend Ron Goldman.

11. C. Vontress, "Counseling Black," *Personal Guidance Journal* 48: 713–19; Russell, Wilson, and Hall, *The Color Complex*, 38; Hall, "The Color Complex" 103.

12. Itabari Njeri, "Colorism: In American Society Are Light-Skinned Blacks Better Off? *Los Angeles Times*, April 24, 1988, F1, F10, F12–F13, Russell, Wilson, and Hall, *The Color Complex*, 134–62.

13. ABC *Nightline*, "Light and Dark."

14. Russell, Wilson, and Hall, *The Color Complex*, 134–62.

15. *Nightline*, "Light and Dark,"; Frank Deford, *There She Is: The Life and Times of Miss America* (New York: Viking, 1971), 249; duCille, *Skin Trade*, 27–28; Sarah Banet-Weiser, *The Most Beautiful Girl in the World: Beauty Pageants and National Identity* (Berkeley: University of California Press, 1999), 123–52.

16. duCille, *Skin Trade*, 27–28; Banet-Weiser, *The Most Beautiful Girl in the World* 123–52.

17. duCille, *Skin Trade*, 27–28.

18. Graham, *Our Kind of People*, 393; Margo Okazawa-Rey, Tracy Robinson, and Janie V. Ward, "Black Women and the Politics of Skin Color and Hair," in *Women, Power, and Therapy*, ed. Marjorie Braude (New York: Haworth Press, 1987), 91–92; Michel Marriott, "Colorstruck," *Essence* (November 1991), 93.

19. West and Fenstermaker, 13–16, 19, 31–33; Peggy McIntosh, "White Privilege and Male Privilege: A Personal Account of Coming to See Correspondence through Work in Women Studies," in *Race, Class, and Gender: An Anthology*, ed. Margaret Anderson and Patricia Hill Collins (Belmont, Calif.: Wadsworth, 1992), 70–73; Feagin and Feagin, *Racial and Ethnic Relations*, 53–54.

20. Denise Segura, "Chicanas and Triple Oppression in the Labor Force," in *Chicana Voices: Intersections of Class, Race, and Gender*, ed. Teresa Córdova et al. (Austin: Center for Mexican American Studies, 1986), 48; Patricia Hill Collins, *Black Feminist Thought: Knowledge, Consciousness, and the Politics of Empowerment* (Boston: Unwin Hyman, 1990), 40–48; Russell, Wilson, and Hall, *The Color Complex*, 39, 131.

21. Russell, Wilson, and Hall, *The Color Complex*, 39, 131.

22. Ibid.

23. Milton Yinger, "Toward a Theory of Assimilation and Dissimilation," *Ethnic and Racial Studies* 4 (3): 249–63.

24. Thomas D. Boston, *Race, Class and Conservatism* (Boston: Unwin Hyman, 1988), 1–53; Richard Lacayo, "Between Two Worlds: The Black Middle Class Has Everything the White Middle Class Has, Except a Feeling That It Really Fits In," *Newsweek* (March 13, 1989), 58–68; Stephen Small, *Racialized Barriers: The Black Experience in the United States and England in the 1980s* (New York: Routledge, 1994), 50–51, 117–27; Isabel Wilkerson, "Middle-Class Blacks Try to Grip a Ladder While Lending a Hand," in *Race, Class, and Gender: An Integrated Study*, 4th ed. (New York: St. Martins Press, 1998), 226.

25. In several books, notably *Race and Economics* (1975), *The Economics and Politics of Race* (1982), and *Civil Rights: Rhetoric or Reality?* (1984), African American economist Thomas Sowell contends that a free market can eliminate racial discrimination if the market is truly free or uncontrolled and educational opportunities are reasonably equal for all groups. African American sociologist William Julius Wilson, in his two books entitled *The Declining Significance of Race* (1978, 1980) and *The Truly Disadvantaged* (1987), makes a similar argument. It should be pointed out, however, that when Wilson speaks of the declining significance of race, he is neither ignoring the legacy of previous racial discrimination nor suggesting that racial discrimination no longer exists. Rather, his central argument is that there has been a change in the "relative role" that race plays in determining African American life chances in the modern industrial period, as reflected in the changing impact of race in the economic

sector—and, in particular, the changing importance of race versus class for social mobility—that has led to the increasing significance of class. See Small, *The Black Experience*, 117–27.

26. Reynold Farley and Walter Allen, *The Color Line and the Quality of Life in America* (New York: Russell Sage Foundation, 1987), 209–361; William Julius Wilson, *The Declining Significance of Race*, 2d ed. (Chicago: University of Chicago Press, 1980), 19–23, 122–54, 167–79; Thomas W. Sowell, *Civil Rights: Rhetoric or Reality?* (New York: William Morrow, 1984), 76–77, 139; Joe Feagin and Melvin P. Sikes, *Living with Racism: The Black Middle-Class Experience* (Boston: Beacon Press, 1994), 26–28.

27. Wilson, *The Declining Significance of Race*, 19–23, 122–54; William Julius Wilson, *The Truly Disadvantaged: The Inner City, the Underclass, and Public Policy* (Chicago: University of Chicago Press, 1987), 3–19; Sowell, *Civil Rights: Rhetoric or Reality*, 76–77, 139.

28. Kovel, *White Racism*, xi, xxix, xxx–xxxiii, liv–lv, 211–30, 234, 247.

29. Daniel, "Beyond Black and White," 333–41; Boston, *Race, Class, and Conservatism*, 8, 41–53; Omi and Winant, *Racial Formation*, 113–36; Howard Winant, *Racial Conditions: Politics, Theory, Comparisons* (Minneapolis: University of Minnesota Press, 1994), 62–64, 166.

30. Boston, *Race, Class, and Conservatism*, 8, 41–53; Lacayo, "Between Two Worlds," 58–68.

31. Farley and Allen, *The Color Line and the Quality of Life in America*, 209–361; Andrew Hacker, *Two Nations: Black and White, Separate, Hostile, Unequal* (New York: Charles Scribner's, 1992), 93–133; Landry, *The New Black Middle Class*, 78–93; Benjamin R. Ringer and Elinor R. Lawless, *Race-Ethnicity and Society* (New York: Routledge, Chapman, and Hall, 1989), 168–69; Wilson, *The Declining Significance of Race*, 122–54; Wilson, *The Truly Disadvantaged*, 3–19; Dalton Conley, *Being Black, Living in the Red* (Berkeley: University of California Press, 1999), 11.

32. Jennifer L. Hochschild, *Facing Up to the American Dream: Race, Class, and the Soul of the Nation* (Princeton: Princeton University Press, 1995), 39–43.

33. Ibid.; Martin Carnoy, *Faded Dreams: The Politics and Economics of Race in America* (New York: Cambridge University Press, 1994), 13–21.

34. Lawrence Bobo, James R. Kluegel, and Ryan A. Smith, "Laissez-Faire Racism: The Crystallization of a 'Kindler, Gentler' Anti-Black Ideology," in *Racial Attitudes in the 1990s: Continuity and Change*, ed. Steven A. Tuch and Jack K. Martin (Westport, Conn.: Praeger), 18; Daniel T. Lichter, "Racial Difference in Underemployment in American Cities," *American Journal of Sociology* 93 (1988): 771–92.

35. Bobo, Kluegel, and Smith, "Laissez-Faire Racism," 18.

36. Julianne Malveaux, *Wall Street, Main Street, and the Side Street: A Mad Economist Takes A Stroll* (Los Angeles: Pines One Publications, 1999), xiii–xv.

37. Bobo, Kluegel, and Smith, "Laissez-Faire Racism," 18; Roger Waldinger and Tom Bailey, "The Continuing Significance of Race: Racial Conflict and Racial Discrimination in Construction," *Politics and Society* 19 (1991): 291–323.

38. Bobo, Kluegel, and Smith, "Laissez-Faire Racism," 18; Melvin L. Oliver and Thomas M. Shapiro, *Black Wealth, White Wealth: A New Perspective on Racial Inequality* (New York: Routledge, 1995), ix–52; Conley, *Being Black, Living in the Red*, 1–13; Feagin and Feagin, *Racial and Ethnic Relations*, 256–57.

39. Bobo, Kluegel, and Smith, "Laissez-Faire Racism," 18.

40. Paul Starr, "Civil Reconstruction: What to Do without Affirmative Action," *American Prospect* (winter 1992): 7–16.

41. Feagin and Feagin, *Racial and Ethnic Relations*, 256–57.

42. Bobo, Kluegel, and Smith, "Laissez-Faire Racism," 18; Douglas S. Massey and Nancy A. Denton, *American Apartheid: Segregation and the Making of the Underclass* (Cambridge: Harvard University Press, 1993), 1–10, 74–78, 81, 83, 144, 148.

43. Massey and Denton, *American Apartheid*, 9, 73, 85–87, 144; Reynolds Farley and William H. Frey, "Changes in the Segregation of Whites from Blacks during the 1980s: Small Steps toward a More Integrated Society," *American Sociological Review* 59 (1992): 23–25; Nancy A. Denton, "Are African Americans Still Hypersegregated in 1990?" in *Residential Apartheid: The American Legacy*, ed. R. Bullard, C. Lee, and J. E. Grigsby (Los Angeles: UCLA Center for African American Studies, 1994), 49–81; Farley and Allen, *The Color Line and the Quality of Life in America*, 146–50.

44. Leonard Steinhorn and Barbara Diggs-Brown, *By the Color of Our Skin: The Illusion of Integration and the Reality of Race* (New York: Dutton, 1999), 36–37; Joe T. Darden, "African American Residential Segregation: An Examination of Race and Class in Metropolitan Detroit," in *Residential Apartheid*, 85–90; Feagin and Sikes, *Living with Racism*, 243–48, 264–71.

45. Bobo, Kluegel, and Smith, "Laissez-Faire Racism," 19.

46. Douglass Massey, A. B. Gross, and M. L. Eggers, "Segregation, the Concentration of Poverty, and the Life Chances of Individuals," *Social Science Research* 20 (1991): 397–420; Massey and Denton, *American Apartheid*, 1–10, 74–78, 83–87, 144, 148; Feagin and Sikes, *Living with Racism*, 249–52; Farley and Frey, "Changes in the Segregation of Whites from Blacks," 23–25; Nancy A. Denton, "Are African Americans Still Hypersegregated," 49–81; Farley and Allen, *The Color Line and the Quality of Life in America*, 146–50; Bobo, Kluegel, and Smith, "Laissez-Faire Racism," 18; Margery Austin Turner, "Discrimination in Urban Housing Markets: Lessons from Fair Housing Audits," *Housing Policy Debates* 3 (1992): 185–215; William E. Jackson, "Discrimination in Mortgage Lending Markets as Rational Economic Behavior: Theory, Evidence, and Public Policy," in *African Americans and the New Policy Consensus: Retreat of the Liberal State?* ed. M. E. Lashley and M. N. Jackson (Westport, Conn.: Greenwood Press, 1994), 157–78.

47. Bobo, Kluegel, and Smith, "Laissez-Faire Racism," 19; Douglas S. Massey and Zoltan L. Hajnal, "The Changing Geographic Structure of Black-White Segregation in the United States," *Social Science Quarterly* 76 (1995): 527–42.

48. Hacker, *Two Nations*, ix; Steinhorn and Diggs-Brown, *By The Color of Our Skin*, 3–28.

49. Steinhorn and Diggs-Brown, *By the Color of Our Skin*, 143–53, 176.

50. Ibid., 222–41.

51. Farley and Allen, *The Color Line*, 408–19; Johnson and Farrell, "Race Still Matters," A48; Boston, *Race, Class, and Conservatism*, 158–59.

52. Omi and Winant, *Racial Formation*, 109–36; Feagin and Feagin, *Racial and Ethnic Relations*, 253–54, 262, 266–67; Charles T. Banner-Haley, *The Fruits of Integration: Black Middle-Class Ideology and Culture, 1969–1990* (Jackson: University of Mississippi Press, 1994), 46–47, 54, 68.

53. Omi and Winant, *Racial Formation*, 28, 73, 116, 128.

54. This was most vividly borne out in the March 1988 *Newsweek* special report entitled "Black and White: How Integrated is America?" which cited only 29 percent of European

Americans as believing that the federal government has not done enough to aid African Americans, while 71 percent of African Americans had this same belief. More important, 53 percent of European Americans believed that affirmative action programs had in fact gone too far in their attempts to equalize the scales by giving less qualified racial minorities priority over more qualified European Americans. David Gelman, Karen Springen, Karen Brailsford, and Mark Miller, "Black and White in America," *Newsweek* (March 7, 1988), 18–23.

55. Small, *The Black Experience*, 117–27; Boston, *Race, Class and Conservatism*, 54–92; Feagin and Sikes, *Living with Racism*, 12–26; Thomas Sowell, *Civil Rights: Rhetoric or Reality?* (New York: William Morrow, 1984), 76–77, 139; Wilson, *The Declining Significance of Race*, 19–23, 122–54; Daniel, "Beyond Black and White," 333–41; Omi and Winant, *Racial Formation*, 109–35.

56. Lawrence H. Fuchs, *The American Kaleidoscope*, 189; Jonathan Peterson, "Times Get Hard for the Poor," *Los Angeles Times*, March 16, 1992, A13–A15.

57. "Backlash," Louisiana Broadcasting, 1991; Bobo, Kluegel, and Smith, "Laissez-Faire Racism," 17; Steven Steinberg, *Turning Back: The Retreat from Racial Justice in American Thought and Policy* (Boston: Beacon Press, 1995), 141–55.

58. Gunnar Myrdal, *An American Dilemma: The Negro Problem and Modern Democracy* (New York: Harper and Brothers, 1944), 4.

59. Ringer and Lawless, *Race-Ethnicity and Society*, 68–72; Steinberg, *Turning Back*, 42–43.

60. Banner-Haley, *The Fruits of Integration*, 55, 70.

61. Omi and Winant, *Racial Formation*, 113–36; Banner-Haley, *The Fruits of Integration*, 58, 68.

62. Steinberg, *Turning Back*, 116; Banner-Haley, *The Fruits of Integration*, 54, 70.

63. Edna Bonacich, "Inequality in America: The Failure of the American System for People of Color," in *Sources: Notable Selections in Race and Ethnicity*, ed. Adalberto Aguirre, Jr. and David V. Baker (Guilford, Conn.: Duskin Publishing Group, 1995), 138–43.

64. Ibid.; Banner-Haley, *The Fruits of Integration*, 10.

65. Okazawa-Rey, Robinson, and Ward, "Black Women and the Politics of Skin Color and Hair," 98–99; Marriott, "Colorstruck," 58; Banet-Weiser, *The Most Beautiful Girl in the World*, 123–31.

66. Feagin and Feagin, *Racial and Ethnic Relations*, 404, 406, 419, 444.

67. Omi and Winant, *Racial Formation*, 66–69, 84, 115, 148; Winant, *Racial Conditions*, 29–36, 112–15, 119–21, 125–29; James Scott, *Domination and the Arts of Resistance: Hidden Transcripts* (New Haven: Yale University Press, 1990), 70–96; Howard Winant, "Racial Formation and Hegemony: Global and Local Developments," in *Racism, Modernity and Identity: On the Western Front*, ed. Ali Ratanssi and Sallie Westwood (Cambridge: Polity Press, 1994), 266–87.

68. Daniel, "Multiracial Identity in Brazil and the United States," 153–78; Robert Brent Toplin, *Freedom and Prejudice: The Legacy of Slavery in The United States and Brazil* (Westport Conn.: Greenwood Press, 1981), 91–101; Winant, *Racial Conditions*, 166.

69. Carlos Arce, Edward Murguía, and W. Parker Frisbie, "Phenotype and Life Chances among Chicanos," *Hispanic Journal of Behavioral Sciences* 9 (1987): 19–33; Terry Wilson, "Blood Quantum: Native American Mixed Bloods," in *Racially Mixed People in America*, ed. Maria P. P. Root (Thousand Oaks, Calif.: Sage Publications, 1992), 108–25; Edward E. Telles

and Edward Murguia, "Phenotypic Discrimination and Income Differences among Mexican Americans," *Social Science Quarterly* 7 (December 1990), 682–96.

70. Some have argued that the lower rates of interracial marriage between European Americans and African Americans, as compared to rates of intermarriage between European Americans and various other Americans of color, as well as the lower rates of intraracial marriages between African Americans and other communities of color, is indicative of the continuing greater social distance and less mutual receptivity toward interracial marriage. This may be attributable to the fact that African Americans diverge more from the dominant European American somatic norm as compared to Native Americans, Asian Americans, Pacific Islanders, and Latinos that are of a more "intermediate" phenotype.

The comparatively higher rates of interracial marriages between European Americans and Americans of color—including African Americans—along with the lower rates of intraracial marriage among the various communities of color, can be also be attributed to the fact that all communities of color have European Americans as their primary significant "other," more so than each other. Consequently, they necessarily have internalized some of the beliefs, ideals, values, and customs of the dominant European Americans and are therefore somewhat "bicultural" (or at least bi-referential) with European Americans and their own individual communities of color. This intraracial pluralism among various communities of color is in part derivative of the long history of spatial distance, as well as social structural separation from each other in terms of inequality perpetuated by the dominant European Americans.

This differentiation also originates in egalitarian pluralism within these individual communities wherein they seek to retain their own communal patterns behavior and beliefs, ideals, values, and customs. This fosters greater differentiation among these communities of color, and thus less mutual "biculturation" with each other, as compared to their differentiation from and biculturation with the dominant European Americans. Increased contact among these communities of color in both the public and private spheres over the last few decades has brought with it new forms of conflict but has also led to the increased formation of primary relationships (friendships, dating, and intermarriage) across this intraracial divide. Inevitably, this will lead to increased intraracial marriages among the various communities of color. McDaniel, "The Dynamic Racial Composition of the United States," 282; Sanjek, "Intermarriage and the Future of Races," 105, 113–14; Spickard, *Mixed Blood*, 6–19, 343–72.

71. Douglass, "Socio-political Consequences," 1–31; Daniel, "Beyond Black and White," 333–41; Daniel, "Multiracial Identity in Brazil and the United States," 153–78; Jon Michael Spencer, *The New Colored People: The Mixed-Race Movement in America* (New York: New York University Press, 1997).

72. Douglass, "Socio-political Consequences," 1–31; Njeri, "Colorism," F1, F10, F12–F13; Radcliffe, "Round One Lost," 1–2.

73. Yinger, "Toward a Theory of Assimilation and Dissimilation," 249–63.

74. Davis, *Who Is Black?*, 73–77.

75. Daniel, "Beyond Black and White," 333–41.

76. Davis, *Who Is Black?* 12, 14. Native Americans have already set a precedent for this trend. This is indicated by their high rates of integration in outmarriage patterns (most specifically among urban Native Americans). In addition, successive generations of individuals whose blended lineage has included Native American ancestry and European American ancestry have not invariably been designated exclusively, or even partially, as Native

Americans. Consequently, these individuals have been extended a white racial identity and the privileges that accompany that status. In addition, self-identification with the background of color has been more a matter of choice.

However, Native Americans also experience greater continuing racial discrimination in terms of education, occupation, and income, and are even more significantly underrepresented than Asian Americans, generally speaking, in the most powerful and prestigious levels of the secondary structural sphere. They are among the most residentially segregated populations in the United States, in terms of urban populations—and particularly among rural populations living on reservations, which are by their very nature extreme forms of exclusion, notwithstanding the fact that some of this is by choice as a form of resistance to assimilation. Accordingly, the overall integration of Native Americans as compared to Asian Americans—specifically Japanese Americans—is significantly lower. This would disqualify them as the most rapidly integrating non-white group in the United States, despite a 60 to 70 percent outmarriage rate, particularly among women. Feagin and Feagin, *Racial and Ethnic Relations*, 195–233, 377–410. Similar trends have prevailed with other backgrounds as well. Jonathan W. Warren and France Winddance Twine, "White Americans, The New Minority?: Non-Blacks and the Ever-Expanding Boundaries of Whiteness," *Journal of Black Studies* 28 (November 1997): 200–218; Vilna Bashi and Antonio McDaniel, "A Theory of Immigration and Racial Stratification," *Journal of Black Studies* 27 (May 1997): 668–82; Eugene J. Cornacchia and Dale C. Nelson, "Historical Differences in the Political Experiences of American Blacks and White Ethnics: Revisiting an Unresolved Controversy," *Ethnic and Racial Studies* 15 (January 1992), 102–24; Stanley Lieberson, *A Piece of the Pie: Blacks and White Immigrants* (Berkeley: University of California Press, 1980), 1–15, 363–83; Feagin and Feagin, *Racial and Ethnic Relations*, 290–376.

77. Barbara Murray and Brian Duffy, "Did the Author of the Declaration of Independence Take a Slave for His Mistress/DNA Tests Say Yes," *U.S. News and World Report* (November 9, 1998), 59–64; Lynn Rosellini, "Cutting the Great Man Down to Size," *U.S. News and World Report* (November 9, 1998), 66; Joseph J. Ellis, "When a Saint Becomes a Sinner," *U.S. News and World Report* (November 9, 1998), 67–69; Barbara Murray, "Clearing the Heirs: We May Soon Know If Jefferson Had Black Children," *U.S. News and World Report* (December 22, 1997); Lucian K. Truscott IV, "Tom and Sally and Frank and Me: A Jefferson Descendent On Luck, Ancestry, and the Meaning of the DNA Findings," *American Heritage* (February/March 1999): 82–84; Emory Curtis, "Technology Uncovers Jefferson," *Interracial Voice Home Page*, <http://www.webcom.com/intvoice>.

78. Jillian A. Sim, "Fading to White: One Woman's Journey into Her Family's Past Uncovers A Story That Affects Every American," *American Heritage* (February/March 1999): 68–78.

79. "Black Women Who Look White," *Maury Povich Show* (July 27, 1993).

80. Daniel, "Beyond Black and White," 333–41; Rhett S. Jones, "The End of Africanity?: The Bi-Racial Assault on Blackness," *Western Journal of Black Studies* 18 (1994): 201–10.

Chapter Nine

1. Others make a distinction between individual racism, which is defined as everyday individual antipathy based on race, and institutional racism, which has larger social structural implications in terms of the distribution of wealth, power, privilege, and prestige.

Molefi Asante, *Kemet, Afrocentricity, and Knowledge*, 17–22; Werner Sollors, "The Idea of Ethnicity," in *The Truth about the Truth: De-Confusing and De-Constructing the Postmodern World*, ed. Walter Truett Anderson (New York: Putnam Books, 1995), 58–65; Ali Rattansi, " 'Western' Racisms, Ethnicities and Identities in a 'Postmodern' Frame," in *Racism, Modernity and Identity: On the Western Front*, ed. Ali Rattansi and Sallie Westwood (Cambridge: Polity Press, 1994), 57; Christie Farnham Pope, "The Challenge Posed by Radical Afrocentrism: When a White Professor Teaches Black History," *Chronicle of Higher Education*, (March 30, 1994), B1; Gerald Early, "Understanding Afrocentrism: Why Blacks Dream of a World without Whites," *Civilization* (July/August 1995), 31–39.

2. hooks, "Postmodern Blackness," 23–31; Marable, *Beyond Black and White*, 121–22; Schiele, "Afrocentricity for All," 27; Nantambu, "Pan-Africanism Versus Pan-African Nationalism," 561–74.

3. Manning Marable, *Beyond Black and White*, 122; Rattansi, " 'Western' Racisms, Ethnicities and Identities," 57; Molefi Asante, *Afrocentricity: The Theory of Social Change*, 105–8; Asante, *Kemet, Afrocentricity, and Knowledge*, 17–22.

4. Marable, *Beyond Black and White*, 122.

5. Mary Lefkowitz, *Not Out of Africa: How Afrocentrism Became an Excuse to Teach Myth As History* (New York: Basic Books, 1996), 161; Molly Myerowitz Levine, "Review Article, The Use and Abuse of *Black Athena*," in *American Historical Review* (April 1992): 440–64; George Will, "Intellectual Segregation: Afrocentrism's Many Myths Constitute Condescension toward African-Americans," *Newsweek* (February 19, 1996), 78.

6. G. Reginald Daniel, "Eurocentrism, Afrocentrism, or Holocentrism?" *Interrace* (May/June), 33; Cornel West, *Beyond Eurocentrism and Multiculturalism*, vol. I (Monroe, Maine: Common Courage Press, 1993), 1–30.

7. hooks, "Postmodern Blackness," 23–31.

8. Charles Lemert, *Sociology after the Crisis* (Boulder: Westview Press, 1996) 86; Pauline Marie Rosenau, *Postmodernism and the Social Sciences: Insights, Inroads, and Intrusions* (Princeton: Princeton University Press, 1992), 52; John Michael Spencer, "Trends of Opposition to Multiculturalism," *Black Scholar* 23 (1993): 2–5.

9. Spencer, "Trends of Opposition," 2–5.

10. hooks, "Postmodern Blackness," 23–31; Patricia Hill Collins, "Setting Our Own Agenda," 52–55; Anderson, *Beyond Ontological Blackness*, 11–19.

11. Schiele, "Afrocentricity for All," 27.

12. Ibid., 27; Molefi Asante, *The Afrocentric Idea* (Philadelphia: Temple University Press, 1987), 3–18; Linda James Myers, "The Deep Structure of Culture: Relevance of Traditional African Culture in Contemporary Life," in *Afrocentric Visions: Studies in Culture and Communication*, ed. Janice D. Hamlet (Thousand Oaks, Calif.: Sage Publications, 1998), 1–14; Norman Harris, "A Philosophical Basis for an Afrocentric Orientation," in *Afrocentric Visions: Studies in Culture and Communication*, ed. Janice D. Hamlet (Thousand Oaks, Calif.: Sage Publications, 1998), 15–26; Terry Kershaw, "Afrocentrism and the Afrocentric Method," in *Afrocentric Visions: Studies in Culture and Communication*, 27–44.

13. Hochschild, *Facing Up to the American Dream*, 137–38; Asante, *The Afrocentric Idea*, 3–18; Jerome H. Schiele, "Rethinking Organizations From an Afrocentric Viewpoint, in *Afrocentric Visions: Studies in Culture and Communication*, 73–88; Linda James Myers, *Under-*

standing an Afrocentric World View: Introduction to an Optimal Psychology (Dubuque, Iowa: Kendall/Hunt Publishing, 1988), 1–28.

14. Schiele, "Afrocentricity for All," 27; Asante, *Kemet, Afrocentricity, and Knowledge*, 5, 26, 28, 39.

15. hooks, "Postmodern Blackness," 23–31.

16. Ibid., 23–31; Anderson, *Beyond Ontological Blackness*, 9–11; Paul Connolly, "Racism and Postmodernism: Towards A Theory of Practice," in *Sociology after Postmodernism*, ed. David Owen (Thousand Oaks, Calif.: Sage Publications, 1997), 65–80; Rattansi, " 'Western' Racisms, Ethnicities and Identities," 30; Steven Seidman, "Introduction," in *The Postmodern Turn: New Perspectives on Social Theory*, ed. Steven Seidman (New York: Cambridge University Press, 1994), 8–9; Rosenau, *Postmodernism and the Social Sciences*, 5–7.

17. Marable, *Beyond Black and White*, 121.

18. David Slater, "Exploring Other Zones of the Postmodern: Problems of Ethnocentrism and Difference Across the North-South Divide," in *Racism, Modernity and Identity: On the Western Front*, ed. Ali Ratanssi and Sallie Westwood (Cambridge: Polity Press, 1994), 88–90.

19. Shohat and Stam, *Unthinking Eurocentrism*, 1–54; Williams and Chrisman, "Colonial Discourse and Post-Colonial Theory," 1–19; Tiffin, "Introduction," vii–xvi.

20. Shohat and Stam, *Unthinking Eurocentrism*, 1–54.

21. Ibid., 39.

22. Ibid.

23. Ibid.

24. Ibid.

25. Ibid., 42.

26. Ibid.; Williams and Chrisman, "Colonial Discourse and Post-Colonial Theory," 17; Albert J. Paolini, *Navigating Modernity*, 91–128; Chris Bongie, *Islands and Exiles: The Creole Identities of Post/Colonial Literature* (Stanford: Stanford University Press, 1998), 3–24; Tiffin, "Introduction," in *Past the Last Post*, vii–xvi.

27. Shohat and Stam, *Unthinking Eurocentrism*, 41.

28. Pieterse, "Unpacking the West," 130–46; Shohat and Stam, *Unthinking Eurocentrism*, 1–54.

29. Shohat and Stam, *Unthinking Eurocentrism*, 1–54; Pieterse, "Unpacking the West," 130–46.

30. Pieterse, "Unpacking the West," 144.

31. Ibid.

32. Eric Wolfe, *Europe and the People without History* (Berkeley: University of California Press, 1982), x.

33. Robert Hollinger, *Postmodernism and the Social Sciences: A Thematic Approach* (Thousand Oaks, Calif.: Sage Publications, 1994), 126–27; Steven Connor, *Postmodern Culture: An Introduction to Theories of the Contemporary* (Oxford: Blackwell, 1989), 224–37; Seidman, *Postmodern Turn*, 7; Huston Smith, *Beyond the Post-Modern Mind*, rev. ed. (Wheaton, Ill.: Theosophical Publishing House, 1989), 238–39.

34. hooks, "Postmodern Blackness," 23–31; Paolini, *Navigating Modernity*, 63–90.

35. Williams and Chrisman, "Colonial Discourse and Post-Colonial Theory," 1–19; Rainier Spencer, *Spurious Issues: Race and Multiracial Identity Politics in the United States* (Boulder: Westview Press, 1999), 1–48; 189–97; Zack, *Race and Mixed Race*, xi–xiv; Naomi Zack,

"Introduction," *American Mixed Race* (Lanham, Md.: Rowan and Littlefield: 1995), xv–xviii; Omi and Winant, *Racial Formation*, 55–61; John M. Murphy, "The Importance of Social Imagery for Race Relations," in *Postmodernism and Race*, ed. Eric Mark Kramer (Westport, Conn.: Praeger, 1997), 17–31; Jund Min Joi, "Racist Ontology, Inferiorization, and Assimilation," in *Postmodernism and Race*, ed. Eric Mark Kramer (Westport, Conn.: Praeger, 1997), 117–27; George Wilson and Jomills Braddock, "Analyzing Racial Ideology: Post-1980 America," in *Postmodernism and Race*, 129–43; Kwame Anthony Appiah, *In My Father's House: Africa in the Philosophy of Culture* (New York: Oxford University Press, 1992), 28–46, 137–57; Smedley, *Race in North America*, 2d ed., 331–32; Yehudi Webster, *The Racialization of America* (New York: Saint Martin's Press, 1992), 1–23; Yehudi Webster, *Against the Multicultural Agenda: A Critical Thinking Alternative* (Westport, Conn.: Praeger, 1997), 1–11, 80–81, 122–27.

36. Omi and Winant, *Racial Formation*, 55–61.

37. Václav Havel, "The Need for Transcendence in the Postmodern World," speech by Václav Havel, president of the Czech Republic, in Independence Hall, Philadelphia, July 4, 1994; Václav Havel, "The Search for Meaning in a Global Civilization," in *The Truth about the Truth*, 232–38; Sorokin, *Social and Cultural Dynamics*, 623–28, 699–704.

38. Joseph Natoli and Linda Hutcheon, "Introduction," in *A Postmodern Reader*, ed. Joseph Natoli and Linda Hutcheon (Albany: State University of New York Press, 1993), ix–xiv; Richard Lowy, "Development Theory, Globalism, and the New World Order: The Need for a Postmodern, Antiracist, and Multicultural Critique," *Journal of Black Studies* 28 (May, 1998): 594–615.

39. Rattansi, "Modern Racisms, Racialized Identities," 30; Seidman, *The Postmodern Turn*, 8–9; Rosenau, *Postmodernism and the Social Sciences*, 5–7.

40. Hollinger, *Postmodernism and the Social Sciences*, 1–19; Rattansi, "'Western' Racisms, Ethnicities and Identities, 28; Rosenau, *Postmodernism and the Social Sciences*, 128–33; Seidman, *The Postmodern Turn*, 1–21; Slater, "Exploring Other Zones of the Postmodern," 87.

41. Natoli and Hutcheon, "Introduction," ix–xiv; Rosenau, *Postmodernism and the Social Sciences*, 6–7.

42. Steven Connor, *Postmodernist Culture: An Introduction to Theories of the Contemporary* (Oxford: Blackwell Publishers, 1989), 27–64; Hollinger, *Postmodernism and the Social Sciences*, xii, 35, 47; Rosenau, *Postmodernism and the Social Sciences*, 12; Hans Bertens, "The Sociology of Postmodernity," in *International Postmodernism: Theory and Literary Practice*, ed. Hans Bertens and Douwe Fokkema (Amsterdam: John Benjamins Publishing, 1997), 103–20; Hans Bertens, "The Postmodern *Weltanschauung* and Its Relations to Modernism: An Introductory Survey," in *A Postmodern Reader*, ed. Joseph Natoli and Linda Hutcheon (Albany: State University of New York Press, 1993), 25–70; George Trey, *Solidarity and Difference: The Politics of Enlightenment in the Aftermath of Modernity* (Albany: State University of New York Press, 1998), 31–68; John R. Searle, "Postmodernism and the Western Rational Tradition," in *Campus Wars: Multiculturalism and the Politics of Difference*, ed. John Arthur and Amy Shapiro (Boulder: Westview Press), 28–48.

43. Natoli and Hutchinson, "Introduction," ix–xiv; Rosenau, *Postmodernism and the Social Sciences*, 6–7.

44. Rattansi, "'Western' Racisms, Ethnicities, and Identities in a 'Postmodern' Frame," 17.

45. Rosenau, *Postmodernism and the Social Sciences*, 4–7; Reincourt, *Sex and Power*, 17–41; Riane Eisler, *The Chalice and the Blad: Our History, Our Future* (San Francisco: Harper & Row,

1988), 42–44, 66–69, 73–77; Shulamith Firestone, *The Dialectic of Sex: The Case for Feminist Revolution* (New York: William Morrow, 1970), 172–191; Eric Neumann, *The Origins and History of Consciousness*, trans. R.F.C. Hull (Princeton: Princeton University Press, 1970, c. 1954), 340.

46. Rosenau, *Postmodernism and the Social Sciences*, 124; Wyle Sypher, *Four Stages of the Renaissance: Transformations in Art and Literature 1400–1700* (New York: Doubleday, 1955), 32–80, 180–200; Charles Jencks, *The Post-Modern Reader* (New York: Saint Martin's, 1995), 30.

47. Robert Harrison, *Deliberate Regression: The Disastrous History of Romantic Individualism in Thought and Art, from Jean-Jacques Rousseau to Twentieth Century Fascism* (New York: Knopf, 1980); Rosenau, *Postmodernism and the Social Sciences*, 6–7.

48. Hollinger, *Postmodernism and the Social Sciences*, xiii, 31–32; Ken Wilber, *A Brief History of Everything* (Boston: Shambhala Publications, 1996), 131, 159.

49. Wilber, *A Brief History*, 166; Seidman, *The Postmodern Turn*, 4; Rosenau, *Postmodernism and the Social Sciences*, 5–7.

50. Wilber, *A Brief History*, 166, 187–92, 261–72; Rattansi, "'Western' Racisms, Ethnicities and Identities," 30; Seidman, *The Postmodern Turn*, 8–9; Rosenau, *Postmodernism and the Social Sciences*, 5–7.

51. Sometimes this distinction between holarchy and hierarchy is described as the difference between a normative hierarchy and a pathological (or dominator) hierarchy.

52. Wilber, *A Brief History*, 27–32, 332.

53. Berman, *Coming to Our Senses*, 72–78; Hollinger, *Postmodernism and the Social Sciences*, 25–26; Hoogvelt, *Sociology of Developing Societies*, 25–26.

54. Margaret Wertheim, *The Pearly Gates of Cyberspace: A History of Space from Dante to the Internet* (New York: Norton, 1999), 43.

55. Ibid., 17–43.

56. Smith, *Beyond the Post-Modern Mind*, 7–8; Fritjof Capra, *The Turning Point: Science, Society, and the Rising Culture* (New York: Simon and Schuster, 1981), 15–49, 53–98; Dana Zohar, *The Quantum Self: Human Nature and Consciousness Defined by the New Physics* (New York: William Morrow, 1990), 17–49.

57. Rosenau, *Postmodernism and the Social Sciences*, 92–108; Wilber, *A Brief History*, 58–61.

58. Wilber, *A Brief History*, 59.

59. Walter Truett Anderson, "Introduction," in *The Truth about the Truth*, 4; Rosenau, *Postmodernism and the Social Sciences*, 78–91.

60. Smith, *Beyond the Post-Modern Mind*, 9; Wilber, *A Brief History*, 65–66.

61. Wilber, *A Brief History*, 58–61.

62. Anderson, "Introduction," 8, 10; Stanley Krippner and Michael Winkler, "Studying Consciousness in the Postmodern Age," in *The Truth about the Truth*, 163; Seidman, *The Postmodern Turn*, 1–23; Hollinger, *Postmodernism and the Social Sciences*, 28, 91; Rosenau, *Postmodernism and the Social Sciences*, 12–14, 67–76, 112.

63. Smith, *Beyond the Post-Modern Mind*, 240.

64. Hillel Schwartz, *Century's End: A Cultural History of the Fin de Siècle from the 990s through the 1990s* (New York: Doubleday, 1990), 217–19.

65. Ibid., 217

66. Anderson, "Epilogue," *The Truth about the Truth*, 238–39.

67. Jamake Highwater, *The Primal Mind: Vision and Reality in Indian America* (New York: Harper & Row, 1981), 68–69, 168–71; Anderson, "Introduction," 5–6.

68. Zygmunt Bauman, "Modernity and Ambivalence," in *Global Culture: Nationalism, Globalization, and Modernity,* ed. Mike Featherstone (Thousand Oaks, Calif.: Sage Publications, 1990), 154; Anderson, "Introduction, 5–6.

69. Smith, *Beyond the Post-Modern Mind,* 232–34.

70. Benjamin R. Barber, "Jihad Vs. McWorld," *Atlantic Monthly* (March 1992), 53–65.

71. Havel, "The Need for Transcendence in the Postmodern World"; Havel, "The Search for Meaning in a Global Civilization," 232–38; Sorokin, *Social and Cultural Dynamics,* 623–28, 699–704; Anderson, "Introduction," 7; Johann P. Arnason, "Nationalism, Globalization and Modernity," in *Global Culture: Nationalism, Globalization, and Modernity,* ed. Mike Featherstone (Thousand Oaks, Calif.: Sage Publications, 1990), 220; Riane Eisler, *The Chalice and the Blade,* 42–44, 66–69, 73–77; Mike Featherstone, "Introduction," in *Global Culture: Nationalism, Globalization, Modernity,* ed. Mike Featherstone (Thousand Oaks, Calif.: Sage Publications, 1990), 11; Ulf Hannerz, "Cosmopolitans and Locals in World Culture," in *Global Culture: Nationalism, Globalization, and Modernity,* 237; Rosenau, *Postmodernism and the Social Sciences,* 54.

72. Wilber, *A Brief History,* 27-32, 332.

73. Havel, "The Need For Transcendence"; Havel, "The Search for Meaning in a Global Civilization," 232–38.

74. Berman, *Coming to Our Senses,* 304–6; Toffler, *The Third Wave,* 300–303.

75. Seidman, *The Postmodern Turn,* 2.

76. Anderson, "Introduction," 10.

77. Ibid., 1–17; Seidman, *The Postmodern Turn,* 2.

78. Anderson, "Introduction," 8–10; Steiner Kvale, "Themes of Postmodernity," in *The Truth about the Truth,* 19; Alvin Tofler, *The Third Wave* (New York: Bantam Books, 1980), 300–303; Capra, *The Turning Point,* 15–49, 53–98; Marilyn Ferguson, *The Aquarian Conspiracy: Personal and Social Transformation in the 1980s* (Los Angeles: J. P. Tarcher Books, 1980), 57–63; Peter Russell, *The Global Brain: Speculations on the Evolutionary Leap to Planetary Consciousness* (Los Angeles: J. P. Tarcher Books, 1982), 160–78.

79. Wertheim, *The Pearly Gates of Cyberspace,* 17–43.

80. Tofler, *The Third Wave,* 301.

81. Ibid., 300–303; Rosenau, *Postmodernism and the Social Sciences,* 56, 124, 128, 171; Houston Smith, "Postmodernism and the World Religions," in *The Truth about the Truth,* 204–14.

82. Emmanual Wallerstein, "Differentiation and Reconstruction in the Social Sciences," letter from the president presented at International Sociological Association, October 1997. (This letter is an abbreviated version of Wallerstein's presentation at ISA Research Council, Montreal, August 6, 1997); Tofler, *The Third Wave,* 300–303; Rosenau, *Postmodernism and the Social Sciences,* 85–86; Conner, *Postmodernist Culture,* 9–10, 19.

83. Rosenau, *Postmodernism and the Social Sciences,* 6–7; Seidman, *The Postmodern Turn,* 2.

84. Ibid., 148–52; Toffler, *The Third Wave,* 300–303.

85. Rosenau, *Postmodernism and the Social Sciences,* 148–52; Anderson, "Epilogue," in *The Truth about the Truth,* 242; Tofler, *The Third Wave,* 300–303; Rosenau, *Postmodernism and the*

Social Sciences, 148–52; Ferguson, *The Aquarian Conspiracy,* 361–86; Ian Barbour, *Religion in an Age of Science* (San Francisco: Harper Collins, 1990), 81, 86.

86. Ferguson, *The Aquarian Conspiracy,* 241–77.

87. Anderson, "Self, Sex, and Sanity," in *The Truth about the Truth,* 128; Maureen O'Hara, "Constructing Emancipatory Realities," in *The Truth about the Truth,* 151–55; William Simon, "The Postmodernization of Sex and Gender," in *The Truth about the Truth,* 156–60; Tofler, *The Third Wave,* 300–303.

88. Kenneth J. Gergen, "The Healthy, Happy Human Being Wears Many Masks, in *The Truth about the Truth,* 136–44; Connie Zweig, "The Death of the Self," in *The Truth about the Truth,* 145–50; Maureen O'Hara and Walter Truett Anderson, "Psychotherapy's Own Crisis," in *The Truth about the Truth,* 170–76.

89. Rosenau, *Postmodernism and the Social Sciences,* 59.

90. Ibid., 57–61.

91. Hollinger, *Postmodernism and the Social Sciences,* xiii, 28; Frederic Jameson, *Postmodernism, or the Cultural Logic of Late Capitalism* (Durham: Duke University Press, 1991), xviii–xxi; Schwartz, *Century's End,* 217; conversation with sociologist John Baldwin, Department of Sociology, University of California, Santa Barbara, February 19, 1998.

92. Terry Mollner, "The Third Way Is Here," *In Context* 19, (autumn 1988), 54–63; Willis Harman and John Renesch, "Twenty-first-Century Business: A Background for Dialog," *City Planet* (August 1992), 4–5.

93. Ibid.

94. Havel, "The Need For Transcendence"; Havel, "Search for Meaning in a Global Civilization," 232–38; Berman, *Coming to Our Senses,* 302–3; Charles Davy, *Toward a Third Culture* (London: Faber and Faber, 1961), 73; Wilber, *A Brief History,* 69–70.

95. Wilber, *A Brief History,* 264.

96. Eisler, *The Chalice and the Blade,* xviii–xxiii; Hannerz, "Cosmopolitans and Locals," in *Global Culture: Nationalism, Globalization, and Modernity,* 239; Featherstone, "Introduction," *Global Culture: Nationalism, Globalization, and Modernity,* 2, 10; Anthony Smith, "Toward a Global Culture," in *Global Culture: Nationalism, Globalization, and Modernity,* 175; Rosenau, *Postmodernism and the Social Sciences,* 5–6; Charles Jencks, "What Is Postmodernism" in *The Truth about the Truth,* 27; Connor, *Postmodernist Culture,* 9–10, 19; Hollinger, *Postmodernism and the Social Sciences,* xiii; Steinar Kvale, "Themes of Postmodernity," 18–25; Seidman, *The Postmodern Turn,* 2; Richard Shweder, "Santa Claus on the Cross," in *The Truth about the Truth,* 78; Wilber, *A Brief History,* 166.

97. Wilber, *A Brief History,* 70.

Epilogue

1. Daniel, "Beyond Black and White," 333–41.

2. Paul R. Spickard, Rowena Fong, and Patricia L. Ewalt, "Undermining the Very Basis of Racism—Its Categories," *Social Work* 4 (1995): 581–84.

3. John Higham, *Send These To Me: Jews and Other Immigrants in Urban America* (New York: Atheneum, 1975), 242–46.

4. John Cruz, *Culture on the Margins: The Black Spiritual and the Rise of American Cultural Interpretation* (Princeton: Princeton University Press, 1999), 3–4, 68.

5. Richard Merelman, *Representing Black Culture: Racial Conflict and Cultural Politics in the United States* (New York: Routledge, 1995), 284–99.

6. Ibid.

7. Steele, *The Content of Our Character: A New Vision of Race in America* (New York: St. Martin's Press, 1990), 66–68.

8. Hacker, *Two Nations*, 60.

9. Merelman, *Representing Black Culture*, 284–99.

10. Ibid.

11. Ibid.

12. Patterson, *Ethnic Chauvinism*, 154–61.

13. Higham, *Send These To Me*, 242–46.

14. Ibid., 242–46; Steinhorn and Diggs-Brown, *By the Color of Our Skin*, 235; Orlando Patterson, *Ethnic Chauvinism: The Reactionary Impulse* (New York: Stein and Day, 1977), 178–85.

15. Merelman, *Representing Black Culture*, 284–99.

16. Ibid.

17. Steinhorn and Diggs-Brown, *By the Color of Our Skin*, 222–23.

18. Ibid.

19. Ibid.

20. Ibid.

21. Banner-Haley, *The Fruits of Integration*, 55, 67–69.

22. Mark A. Chesler, "Creating and Maintaining Interracial Coalitions," in *The Impacts of Racism on White Americans*, ed. Benjamin P. Bowser and Raymond G. Hunt (Thousand Oaks, Calif.: Sage Publications, 1981), 217–43; Ervin Laszlo, *Evolution: The Grand Synthesis* (New Science Library: Shambhala, 1987), 133–49; Higham, *Send These to Me*, 242–46; Richard W. Thomas, *Understanding Interracial Unity: A Study of Race Relations* (Thousand Oaks, Calif.: Sage Publications, 1996), 195–211; Merelman, *Representing Black Culture*, 284–99; Loriane Hutchins and Lani Kaahumanu, "Bicoastal Introduction," in *Bi Any Other Name: Bisexual People Speak Out* (Boston: Alyson Publications, 1991), xxii–xxiv.

23. Correspondence with Ken Wilber, December 23, 1998; Wilber, *A Brief History*, 188–90.

24. Merelman, *Representing Black Culture*, 284–89.

25. Ibid.; Louise Derman-Sparks, *Anti-Bias Curriculum: Tools for Empowering Young Children* (Washington, D.C.: National Association of the Education of Young Children, 1989), ix–10, 31–38; Yehudi Webster, *Against the Multicultural Agenda*, 5–10, 101–67; Shelby Steele, *The Content of Our Character*, 127–48; Arthur Schlesinger, Jr., *The Disuniting of America: Reflections on A Multicultural Society* (Whittle Direct Books, 1991), 1–3, 20–57; Dinesh D'Sousa, *Illiberal Education: The Politics of Race and Sex on Campus* (New York: Free Press, 1991), 1–23, 59–123, 194–228; Wilber, *A Brief History*, 188–90; Diane Ravitch, "Multiculturalism Yes, Particularism No," *Chronicle of Higher Education* (October 24, 1990), A44; Martin Cross, *The End of Sanity: Social and Cultural Madness in America* (New York: Avon Books, 1997), 144–73; Sam Allis, Jordon Bonfante, Cathy Booth, "Whose America?: A Growing Emphasis on the

Nation's 'Multicultural' Heritage Exalts Racial and Ethnic Pride At The Expense of Social Cohesion," *Time Magazine* (July 8, 1991), 12–17; Sharon Bernstein, "Multiculturalism: Building Bridges or Burning Them?" *Los Angeles Times*, A1; Chester E. Finn, Jr., "Why Can't Colleges Convey Our Diverse Culture's Unifying Themes?" *Chronicle of Higher Education* (June 13, 1990), A40; Larry Gordon and David Treadwell, "On Race Relations, Colleges Are Learning Hard Lessons," *Los Angeles Times*, A1; Peter I. Rose, *They and We: Racial and Ethnic Relations in the United States*, 5th ed. (New York: McGraw-Hill, 1997), 239–56; John Brooks Slaughter, "The Search for Pluralism in Higher Education," keynote address at the eighth annual Naumburg Memorial Lecture, University of California, Los Angeles (April 18, 1989); William A. Henry, Jr., "Beyond the Melting Pot," *Time Magazine* (April 9, 1990), 28–31; Richard Leviton, "Reconcilable Differences," *Yoga Journal* (September/October 1992): 50–55, 100.

26. Janet E. Helms, "An Overview of Black Racial Identity Theory," in *Black and White Identity: Theory, Research, and Practice*, ed. Janet E. Helms (Westport, Conn.: Greenwood Press, 1990), 9–32; Janet E. Helms, "Toward a White Racial Identity Development," in *Black and White Identity: Theory, Research, and Practice*, 49–66; Steele, *The Content of Our Character*, 48–49, 77–109.

27. Hutchins and Kaahumanu, "Bicoastal Introduction," xxii–xxiv.

28. Hacker, *Two Nations*, ix–xiii; Wilber, *A Brief History*, 188–90.

Index

Page numbers followed by *f* indicate figures.